GEORGE ORWELL NOW!

Mass
Communication
and
Journalism

Lee B. Becker
GENERAL EDITOR

Vol. 18

The Mass Communication and Journalism series
is part of the Peter Lang Media and Communication list.
Every volume is peer reviewed and meets
the highest quality standards for content and production.

PETER LANG
New York • Bern • Frankfurt • Berlin
Brussels • Vienna • Oxford • Warsaw

GEORGE ORWELL NOW!

EDITED BY RICHARD LANCE KEEBLE

PREFACE BY RICHARD BLAIR, SON OF GEORGE ORWELL

PETER LANG
New York • Bern • Frankfurt • Berlin
Brussels • Vienna • Oxford • Warsaw

Library of Congress Cataloging-in-Publication Data

George Orwell Now! / edited by Richard Lance Keeble.
pages cm. — (Mass communication and journalism; Vol. 18)
Includes bibliographical references and index.
1. Orwell, George, 1903–1950—Criticism and interpretation.
2. Orwell, George, 1903–1950. Nineteen eighty-four.
3. Orwell, George, 1903–1950—Influence. 4. Journalism and literature.
5. Mass media and literature. 6. Totalitarianism and literature.
I. Keeble, Richard, editor.
PR6029.R8Z675   828'.91209—dc23   2015019986
ISBN 978-1-4331-2983-4 (hardcover)
ISBN 978-1-4331-2982-7 (paperback)
ISBN 978-1-4539-1669-8 (e-book)
ISSN 2153-2761

Bibliographic information published by **Die Deutsche Nationalbibliothek**.
Die Deutsche Nationalbibliothek lists this publication in the "Deutsche
Nationalbibliografie"; detailed bibliographic data are available
on the Internet at http://dnb.d-nb.de/.

The paper in this book meets the guidelines for permanence and durability
of the Committee on Production Guidelines for Book Longevity
of the Council of Library Resources.

© 2015 Peter Lang Publishing, Inc., New York
29 Broadway, 18th floor, New York, NY 10006
www.peterlang.com

Printed in the United States of America

Dedicated
to Margaret

Table of Contents

Preface

An In-Depth Look into Orwell's Complex Mind

RICHARD BLAIR

Although my father, George Orwell, died in January 1950 at the comparatively early age of forty-seven, his writing continues to provoke discussion and comment to this day. Indeed, his legacy expands with the passage of time, and he has been widely read and argued over by academics, writers and readers ever since.

The genesis of this outpouring of material about Orwell began in the early seventies as unauthorized biographers, frustrated by the refusal of his widow, Sonia, to allow anything to be written about him, for fear of saying something controversial, finally started to write *unauthorized biographies*. Eventually Sonia had to give in and go against his wishes as laid down in his will, that *no biography be written* and commission the late Professor Sir Bernard Crick to undertake his 'official biography.' Although he had full access to all his papers and the result was an outstanding success, Sonia was not happy with the outcome. But then, in 1980, Sonia, having just fought and won a legal battle to regain full control of Orwell's copyright, died—and this freed up the literary executor of the estate to fully exploit the copyright to responsible writers such as Crick, publishers and film makers.

Amongst all these new opportunities were many writers who wanted to do their own biographies, and this has led to a plethora of new and interesting interpretations of Orwell's work. Perhaps the most prolific scholar of Orwell has been Professor Peter Davison, whose masterly editing of all Orwell's novels, essays and collected works was a labor of love. This has been followed by subsequent editions of particular aspects of Orwell's prodigious output, such as his essays and diaries. In the last decade or so there have been many other publications on various aspects of his life and writings.

One would, therefore, think that after all this time there would be little else to discover about the workings of Orwell's mind. How wrong can one be because Professor Richard Lance Keeble, of the University of Lincoln, has put together and contributed to an anthology of essays written by enthusiastic and knowledgeable scholars of Orwell. This collection, which ranges from analysis of his novels to the relevance of what he wrote all those years ago to today's world of intrusive surveillance, is an in-depth look at how his mind worked and why he is still so widely read.

Although Orwell has become an 'icon,' many people may argue that perhaps he was not always right. Informed argument is no bad thing and can lead to lively debate. There are some writers who like to misinterpret his works, either deliberately or otherwise, in order to further their own interests and this can mislead readers. Once the genie is out of the bottle, it is very difficult to put it back again. But they have to ask themselves the question: 'Will I be remembered in years to come?' The answer may well be: 'Not in the same way as Orwell has been remembered.'

Indeed, Orwell was a man who set out to inform the world of what people didn't want to know in a simple, clear message in order to alert them to the dangers of not questioning the motives of governments and large organizations who wish to manipulate events for their own benefit. This anthology is, therefore, another important piece of the jigsaw that helps us to understand the complex mind of the man that was George Orwell.

Introduction

Orwell Now: Nothing Less Than a Cultural Icon

RICHARD LANCE KEEBLE

George Orwell today is nothing less than a cultural icon. Indeed, the persistence of George Orwell and 'Orwellian' as reference points in contemporary mass media is remarkable. I typed a number of names into the LexisLibrary database of London-based 'broadsheet' newspapers covering three months of issues of the *Guardian, Observer, Times, Sunday Times, Daily Telegraph, Sunday Telegraph* and *Independent on Sunday*. These were the results:

William Shakespeare 1,342; J. K. Rowling 502; George Orwell 358; Virginia Woolf 204; Will Self 171; Hilary Mantel 163; Charles Dickens 161; Salman Rushdie 112; Margaret Atwood 93; Nick Davies 91; Leo Tolstoy 88; George Eliot 67; Ian Fleming 57; Margaret Drabble 49; John Updike 44; Gore Vidal 33; Erich Maria Remarque 23; John Berger 22; Noam Chomsky 20; Doris Lessing 15; Simone de Beauvoir 15; E. L. James 8; P. D. James 7; Jack London 7; Arundhati Roy 2.

While the LexisLibrary results have to be seen as not 100 per cent reliable, these figures are still fascinating. Orwell's position is high—and his presence in the media is enhanced still further in other ways. For instance, the word 'Orwellian' is very prominent: it is used as a pejorative adjective to evoke totalitarian terror, the falsification of history by state organized lying; the use of euphemistic language to camouflage morally outrageous ideas and actions. Occasionally 'Orwellian' is used as a complimentary adjective to mean 'displaying outspoken intellectual honesty, like Orwell.' I typed 'Orwellian' into LexisLibrary for the same period and it came up 77 times; in Google it registered 1,350,000 hits (see Keeble 2014a).

For instance, on 9 July 2014, the *Guardian* columnist Owen Jones wrote: 'Twenty-seven Palestinians are reported to have died in Gaza and mercifully no Israelis have been killed by Hamas rockets—and yet the BBC opts for the Orwellian "Israel under renewed Hamas attack."' On 1 August, an obituary of the novelist Dan Jacobson, in *The Times*, spoke of his 'Orwellian aversion to jargon and frivolous writing.' In *The Times* on the following day, Janice Turner wrote about seeking seats in a train 'where Orwellian screens won't blast me with entertainment packages.' And in the *Daily Telegraph*, of 16 August 2014, a report by Jeremy Warner was headlined 'Amazon facing Orwellian nightmare' (ibid.).

After the NSA contractor and whistleblower Edward Snowden in June 2013 revealed through the London-based *Guardian* and other international news media details of the massive global surveillance systems operated by intelligence agencies in the United States and United Kingdom, Orwell's *Nineteen Eighty-Four*—and its description of a Big Brother society in which the state intrudes into the innermost parts of everyday life—was a constant reference point globally. Sales of the book, in fact, rose 6,000 per cent on Amazon immediately after the revelations (Capon 2013).

ORWELL AND TODAY'S MASS MEDIA

Orwell's legacy can still cause heated controversies in the media. In a highly publicized spat in his BBC 'Points of View' contribution on 31 August 2014, the award-winning novelist Will Self took issue with Orwell when he wrote (in the essay, 'Politics and the English language,' of 1946): 'Most people who bother with the matter at all would admit that the English language is in a bad way, but it is generally assumed that we cannot by conscious action do anything about it. Our civilisation is decadent and our language—so the argument runs—must inevitably share in the general collapse.' As I argued at the time (Keeble 2014b):

> For Self to dare to accuse Orwell of being a 'talented mediocrity' backed by a present-day 'language police' who seek to impose 'good old-fashioned prejudices' on a 'living, changing' tongue adds just that necessary bit of controversy to thrust the whole kerfuffle high into the headlines.

Bruno Waterfield, Brussels correspondent of the *Daily Telegraph*, claimed Self's tirade mixed 'ignorance with snobbish disdain for the public' (Waterfield 2014). Self rightly highlighted the way in which the English language, far from declining and being in a 'bad way,' is being constantly invigorated with the addition of new words and neologisms.[1] Yet paradoxically Orwell himself gave to the English language a whole host of new words, phrases and striking aphorisms. He was the first person to use the phrase 'Cold War.' Other phrases and words he invented which have slipped effortlessly into everyday English include 'Big Brother,' 'newspeak' (and variants such as 'nukespeak' and 'massacrespeak'); 'doublethink' (and variants such as 'groupthink'); even 'Room 101' (the name of a television series of dubious quality)—all from his famous dystopian novel *Nineteen Eighty-Four* (of 1949).

Moreover, many of his aphorisms are regularly referred to in the media. For instance, there's 'During times of universal deceit, telling the truth becomes a revolutionary act' and 'Early in life I had noticed that no event is ever correctly reported in a newspaper.' Others include: 'Every war when it comes, or before it comes, is represented not as a war but as an act of self-defence against a homicidal maniac.' 'Freedom is the right to tell people what they do not want to hear,' and 'In our age there is no such thing as "keeping out of politics." All issues are political issues, and politics itself is a mass of lies, evasions, folly and hatred.' And there's 'The great enemy of clear language is insincerity.' Indeed, while Orwell acquired international fame for his great novels *Animal Farm* (1945) and *Nineteen Eighty-Four*, he is perhaps best seen first and foremost as a journalist. All those aphorisms certainly combine some of the best elements of journalism: conciseness, originality and a sense of moral and political urgency.

THE EVER-EXPANDING FIELD OF ORWELL STUDIES

Orwell is one of the most commented on and researched writers of all times. And yet Orwellian scholarship continues to thrive: 2013 saw the publication of a major new biography by Robert Colls, *George Orwell: English Rebel* (Oxford: Oxford University Press). While Orwell's 'Englishness' may be considered an already over-worked theme, Colls's text drew overall highly positive reviews. In the *Guardian*, another Orwell biographer, D. J. Taylor praised it as an 'excellent, provocative addition to Orwell studies.'[2] And in a 5,000-word essay in the *New Left Review*, Francis Mulhern commented that the book

> ... joins an already substantial body of commentary—his introduction lists some twenty predecessors, who themselves are only a sub-set of the much larger corpus of writing devoted to the man, the works and their afterlife. Where he differs from these is in his particular interest in Englishness, which has been his speciality as a historian over the past thirty-odd years. That too has been a busy field, and the result is a book of conspicuous learning, more than a quarter of its length given over to the scholarly apparatus. It is also, within its simple chronological scheme, a digressive book, here taking off to explore some aspect of a general situation, there pausing over some circumstance or consideration, as if wanting to find room for everything (Mulhern 2014).

Peter Davison's magisterial 20-volume collection of Orwell's writings continues to form the basis for a range of complementary texts: 2014 saw the publication of Davison's *Seeing Things as They Are: George Orwell's Selected Journalism and Other*

Writings (London: Harvill Secker) which Alan Massie, reviewing in the *Daily Telegraph*, said provided a 'treat on almost every page' (Massie 2014). In my own review, I commented:

> Orwell tended to look down on his journalism as 'mere pamphleteering' and a 'lesser' form of literature. He had a horror of hack reporting, despised the 'dreary sub-world of the freelance journalist' and maintained a constant attack on journalists as professionals … Yet in his essay 'Why I write' (of 1946) Orwell said he wanted 'to make political writing into an art.' This volume proves conclusively that Orwell succeeded in achieving just that (Keeble 2014c).

ORWELL'S *NINETEEN EIGHTY-FOUR* IN 2015

This particular volume sprang out of a symposium I organised at the University of Lincoln on Orwell's life and works funded by some of the money from a National Teaching Fellowship award I had won in 2011. The first section incorporates a range of fascinating approaches to Orwell's dystopian masterpiece *Nineteen Eighty-Four*. Peter Marks (who travelled over from Sydney, Australia, for the conference) examines the impact the text has had on the development of surveillance studies—particularly in the work of David Lyon, James Rule, David Rosen and Aaron Santesso, Sébastien Lefait, Simon Davies, Thomas Levin and John McGrath. But Marks points out that not all the responses from surveillance scholars have been positive: 'Critics and theorists such as Gilliom and Monahan, Rosen and Santesso, and Goold and others come less to praise Big Brother than to chase away his specter as misleading or redundant, a distraction from the reality of a world dominated instead by Big Data.' Against this, Marks argues that the novel still retains the power to provoke and instruct.

Next, Florian Zollmann argues that contemporary Western societies, politics and military strategies in many respects mirror the features as described in *Nineteen Eighty-Four*. He says:

> Western democracies are afflicted by extreme wealth inequalities and poverty. Governance is conducted in agreement with the interests of the corporate-business elites and wealthy view. Power is subtly exercised by a deep state which represents the overarching interests of the business community—'The Party.'

Moroever, Zollmann suggests, Western governments have been pursuing an extreme military agenda under the guise of liberal interventionism. NATO's aggressive expansion into Eastern Europe and the Middle Eastern hemisphere has even evoked the possibility of a 'World War III scenario' in the not-so-distant future. 'In short, does not all this suggest that we are living in times that warrant a comparison with *Nineteen Eighty-Four*?'

Henk Vynckier, of Tunghai University, Taiwan, in March 2014 jointly edited with his colleague John Rodden, a special edition of *Concentric: Literary and Cultural Studies* (Vol. 40, No. 1) devoted to Asian and global perspectives on Orwell.[3] Here he examines the ways in which Orwell's fascination with collecting things (everything from books, political pamphlets, and comic postcards to candle-holders and Victorian commemorative mugs) was reflected in his novels culminating in the representation of his anti-hero of *Nineteen Eighty-Four*. Winston Smith, Vynckier says, is a belated urban collector and *flâneur* stranded in an age of collectivism, who endeavors to construct a private sphere with the help of beautiful objects from the past: 'In sum, whereas James Joyce offered *A Portrait of the Artist as a Young Man* (1916), I intend to sketch *A Portrait of the Artist as a Collector.'*

Finally in this section, Adam Stock aims to re-cast the term 'Orwellian' as referring not only to a description of tyranny, lies and fear, but to a particular narrative way of explaining individual experience of the modern world. He thus explores *Nineteen Eighty-Four*'s varied influence on a range of texts including Marge Piercy's *Woman on the Edge of Time* (1979), Cory Doctorow's Young Adult (YA) novel *Little Brother* (2008) and David Mitchell's acclaimed novel *Cloud Atlas* (2004). Stock concludes by arguing that Orwell's most perceptive followers 'have engaged with the novel not only as a presentation of ideas or as a means of invoking an atmosphere of fear and tyranny, but as a work concerned with the alienating experience of modernity.'

ORWELL, THE LITERARY CANON—AND FURTHER EXPLORATIONS

The second section brings together an eclectic range of new Orwellian perspectives. Paul Anderson begins by suggesting that the best description of Orwell's mature politics is still that given by the late Bernard Crick in his seminal biography more than 30 years ago: that Orwell was 'a pretty typical *Tribune* socialist.' He thus takes issue with Peter Wilkin (2013), who has argued that Orwell is best viewed as a 'Tory anarchist,' with John Newsinger (1999), who, he says, exaggerates his dissidence from Labour, and with Robert Colls (2013), who plays it down too much.

Luke Seaber focuses on the 'London' section of *Down and Out in Paris and London* to show how, in an ostensibly documentary, yet certainly partially fictionalized, form Orwell was able to suggest to his readers that what they were reading was reasonably pure non-fiction. Moreover, drawing on the evidence of the Register of the Court of Summary Jurisdiction sitting at Old Street Police Court for December 1931, Seaber argues that Orwell's account of being picked up drunk, taken to Bethnal Green police station and then to Old Street Police Court to be seen by a magistrate was 'consistently accurate.' He concludes:

> The 'London' section of *Down and Out in Paris and London* in the ultimate analysis shows a far greater degree of rhetorical subtlety than the book's reputation as a simple, perhaps even naïf, description might suggest. Orwell's description of the world of the London poor and suburban casual wards shows a level of rhetorical sophistication, in various forms, aimed not so much at convincing the reader of the truth of the tale being told as of the truthfulness of the teller.

John Newsinger next argues that Orwell developed an understanding of socialism out of his experiences during the civil war in Spain (1936–1937) that placed him firmly on the far left and, moreover, he 'remained remarkably consistent in adhering to this understanding until his early, indeed sadly premature, death.'

One of the intentions of this text is to draw together a wide range of political perspectives on Orwell: highlighting all and endorsing none. Next, Philip Bounds, author of a controversial political memoir of the left in Wales,[4] suggests that in *The Road to Wigan Pier* (1937) Orwell tried to explain the distressing failure of the inter-war left to win much support for a socialist solution to the crisis. The contemporary relevance of this part of his book, Bounds argues, 'scarcely needs underscoring.' Although many people on the radical left in Britain thought their time had come when international capitalism lurched into crisis in 2008, there has since been no major revival of socialist politics, according to Bounds. The innumerable small Marxist parties and the radical wing of the Labour Party he says, are still weak, fragmented and marginalized. To what extent does *The Road to Wigan Pier* help us to understand the modern left's lack of effectiveness? Does its diagnosis of the left's cultural malaise still speak to our contemporary political practices or should we be seeking new explanations? These are among the questions Bounds attempts to answer in his chapter.

NEW INTERNATIONAL PERSPECTIVES ON ORWELL

The international interest in Orwell continues to expand. I, for instance, was interviewed (along with Michael Radford, director of the 1984 film, *Nineteen Eighty-Four*, and Richard Blair, Orwell's son) for a documentary *Finding 1984*, made by the Japanese pay-TV network Wowow and the Australian production company WildBear Entertainment. The film concentrated on Orwell's great dystopian novel—linking it to the recent revelations by Edward Snowden about global surveillance by the NSA. It appeared in Japan on 27 December 2014 to acclaim and was due for a later showing in Australia.[5] Here, Sorbonne academic Marina Remy draws on an eclectic range of theorists, including Jacques Derrida, Emmanuel

Levinas, Frédéric Regard and Annie Verut-Plichon to explore Orwell's representation of the encounter between the self and the other in his novels *Burmese Days* (1934) and *Keep the Aspidistra Flying* (1936). Remy goes on to argue that Orwell's works 'constantly question clear-cut dichotomies between both self and other, fact and fiction by staging, creating and re-creating encounters with others and considering the time of the other in the temporality of the novel.'

Sreya Mallika Datta and Utsa Mukherjee, students at Presidency University, Kolkata, India, present what they call a 'postcolonial critique' of Orwell's works on colonial Burma—analyzing the interactions between the 'colonizer' and the 'colonized' and examining the gaps and incongruences within this curiously ambivalent sphere. 'Orwell's writings,' they say, 'provide a telescopic view of the multiple possibilities of a colonial encounter, going beyond the pigeon-holes of binaries into a re-examination of the colonial dialogue.'

Shu-chu Wei, Visiting Professor at Tunghai University, Taiwan, explores how the practices of communist dictatorships are exposed and satirized in both Orwell's *Animal Farm* (1945) and *The Execution of Mayor Yin and Other Stories from the Great Proletarian Cultural Revolution* (尹縣長) (1976) by the Taiwanese author Chen Jo-hsi (also spelled as Chen Ruoxi). Shu-chu Wei considers two pairs of representative characters: Mollie in *Animal Farm* and P'eng Yu-lien in 'Residency check' from *The Execution of Mayor Yin*, as well as Boxer in *Animal Farm* and Mayor Yin in *The Execution of Mayor Yin*. She also discusses recurring themes of cover-ups and propaganda in both books. She concludes:

> It is not likely that Chairman Mao and other leading communists in China ever read *Animal Farm*, but it is intriguing that the script they followed when they launched the infamous Cultural Revolution is very similar to that followed in *Animal Farm*. Thanks to Chen Jo-hsi and her stories about Yu-lien, Mayor Yin and Master K'uai, we see clearly how common human characteristics such as good looks and vanity, loyalty and devotion, and love of one's wife are exploited in the name of national expediency and the lust for power.

ORWELL AND THE JOURNALISTIC IMAGINATION

Much recent academic study has been focusing on the various elements that make up the 'journalistic imagination' (see Hartsock 2000; Keeble and Wheeler 2007; Bak and Reynolds 2011; Keeble and Tulloch 2012 and 2014). The book's final section has two chapters which engage with this theoretical debate in very different ways. In the first, Tim Crook argues that Orwell was 'radiophonic' in his writing in that it evoked the sound perspective of radio broadcasting. He continues:

> Indeed, there is a distinct drama-documentary style of prose in books such as *Down and Out in Paris and London* (1933), *The Road to Wigan Pier* (1937) and *Homage to Catalonia* (1938). The first part of Chapter Three of his 1935 novel *A Clergyman's Daughter* reads like

a transcript of the 1934 BBC Manchester feature *'Opping 'Oliday*. Both the chapter and the radio feature deal with the now lost sub-culture of casual hop-pickers traveling to Kent in the late summer. The BBC program was the first documentary feature to use a recording van. The microphone was thus taken out of the studio to record people directly on location.

Finally, my own chapter compares Orwell's account of his fighting alongside Republican militiamen during the Spanish Civil War in *Homage to Catalonia* (1938) with his dispatches for David Astor's *Observer* and *Manchester Evening News* from the European frontline during the final months of World War II in 1945. I argue that *Homage* is a wonderfully confident piece of eye-witness reportage that embraces a wide range of literary techniques. In contrast, the pieces of war reporting from 15 February to the end of May 1945 lacked that assurance and highlighted his difficulties in finding an appropriate voice. Significantly, in writing *Homage* Orwell was in no way constrained by the demands of professionalism: he was an outspoken, activist journalist—but these demands later intruded into his reporting style while on assignment at the end of the Second World War.

Finally, Peter Stansky, of Stanford University, provides a reflective 'Afterword' arguing persuasively why Orwell is more relevant today than ever before.

NOTES

1. For instance, see http://www.telegraph.co.uk/culture/books/booknews/11066483/Will-Self-attacks-literary-mediocrity-George-Orwell.html, accessed on 12 March 2015.
2. See http://www.theguardian.com/books/2013/nov/20/george-orwell-english-rebel-review, accessed on 12 March 2015.
3. See for instance http://www.concentric-literature.url.tw/issues/Orienting%20Orwell%20Asian%20and%20Global%20Perspectives%20on%20George%20Orwell/5.pdf, accessed on 13 March 2015.
4. For a review of *Notes from the End of History: A Memoir of the Left in Wales* see http://www.orwell-society.com/?p=1202, accessed on 13 March 2015.
5. See http://realscreen.com/2014/11/06/wowow-wildbear-ready-orwell-themed-doc-finding-1984/, accessed on 12 March 2015.

REFERENCES

Bak, John S. and Reynolds, Bill (2011) *Literary Journalism across the Globe: Journalistic Traditions and Transnational Influences*, Chicago: University of Massachusetts Press.

Capon, Felicity (2013) Sales of Orwell's *1984* rocket in wake of US Prism surveillance scandal, 12 June, *Daily Telegraph*. Available online at http://www.telegraph.co.uk/culture/books/book-news/10115599/Sales-of-Orwells-1984-rocket-in-wake-of-US-Prism-surveillance-scandal.html, accessed on 12 March 2015.

Colls, Robert (2013) *George Orwell: English Rebel*, Oxford: Oxford University Press.

Hartsock, John C. (2000) *A History of American Literary Journalism: The Emergence of a Modern Narrative Form*, Amherst: University of Massachusetts Press.

Keeble, Richard Lance (2014a) George Orwell: The cultural icon of today, 10 September. Available online at http://www.orwellsociety.com/?p=1105, accessed on 1 March 2015.

Keeble, Richard Lance (2014b) The Orwell/Self spat: What it reveals about contemporary culture, 7 September. Available online at http://www.orwellsociety.com/?p=1101, accessed on 12 March 2015.

Keeble, Richard Lance (2014c) Far beyond mere hackery: Orwell's journalism, 1 December. Available online at http://www.orwellsociety.com/?p=1158, accessed on 12 March 2015.

Keeble, Richard Lance and Tulloch, John (2012) *Global Literary Journalism: Exploring the Journalistic Imagination Volume 1*, New York: Peter Lang.

Keeble, Richard Lance and Tulloch, John (2014) *Global Literary Journalism: Exploring the Journalistic Imagination Volume 2*, New York: Peter Lang.

Keeble, Richard and Wheeler, Sharon (2007) *The Journalistic Imagination: Literary Journalists from Defoe to Capote and Carter*, London: Routledge.

Massie, Alan (2014) George Orwell's idiosyncratic journalism anticipated the age of social media, *Telegraph*, 13 December. Available online at http://www.telegraph.co.uk/culture/books/bookreviews/11287263/Seeing-Things-As-They-Are-Selected-Journalism-and-Other-Writings-by-George-Orwell-review.html, accessed on 12 March 2015.

Mulhern, Francis (2014) Forever Orwell, *New Left Review*, No. 87, May-June. Available online at https://newleftreview.org/II/87/francis-mulhern-forever-orwell, accessed on 12 March 2015.

Newsinger, John (1999) *Orwell's Politics*, Oxford: Oxford University Press.

Waterfield, Bruno (2014) Self, Orwell and the English language, September. Available online at http://www.spiked-online.com/review_of_books/article/self-orwell-and-the-english-language/15774#.VQGY7U1yZy0, accessed on 12 March 2015.

Wilkin, Peter (2013) George Orwell: The English dissident as a Tory anarchist, *Political Studies*, Vol. 61, No. 1, pp. 215–230.

Orwell, Big Brother—AND His Little Nephews

CHAPTER ONE

George Orwell AND THE History OF Surveillance Studies

PETER MARKS

INTRODUCTION

A specter is haunting the academic field of surveillance studies—the specter of Big Brother, the monstrous anti-hero of George Orwell's dystopian novel, *Nineteen Eighty-Four* (1949). The disembodied emblem of the Party (never seen in the flesh, and only ever viewed in posters 'plastered everywhere'), Big Brother remains a potent public symbol of totalitarian power and of invasive monitoring. Loved with disturbing and destructive vigor by members of the Party, Big Brother's simultaneous psychological ubiquity and physical absence make him the stuff of waking dreams and nightmares. His seemingly inescapable gaze, communicated verbally in the phrase 'Big Brother Is Watching You,' has become talismanic in the contemporary world, an overt sign of our 'surveillance society.'

That phrase is embedded in the title of David Lyon's *The Electronic Eye: The Rise of Surveillance Society* (1994), a major early text in surveillance studies, and one of a series of works in which Lyon, perhaps the world's leading surveillance scholar, sets out to track the endlessly morphing reach of monitoring technologies and practices in everyday lives. *The Electronic Eye* spends much of a chapter on *Nineteen Eighty-Four*, and, as we will see, the novel reappears regularly in Lyon's work, including his recent collaboration with Zygmunt Bauman, *Liquid Surveillance: A Conversation* (2013). Lyon is not alone among recent surveillance scholars in referencing Big Brother: John Gilliom and Torin Monahan declaring the fictional character 'probably the most famous bogeyman and symbol of a surveillance society' in their *SuperVision: An Introduction to the Surveillance Society* (2013). David Rosen and Aaron Santesso, in *The Watchman in Pieces: Surveillance, Literature and Liberal Personhood* (2013), and Sébastien Lefait, in *Surveillance on Screen: Monitoring Contemporary Films and Television* (2013), also utilize *Nineteen Eighty-Four* as a point of comparison with either literature over many centuries or films in the last hundred years. Moreover, Simon Chesterman's *One Nation Under Surveillance: A New Social Contract to Defend Freedom Without Sacrificing Liberty* (2011) and Lisa Nelson's *America Identified: Biometric Technology and Society* (2010) begin by quoting these chilling words from *Nineteen Eighty-Four*'s early pages:

> You had to live—did live, from habit that became instinct—in the assumption that every sound you made was overheard, and except in darkness, every movement scrutinized (Orwell 1997: 5).

These lines are among the most quoted words in surveillance studies, justifying sociologist and legal expert Benjamin Goold's comment that 'Looking back over the discourse of surveillance and technology over the last fifty years it is difficult to overestimate the impact of Orwell's novel … on popular and academic imaginations' (Goold 2004: 208). The more recent references and quotations above suggest that the specter of Big Brother remains.

In this chapter, I survey what is now sixty years of impact on the imagination. My primary interest lies in considering academic responses to *Nineteen Eighty-Four*, but the public response will not be neglected entirely; in fact, the two are intertwined. Such an endeavor might focus on the novel's and its author's undoubted influence on English post-war literature, one highlighted in the title of John Brannigan's *Orwell to the Present: English Literature 1945–2000* (2002). Or it might explore the powerful and, for some, disastrous impact *Nineteen Eighty-Four* has had on utopian thinking. Michael Marder and Patrícia Vieira, for example, ask despondently in their introduction to a recent collection:

> Is there still any space, whether conceptual or practical, for the thinking of utopia … in a world marked by a chronic dystopian outlook? … Aesthetically, this dystopian mood has given rise to countless novels and films, the most emblematic of which is perhaps George Orwell's *1984* (sic) (Marder and Vieira 2012: ix).

Their collection's title, *Existential Utopia: New Perspectives on Utopian Thinking*, advertises Marder's and Vieira's conviction that there is conceptual and practical space for such thinking, but the claim that *Nineteen Eighty-Four* remains emblematic of a chronic dystopian outlook speaks to its global importance and its sustained power to provoke academic thinking. My focus in this chapter, though, is the novel's impact on the still-developing field of surveillance studies—a field that can be dated from James Rule's *Private Lives and Public Surveillance* (1973). In surveillance studies, *Nineteen Eighty-Four*'s influence has arguably been even more profound, as illustrated in the titles of Simon Davies's *Big Brother: Britain's Web of Surveillance* (1996), Thomas Levin's *CTRL [Space]: The Rhetorics of Surveillance from Bentham to Orwell* (2002) and John McGrath's *Loving Big Brother: Performance, Privacy and Surveillance Space* (2004). These references, among many others in articles and chapters, might seem a sincere form of flattery, but not all the responses from surveillance scholars have been positive. Critics and theorists such as Gilliom and Monahan, Rosen and Santesso, and Goold and others come less to praise Big Brother than to chase away his specter as misleading or redundant, a distraction from the reality of a world dominated instead by Big Data. Against this dismissal by some, I argue that the novel still retains the power to provoke and instruct, and I sense that any future history of surveillance and surveillance studies will need to account for *Nineteen Eighty-Four's* durable legacy.

THE PUBLIC LOOKS AT BIG BROTHER

Goold's recognition that Orwell's novel has had a massive impact on both popular and academic understanding of surveillance to some extent obscures the different impact the novel has had on the public and on scholars. It provided a powerful early model for researchers wishing to deal systematically with the emerging reality of a surveillance society, and in some instances, such as with James Rule, it supplied the initial motivation for that scholarly interest: 'As with most people,' Rule admits, 'my first sensitivity to the issues [surrounding surveillance] came on reading Orwell's *1984*' (1973: 18). Beyond sparking his interest in surveillance, the novel provided Rule with a vivid means with which to measure the distance between Orwell's fiction and the reality of 1970s Britain and the United States. His assessment that the 1970s did not yet approximate to the world imagined by Orwell is less surprising for what it says about that world than for the fact that a social scientist attempting to observe and assess his contemporary society objectively, extensively and in great detail (*Private Lives, and Public Surveillance* runs to almost 400 pages) would use a piece of fiction as a principal point of comparison. Yet Rule does use *Nineteen Eighty-Four* as that point, indicating how, by the time the first researchers who might be called surveillance scholars appeared in the 1970s and 1980s, the novel was firmly established in the *zeitgeist*. From the outset, it had been an international bestseller. More than this, it quickly became a global cultural phenomenon, taught in high schools and translated into dozens of languages. Key phrases and motifs from the novel such as 'Big Brother,' 'telescreens' and the 'Thought Police,' all with surveillance implications, found their way into the public mindset, employed and debated even by those who had not read the novel. The text generated the adjective 'Orwellian,' a multi-purpose adjective useful for describing totalitarian forces, possibilities and dangers in the 'real world.'

It became synonymous with intrusive state monitoring, threats to privacy and to individual autonomy.

More remarkable still a novel published in a world where metadata, Facebook and mobile phones were undreamt of, maintained its relevance in the twentieth-first century, retaining sufficient cultural purchase to be worth dismissing by some surveillance scholars after six decades. It is regularly, indeed almost automatically, invoked today when questions are raised in the media about the invasion of privacy, tensions between national and personal security, technology function creep, and the protection of freedoms. Politicians, journalists and the public continue to use the book as shorthand for myriad surveillance issues, even when, as with the selling of customer data for commercial profit, the circumstances bear no relationship to the situation described in the book. Brand recognition for *Nineteen Eighty-Four* is such that the internet watchdog, Privacy International, gives its annual Big Brother Awards 'to government agencies, private companies and individuals who have excelled in the violation of our privacy,' and the British television show *Room 101* has celebrities talking comically about their greatest fears, alluding to the room in the novel that holds 'the worst thing in the world' (Orwell 1997: 296) for its endless sequence of occupants. When the NSA contractor Edward Snowden revealed the extent of data monitoring by security agencies in the United States and the United Kingdom in 2013, sales of *Nineteen Eighty-Four* 'enjoyed a massive spike in sales' in the United States (*New Yorker* 2013). Typing the words 'Big Brother' and 'surveillance' into Google (a quick, if admittedly approximate, gauge of cultural impact) produces over eight million hits—this novel still matters.

An outward, if ironic, signal of *Nineteen Eighty-Four*'s continuing and massive hold on the contemporary imagination is the internationally successful 'reality' television show named in its honor, *Big Brother*. There, in a direct inversion of the speculative reality of Airstrip One where telescreens, spies and the Thought Police enforce maximum surveillance on Party members especially, contestants on *Big Brother* compete to be constantly monitored, believing that intrusive scrutiny by dozens of cameras and millions of viewers offers a fast track to easy fame and outrageous fortune. First produced in the Netherlands in 1999, *Big Brother* quickly became a global phenomenon. Surprisingly, it still flourishes, in countries as culturally distinct as Albania and Argentina, Brazil and France, Germany and Israel, Portugal, Canada and Australia. *Big Brother* could well be the exemplar of the so-called 'spectator society,' in which people want to and actively work towards being seen, often by complete strangers to whom they transmit aspects of their identity or perform fantasy versions of themselves. The cultural theorist Slavoj Žižek detects a more ominous or darkly comic dimension to this desperate need to be seen:

> What we obtain here is the tragi-comic reversal of the Bentham-Orwellian notion of the Panopticon-society in which we are (potentially) 'observed always' and have no place to hide from the omnipotent gaze of the Power: today, anxiety seems to arise from the

prospect of NOT being exposed to the Other's gaze all the time, so that the subject needs the camera's gaze as a kind of ontological guarantee of his/her being (Žižek 2002: 225).

The connection to Jeremy Bentham and his Panopticon building, the other early model for surveillance studies, will be considered in the following section. For now it is enough to register that Žižek's comment suggests that the situation described in *Nineteen Eighty-Four* can even help us make sense of a contemporary cultural phenomenon very different from that in the novel itself, one tied not to the totalitarian power of the state so much as the enveloping power of consumer capitalism. If, as Karl Marx and Friedrich Engels announced in the *Communist Manifesto* of 1848, communism is the specter haunting capitalism, *Big Brother* the show seems like capitalism's embarrassing and profitable dark secret.

BIG BROTHER AND THE BIRTH OF SURVEILLANCE STUDIES

The modern commercialization of surveillance that *Big Brother*, the reality show, embodies is radically at odds with the world depicted by Orwell—though closer to the narcissism and materialism of Aldous Huxley's *Brave New World* (of 1932). As already noted, though, *Nineteen Eighty-Four* was a critical yardstick for Rule's *Private Lives and Public Surveillance*, the text recognized (Marx 2012: xxii) as foundational to surveillance studies. As I state in *Imagining Surveillance: Eutopian and Dystopian Literature and Film*: 'Rule indicates the importance of Orwell's novel clear from the outset, opening with the question: "Why do we find the world of 1984 so harrowing?" Beyond its centrality to the investigation he undertakes, Rule acknowledges the novel's personal impact' (Marks 2015: 14). One answer to Rule's question, and an aspect often underplayed in considering the novel's lasting power to disturb readers who live in modern democracies, is that it situated elements associated with the totalitarian oppression of Nazi Germany and the Soviet Union in Airstrip One, still identifiably London. As Orwell made plain in a statement on *Nineteen Eighty-Four*, the setting 'of the book is laid in Britain in order to emphasize that the English-speaking races are not innately better than anyone else and that totalitarianism, *if not fought against*, could triumph anywhere' (Orwell 1998: 135; emphasis in the original). The world he creates is both provocatively different from those of its 'Western' readers, yet worryingly familiar. Projecting into the future, not so much as prediction than as prospect, Orwell encourages, if not forces, readers to confront the possibility that such a world might eventuate if they allow it.

By placing the novel's action not in some far distant future or fantasy space, but in a modified though recognizable place, Orwell unwittingly set up connections and parallels that surveillance scholars (many of whom were European or North American) could address, adapt or critically examine in studying the actual world rather than its fictional equivalent. *Nineteen Eighty-Four* was not unique in this regard, and novels and films regularly furnish surveillance studies with imaginative and illuminating scenarios and characters through which to investigate actual surveillance. That said, references to *Nineteen Eighty-Four* in surveillance studies far exceed any made about other creative text, even given the clear monitoring components in works such as Margaret Atwood's *The Handmaid's Tale* (1985) or Peter Weir's film, *The Truman Show* (1998).

Most of what can now be understood as surveillance studies emerged after *The Handmaid's Tale*, works such as Stanley Cohen's *Visions of Social Control* (1985) and Gary T. Marx's sociological study *Undercover: Police Surveillance in America* (1988) being early and highly influential pieces that expanded the territory beyond that mapped out by Rule. Both texts were written soon after 1984, referred to by some as 'Orwell's year,' when the novel received unprecedented popular and academic attention, becoming the subject of countless articles, conferences and allusions. John Rodden, the best chronicler of Orwell's literary reputation, records 'the 1984 "countdown"' and says: 'During 1983 and 1984, what the mass media called "Orwellmania" spurred *Nineteen Eighty-Four* alone to sales of almost 4 million copies' (Rodden 1989: 49). Apple computers used the imagery of Big Brother and the 'Two Minute Hate' in a striking advertisement directed by Ridley Scott, the creator of *Blade Runner* (1982) that ended with the pronouncement: 'On January 24th, Apple will introduce the Macintosh. And you'll see why 1984 will not be like *1984*.'

A flurry of critiques argued that the actual 1984, indeed, was far from the fictional *Nineteen Eighty-Four*, the blurring of year and title heightened in the United States by the 1950 Signet edition that had renamed the novel *1984*. The novel cast a long, menacing shadow, and not surprisingly Cohen and Marx individually harked back briefly beyond Atwood to Orwell in their own treatment of surveillance. Cohen made the important general point that it 'is not whether these things could "really" happen. As with Orwell's *Nineteen Eighty-Four*, or any species of anti-utopian thinking, these visions help clarify our values and preferences' (Cohen 1985: 205). Cohen understood the work a fictional text can do in prompting thought that leads to clarified values and preferences, even if the world depicted in that text fails a 'reality test.' Unlike Rule, Cohen's consideration of the novel was not integral to his argument, more a passing comment on a work he clearly assumed his readers at least would be aware of and would likely have read. Gary T. Marx also had larger questions to answer in *Undercover* than any to do with *Nineteen Eighty-Four*, but again the centrality of that novel to public awareness and institutional thinking on surveillance seemed to require some form of mention. Marx was keenly concerned with the reality of policing in the United States in the 1980s, and was developing a subtle and complex model about 'New Surveillance' in which overt and oppressive measures along the lines of *Nineteen*

Eighty-Four were less the norm than a more covert approach that co-opted rather than coerced the public into accepting surveillance procedures. Having studied at length the real conditions of contemporary policing in the United States, Marx reassured his readers that 'George Orwell is not yet around the corner' (Marx 1988: 14), the slight qualification in the phrase 'not yet' indicating that *Nineteen Eighty-Four* was still the popular measure of surveillance after forty years and that elements of it were worth addressing.

THE PANOPTICON AS ALTERNATIVE MODEL

In the 1980s a second more theoretically complex and equally arresting take on surveillance was gaining adherents among surveillance scholars: Michel Foucault's Panopticon model, based on the ideas of the eighteenth-century utilitarian philosopher Jeremy Bentham (1748–1832). Very briefly stated, Bentham planned a building called the Panopticon which, as its name suggests, was designed so that each of its inhabitants could be seen at all times by a central, hidden inspector. The effect of this constant monitoring, Bentham reasoned, would be that those inside the Panopticon inevitably would come to internalize psychologically what Žižek above calls 'the omnipotent gaze of the Power' and would start automatically acting in accord with social laws and regulations. For Bentham, the results would be transformative in a wholly positive way:

> Morals reformed—health preserved—industry invigorated—instruction diffused—public burthens lightened—Economy seated as it were on a rock—the Gordian knot of the Poor-Laws not cut, but untied—all by a simple idea in Architecture (Bentham 1995: 31).

For Michel Foucault, though, the same device and means of organizing or regulating people would lead inexorably to a world in which autonomy was sacrificed for compliance, resulting in a form of 'discipline society' (Foucault 1975). The quick uptake of Foucault's ideas in the 1980s and 1990s provided surveillance studies with an academic base and focus. While not all scholars adopted those ideas, the Panopticon superseded Big Brother as the dominant image in the field. Foucault's use of historical evidence (even if this were challenged by traditional historians) gave his views a grounding in reality that aligned broadly with the perspectives of the social scientists and sociologists who quickly came to dominate surveillance studies. By contrast, the fictional world of Oceania (over which Big Brother rules) was obviously less real or amenable to sociological application. One of the major early works on surveillance, Oscar Gandy's *The Panoptic Sort: A Political Economy of Personal Information* (1993), embedded Foucault's thinking into its title. Gandy made clear his affiliation with Foucault, admitting that the Frenchman's thinking threatened 'to dominate the construction of my arguments about power and social control' (Gandy 1993: 9). The subtitle of *The Panoptic Sort* also identified the gathering, sorting and assessment of personal information as a key element in modern day surveillance. The practice in some ways began in its modern form with the rise of bureaucracies in the late nineteenth century, but the invention and rapid proliferation of computers in the second half of the twentieth century gave governments and corporations unprecedented access to inestimable amounts of information. This new circumstance encouraged such organizations to collect and collate information on whole societies, making decisions that might have momentous effects on the life choices of individuals. The centrality of this 'panoptic sort' to the structure and administration of contemporary society, with the possibility of inbuilt, unacknowledged or undetected biases, was a key concern in Gandy's book, switching focus from the visual surveillance associated with *Nineteen Eighty-Four* to the mass monitoring of information. Big Brother was being supplemented by and to an extent surpassed what would come to be known as Big Data.

Even so, David Lyon in *The Electronic Eye*, published the year after *The Panoptic Sort*, still gave consideration to Orwell and to *Nineteen Eighty-Four*, part of a chapter on 'From Big Brother to the Electronic Panopticon' dealing with the novel's applicability to contemporary conditions. Lyon asserted, however, that the novel was outdated technologically and that the Panopticon was now the major alternative model to Big Brother. The chapter title, with its emphasis on the *Electronic* Panopticon, spoke to the criticism that Foucault, a generation younger than Orwell, who had therefore grown up during the rise of computer culture (whereas Orwell had died in 1950) failed to consider the technological aspects of surveillance that derived from rapidly-developing technology. Lyon goes on to accept that 'limited, but important aspects of [Orwell's] account of a surveillance society still remain relevant today' (1994: 58), noting that in the 1990s 'the majority of surveillance studies is informed by either Orwellian or Foucauldian ideas' (ibid.: 79). The 1990s would see the development of a more systematic academic examination of surveillance, the first signs of a research field that made the monitoring of people and places its focus. But Lyon's use of the phrase 'the majority of surveillance studies' revealed that research in the early 1990s was still relatively piecemeal, so that 'surveillance studies' referred to research projects carried out by a range of individuals and small teams rather than by anything approximating a coherent academic discipline. Critically, *Nineteen Eighty-Four* was a recognized part of the library of sources from which researchers might draw. The reality, though, was that the social science approach quite validly taken by most surveillance researchers privileged the material world over the metaphorical. This comparative neglect of creative texts was understandable given the motivations, research focus and expertise of most surveillance scholars. Orwell's novel might be alluded to, sometimes almost ritualistically in the opening pages of articles and books, but it was less likely to gain sustained and detailed interpretive attention in its own right.

THE ESTABLISHMENT OF SURVEILLANCE STUDIES

If *Private Lives and Public Surveillance* can be treated as the key early text for surveillance studies as an academic field, that field or subfield took a relatively long period to establish itself. Work in the 1980s and 1990s by Lyon, Marx and Gandy quoted in the previous section did much to ask and partly to answer the sorts of questions surveillance scholars would pursue. Lyon's *Surveillance Society: Monitoring Everyday Life* (2001) marked another major intervention on the subject. As the subtitle reflects, Lyon takes an inclusive approach to surveillance in this work, aiming to detail and look objectively at the positive and negative aspects of monitoring. He argues that the tracking and transmission of information allow for many of the disembodied transactions that convey innumerable benefits upon those under scrutiny: social security and credit cards, and forms of identification that allow us access to places, goods and services. Some of the most enabling and attractive features of contemporary life, Lyon declares, are dependent upon forms of surveillance that are neither intrusive nor restrictive. For this reason, he argues against what he takes to be the reductive negativity of dystopian accounts of surveillance, the primary example being *Nineteen Eighty-Four*. Lyon contends that such negative accounts fail to depict the positive side of surveillance, promote a general pessimism, and fail to offer readers any alternative scenario. I subsequently argued against this reading of *Nineteen Eighty-Four* and dystopias as a genre (Marks 2005), but for the purposes of this chapter my argument in itself is less pertinent than the journal in which it appeared: *Surveillance & Society*. New academic fields are rare enough, one sign of intellectual critical mass having been reached being the setting up of a substantial, peer-reviewed scholarly publication. *Surveillance & Society* was such a journal, established in 2002, a year after Lyon's key text, *Surveillance Society*. Lyon was one of the founding editors, along with David Murakami Wood, Kirstie Ball, Clive Norris and Stephen Graham (all of whom would make significant contributions to the development of surveillance studies). In the journal's first editorial Lyon wrote of already existing initiatives in the field. He also proposed the need to:

> … provide new means of networking between some of the key players, in different countries and contexts. The new online journal and resource web site, *Surveillance-and-Society* (sic), is the result. This first issue editorial demonstrates the need for surveillance studies, and comments on some of its dimensions, disciplinary frameworks, and intended audiences and participants (Lyon 2002: 1–2).

Surveillance scholars could find a home and those with similar interests on the site, but Lyon's understanding that surveillance studies was more needed than fully evolved exposés the tentative probing scholars were still making in the area at the start of the twenty-first century. Amidst the usual ground clearing, Lyon also makes initial connections across disciplines, acknowledging the significance of 'computing and information science,' as well as law 'for understanding legal responses' and 'social psychology and anthropology, for exploring the ways in which surveillance is experienced.' He extends the welcoming scholarly hand even further, noting the relevance of 'consumer studies, social movements studies, globalization studies, labor studies, media studies and so on. Of the last, it is worth noting that novels, such as Margaret Atwood's *The Handmaid's Tale* or films, such as *Gattaca* [a futuristic, sci-fi thriller directed by Andrew Niccol, of 1997], offer important insights into surveillance' (ibid.: 5). The first editorial of any new journal is often very much a manifesto, and while aiming to be as inclusive as possible, Lyon also attempted to launch surveillance studies into new territory. To that end, he states that:

> Models and paradigms for surveillance are useful for some periods but not for others. Whatever one may learn from Jeremy Bentham's Panopticon or George Orwell's totalitarian telescreen technologies, it is not clear that these are entirely helpful ways of understanding surveillance today. The kinds of processes we now confront have more in common with the lawn weed 'Creeping Charlie' with its star-shaped shoots or with the Google web search engine—though these lack the cachet of the 'inspection tower' or 'nineteen-eighty-four' (sic) (ibid.: 4).

Despite this dismissal, two of the first four articles in the new journal mentioned Orwell and Big Brother, even if in passing, with Nick Taylor noting in 'State Surveillance and the Right to Privacy' that:

> Throughout the history of policing in Britain, the response to social disorder and rising crime rates has been to adopt the most modern equipment and techniques available. Over the past thirty years in particular, considerable advances in technology have dramatically increased the powers of the state to carry out surveillance upon its citizens. This inevitably brings with it the dystopic vision of an Orwellian society (Taylor 2002: 66).

It is worth recalling that the advances in technology Taylor was thinking of in 2002, including computers and various forms of scanners, were neither invented nor even conceived of when Orwell died. His novel continues to transcend its historical and technological moment, to be applicable to circumstances substantially different from the world it depicts.

That circumstances might change quickly and dramatically was evident to Lyon in the opening *Surveillance & Society* editorial, where he notes the unhappy coincidence between the emergence of surveillance studies and what he could not then know, but what would in time become, one of the most momentous and consequential triggers for a new surveillance environment—the events of 11 September 2001. 'Suddenly,' Lyon writes:

> ... the steady increase in surveillance—and in surveillance studies—received a boost from a world event. September 11 prompted widespread international concern for security in the

face of global terrorism, seen terrifyingly in the suicide plane attack on the World Trade Center in New York, and the damage inflicted on the Pentagon. Already existing surveillance was reinforced at crucial points, with the promise of more to come. Many countries rapidly passed laws permitting unprecedented levels of policing and intelligence surveillance, which in turn draws upon other sources such as consumer records (Lyon 2002: 1).

We live in that world of 'more to come' that Lyon could only guess at in 2002, with the Patriot Act (and its assault on civil rights) in the United States just brought in, and events from the invasion of Iraq (2003) to the deployment of drones, the revelations by Edward Snowden, the NSA contractor, about global—and highly intrusive—surveillance, and the rise of ISIS/Islamic State in the Middle East, and innumerable others, impossible to predict. Not all of these surveillance-enhancing developments were directly the result of 11 September, but undoubtedly they and many other changes to national and global landscapes were accelerated by the horrendous acts on that day. By a sad irony, those acts would also revive elements of *Nineteen Eighty-Four* and Big Brother for both the public and for surveillance scholars.

THE 11 SEPTEMBER EFFECT

One of the signal changes surveillance studies noted about modern monitoring was not just how ubiquitous it had become, encoded in the subtitle of Lyon's *Surveillance Society: Monitoring Everyday Life*, but also how benign and beneficial it had become. Surveillance in the late twentieth century had become commonplace and necessary to the smooth running of advanced capitalism. Unimaginable quantities of personal information were encoded, transmitted, accessed and assessed instantly via computers potentially from anywhere on the planet at any time of day or night. These disembodied actions and transactions enabled us to buy, to travel, to vote, in many senses to *be* modern citizens. Monitoring was now not just carried out by the state, which in any case presented itself in the late-twentieth century as protecting rather than interfering, but also by major and minor corporations, who used information supplied by us to tailor their activities to our needs and desires. That they might make a larger profit as a result of this scrutiny was more happy consequence than sinister. To some degree, these attitudes still prevail with many citizens, and they are certainly encouraged by governments and businesses. But 11 September brought the darker side of state surveillance back before the public eye.

Paradoxically, 11 September was one of the most consequential surveillance failures in modern history, comparable to the Japanese attack on Pearl Harbor in December 1941. Subsequent inquiries disclosed that information about the attackers and their plans was available and that certain individuals or agencies had alerted those higher up about the dangers. The problem, though, was not an absence of monitored information but a surfeit, coupled with the need not simply to respond to terrorist acts, but to prevent them. The complexities of this surveillance maelstrom are beyond the scope of this chapter, but one effect of the events themselves and the government responses to them, was a massive increase, if not overreach, in the scope and intensity of state-based surveillance. In the effort to stop a recurrence of 11 September or its equivalent, governments in many ostensibly liberal nations brought in extremely tough new laws and procedures that entailed unprecedented levels of surveillance. In nations used to overtly oppressive state control, such changes might been accepted with a cynical shrug of the shoulders, but in many Western democracies the abrupt and forceful imposition of state power and state intrusion created various levels of discussion and dissent. Once again, it is beyond the scope of this chapter to describe, let alone analyze the sweep and impact of this dissent, but one general consequence of these government efforts was that they might be linked to Big Brother. Not all citizens made this connection, of course, many taking comfort in the increased security they were promised, but a quotation from Benjamin Franklin, one of the 'founding fathers' of the United States (1706–1790), that 'those who give up *essential* Liberty, to purchase a little *temporary* Safety, deserve neither Liberty nor Safety' (Franklin 1963: 242; emphasis in the original) was regularly revived even as the war of terror gained momentum.

As suspicions of state motives for increased surveillance mounted, another revived quotation was that from the opening of *Nineteen Eighty-Four* cited at the start of this chapter, about having every movement scrutinized. It appeared in Maureen Webb's *Illusions of Security: Global Surveillance and Democracy in the Post-9/11 World* (2007). As we have seen others do in this chapter, Webb uses the iconic power of Orwell's words to consider something *Nineteen Eighty-Four* itself does not depict. Orwell here is describing the situation of living in the gaze of the telescreen, not imagining a world in which electronic communications, let alone financial transactions, might be scrutinized by the NSA. She later admits that the methods that Orwell describes are 'quaint in that they require human beings to spy on each other using auditory or visual devices' (ibid.: 147–148). She immediately excuses this quaintness by changing tack slightly but significantly:

> In the Orwellian society of the twenty-first century, we will be watched and assessed by computers. And the assessment will be based, not on our actual observed involvement in illegal, criminal, or even suspicious activity, but on the probability that we might be engaged in such activity (ibid.: 148).

Switching from the quaint scenario Orwell actually wrote to the technologically advanced society Webb accepts as inevitable and 'Orwellian,' she reconfigures *Nineteen Eighty-Four* for a 'post-9/11 world,' giving it a currency undiminished by seven decades.

David Lyon, despite his 2001 critique of *Nineteen Eighty-Four*'s dystopian negativity in *Surveillance Society*, was willing to rehabilitate Big Brother somewhat two years later in *Surveillance After September 11* (2003). There he concedes that

> Whatever sociologists have to say, it would be foolish to ignore the one name that is always invoked in surveillance studies: George Orwell. His novel, *Nineteen Eighty-Four*, and its monstrous anti-hero, Big Brother, have become bywords within the surveillance genre. And with good reason (Lyon 2003: 29).

Lyon understands that in the changed scenario post-11 September Orwell still has something to say, and that 'it would be naïve to imagine that Big Brother scenarios are a thing of the past' (ibid.: 33). He continues: 'Draconian measures are appearing worldwide as country after country enacts laws and practices purporting to counteract "terrorism"' (ibid.: 34). Lyon, like Webb, uses the adjective 'Orwellian' to explain the new situation created by the attacks on New York and the Pentagon, arguing: 'The Orwellian dimensions of post-9/11 laws, directives and decisions are deepest when one examines the secrecy surrounding these shifts' (ibid.: 55). And he updates Orwell's warning:

> … about a centralized totalitarian surveillance state, in which Big Brother held sway through a regime of fear and uncertainty. This now becomes possible through system integration, not necessarily centralization (ibid.: 95).

Orwell might not have created a way of assessing contemporary surveillance, Lyon intimates, but he still points the way.

THE SURVEILLANCE STUDIES CASE AGAINST ORWELL

Lyon's aside about 'whatever sociologists have to say' in the comment above reveals that while many surveillance theorists have adopted and adapted elements from *Nineteen Eighty-Four*, many more see the novel as a distraction from the reality of surveillance in the twentieth- and twenty-first centuries, an irrelevance given the vastly different surveillance society we inhabit. The complete absence, for example, of computers in Orwell's vision, perhaps the key surveillance technology of the last half-century, renders his speculation—for all its vividness and cultural power—redundant in a world of metadata and social media, microchips and iris scanners. Orwell cannot be blamed for not imagining computers and other innovations that were barely conceived of when he wrote the novel, but for many surveillance scholars these crucial technological deficiencies stop the novel from contributing anything meaningful to contemporary research.

Rather than rehearse the whole surveillance studies case against *Nineteen Eighty-Four*, I return to some of the examples lightly sketched in at the start of this chapter. Benjamin Goold's 2004 comment that 'looking back over the last fifty years it is difficult to overestimate the impact of Orwell's novel ... on popular and academic imaginations,' comes with the counsel for his fellow surveillance scholars against paying too much attention to imagined surveillance societies. Goold worries that the 'theoretical literature of social control will become increasingly divorced from reality' (Goold 2004: 212). Goold's is more methodological advice than total dismissal, but no less insistent or plausible for that. Yet he and his co-editor Daniel Neyland include Mike Nellis's chapter 'Since *Nineteen Eighty-Four*: Representations of surveillance in literary fiction' (Nellis 2009: 178–204) in the collection *New Directions in Surveillance and Privacy*. There they ask:

> ... a brace of questions: we have the opportunity to ask whether writing about the futures of surveillance can be seen as one of the sets of resources through which readers of texts orient their contemplation of surveillance activities. Through fiction can we see the ways in which surveillance concepts are becoming part of the world? (Goold and Neyland 2009: xxiv).

Goold and Neyland seem likely to answer 'yes' to their own questions, and Nellis suggests *Nineteen Eighty-Four* as the starting point for modern literary representations of surveillance.

John Gilliom and Torin Monahan did declare Big Brother 'probably the most famous bogeyman and symbol of a surveillance society,' but they also argued strongly: 'We believe that terms like *Big Brother* and *privacy* are out-of-date and no longer help to describe the dynamic new forms of technology, power and politics' (op. cit.: 7). Gilliom and Monahan retreat for this total dismissal later in the book, accepting that concepts such as Big Brother and privacy:

> ... are meaningful parts of our cultural system that can help us visualize and discuss some aspects of the surveillance society. Orwell's Big Brother reminds us of the danger of totalizing state power and the often subtle interplay of tyranny and 'concern' in surveillance regimes (ibid.: 128).

Their qualified acceptance of *Nineteen Eighty-Four* confirms that while surveillance studies retains a limited place for particular features of Orwell's novel, and somewhat grudgingly recognizes its undeniable and to date unyielding hold on public and media discourse, the rapidly expanding academic field has a range of concerns and approaches that in no way require reflection on or deference to it.

CONCLUSION

For all that, *Nineteen Eighty-Four* still commands the attention of surveillance scholars. David Lyon, in his authoritative *Surveillance Studies: An Overview* (2007), presses the case that most people:

… know about surveillance because we have read about it in a classic novel such as *Nineteen Eighty-Four* (1949) or that we have seen a film depicting surveillance such as *Enemy of the State* (1998). Such movies and novels help us to get our bearings on what surveillance is all about and—because they are usually negative, dystopian—give us a sense of the kind of world we wish to avoid (Lyon 2007: 139).

By including himself in the 'we' who read and come to get 'our bearings,' Lyon gestures to the interlinking of public and academic interests and concerns to which *Nineteen Eighty-Four* still speaks; academics are people, too. He and Zygmunt Bauman cast their net slightly wider in *Liquid Surveillance*, arguing that 'the utopian and dystopian muses still offer scope for imaginative critiques' (Bauman and Lyon 2013: 115), foregrounding *Nineteen Eighty-Four* and Aldous Huxley's *Brave New World* (1932) amongst the key texts. We might see the resilience and applicability of creative texts recognized in Torin Monahan's 2011 article, 'Surveillance as Cultural Practice,' where Monahan writes of an emerging cultural studies of surveillance, one that addresses and creatively interprets literature and films which imagine surveillance in provocative and illuminating ways. The primary texts dealt with in the texts mentioned in the introduction to this chapter, Rosen's and Santesso's *The Watchman in Pieces: Surveillance, Literature and Liberal Personhood* and Lefait's in *Surveillance on Screen*, are instructive examples of this new recognition that creative texts are valuable guides to cultural attitudes to surveillance. Both deal with *Nineteen Eighty-Four* within an array of literary or cinematic works, respectively. My own *Imagining Surveillance* focuses on the longstanding contribution of utopian texts to the depiction and assessment of surveillance from Thomas More's *Utopia* (1516) through to Spike Jonze's movie *Her* (2013). Because of its cultural centrality to the understanding of modern surveillance, *Nineteen Eighty-Four* gets one of the seven chapters in the book. Nonetheless, *Imagining Surveillance* deals with many other pieces of literature and film, situating Orwell's classic within nearly five centuries of utopian speculation. These early instances of Monahan's cultural studies of surveillance promise to seed new and inventive territory for surveillance studies. Given the history of the field over the last four decades, one inaugurated by *Private Lives and Public Surveillance* and its opening question: 'Why do we find the world of *1984* so harrowing?', the specter of Big Brother will not easily go away.

REFERENCES

Atwood, Margaret (1985) *The Handmaid's Tale*, Toronto: McClelland and Stewart.

Bauman, Zygmunt, and Lyon, David (2013) *Liquid Surveillance: A Conversation*, Cambridge: Polity.

Bentham, Jeremy (1995) *Jeremy Bentham: The Panopticon Writings*, edited and introduced by Bozovic, Miran, London: Verso.

Brannigan, John (2002) *Orwell to the Present: English Literature 1945–2000*, London: Palgrave Macmillan.

Chesterman, Simon (2011) *One Nation Under Surveillance: A New Social Contract to Defend Freedom Without Sacrificing Liberty*, Oxford: Oxford University Press.

Cohen, Stanley (1985) *Visions of Social Control*, Cambridge: Polity Press.

Davies, Simon (1996) *Big Brother: Britain's Web of Surveillance and the New Technological Order*, London: Pan Books.

Foucault, Michel (1975) *Discipline and Punish: The Birth of the Prison*, New York: Vintage Books.

Franklin, Benjamin (1963) *The Papers of Benjamin Franklin, Volume 6*, edited by Labaree, Leonard W., New Haven, CT: Yale University Press.

Gandy, Oscar (1993) *The Panoptic Sort: A Political Economy of Personal Information*, Boulder: Westview Press.

Gilliom, John and Monahan, Torin (2013) *SuperVision: An Introduction to the Surveillance Society*, Chicago: Chicago University Press.

Goold, Benjamin J. (2004) *CCTV Policing: Public Surveillance and Police Practice in Britain*, Oxford: Oxford University Press.

Goold, Benjamin J. and Neyland, Daniel (2009) *New Directions in Surveillance and Privacy*, Portland, Oregon: Willan Publishing.

Lefait, Sébastien (2013) *Surveillance on Screen: Monitoring Contemporary Films and Television*, Lanham: Scarecrow Press.

Levin, Thomas (ed.) (2002) *CTRL [Space]: Rhetorics of Surveillance from Bentham to Orwell*, Cambridge, Massachusetts: MIT Press.

Lyon, David (1994) *The Electronic Eye: The Rise of Surveillance Society*, Cambridge: Polity.

Lyon, David (2001a) *Surveillance Society: Monitoring Everyday Life*, Buckingham: Open University Press.

Lyon, David (2001b) Editorial. Surveillance Studies: Understanding visibility, mobility and the phenetic fix, *Surveillance & Society*, Vol. 1, No. 1, pp. 1–7.

Lyon, David (2003) *Surveillance after September 11*, Cambridge: Polity.

Marder, Michael, and Vieira, Patrícia (eds) (2012) *Existential Utopia: New Perspectives on Utopian Thought*, New York: Continuum.

Marks, Peter, (2005) Imagining Surveillance: Utopian Visions and Surveillance Studies, *Surveillance and Society*, Vol. 3, Nos. 2/3, pp. 222–39.

Marks, Peter (2015) *Imagining Surveillance: Eutopian and Dystopian Literature and Film*, Edinburgh: Edinburgh University Press.

Marx, Gary T. (1988) *Undercover: Police Surveillance in America*, Oakland: University of California Press.

Marx, Gary T. (2012) Preface: 'Your papers please': Personal and professional encounters with surveillance, *Routledge Handbook of Surveillance Studies* (ed.) Ball, K. et al., Abingdon: Routledge pp. xx–xxxi.

McGrath, John (2004) *Loving Big Brother: Performance, Privacy and Surveillance Space*, Abingdon: Routledge.

Monahan, Torin (2011) Surveillance as cultural practice, *The Sociological Quarterly*, Vol. 52, No. 4, pp. 495–508.

Nellis, Mike (2009) Since *Nineteen Eighty-Four*: Representations of surveillance in literary fiction, Goold, Benjamin J. and Neyland, Daniel (eds) (2009) *New Directions in Surveillance and Privacy*, Portland, Oregon: Willan Publishing pp. 178–203.

Nelson, Lisa (2010) *America Identified: Biometric Technology and Society*, London: MIT Press.

New Yorker (2013) So are we living in 1984?, 11 June. Available online at http://www.newyorker.com/books/page-turner/so-are-we-living-in-1984, accessed on 10 March 2015.

Orwell, George (1997) *The Complete Works of George Orwell, Volume 9: Nineteen Eighty-Four*, edited by Davison, Peter, London: Secker and Warburg.

Orwell, George (1998) *The Complete Works of George Orwell, Volume 20: Our Job Is To Make Life Worth Living*, edited by Davison, Peter, London: Secker and Warburg.

Rodden, John (1989) *The Politics of Literary Reputation: The Making and Claiming of 'St. George' Orwell*, Oxford University Press: Oxford.

Rosen, David, and Santesso, Aaron (2013) *The Watchman in Pieces: Surveillance, Literature, and Liberal Personhood*, New Haven: Yale University Press.

Rule, James B. (1973) *Private Lives and Public Surveillance*, London: Allen Lane.

Taylor, Nick (2002) State surveillance and the right to privacy, *Surveillance & Society*, Vol. 1, No. 1, pp. 66–85.

Webb, Maureen (2007) *Illusions of Security: Global Surveillance and Democracy in the Post-9/11 World*, San Francisco: City Lights Books.

Žižek, Slavoj (2002) Big Brother, or the triumph of the gaze over the eye, Levin, Thomas (ed.) (2002) *CTRL [Space]: Rhetorics of Surveillance from Bentham to Orwell*, Cambridge, Massachusetts: MIT Press pp. 224–227.

CHAPTER TWO

Nineteen Eighty-Four
IN 2014

Power, Militarism and Surveillance in Western Democracies

FLORIAN ZOLLMANN

> Totalitarianism, if not fought against, could triumph anywhere.
> —GEORGE ORWELL, CITED IN SLATER 2003: 240

In the dystopian novel *Nineteen Eighty-Four* (1949), George Orwell depicted the totalitarian police state Oceana. Orwell went into great detail outlining the features of a Big Brother regime that exercised control over the populace via surveillance, propaganda, cognitive manipulation, censorship, and coercion. Orwell also envisioned how authorities might use a permanent state of war to facilitate patriotism and justify an oppressive war economy in a stratified society ruled by a minority—'The Party.'

According to mainstream academic and popular accounts of *Nineteen Eighty-Four*, the novel can be regarded as a warning against Stalinism and other totalitarian forms of 'socialism.' In contrast, I will argue in this chapter that *Nineteen Eighty-Four* can equally be read as a prophecy for the excesses of what might be termed 'liberal democracy' or 'real existing capitalism.' Indeed, I will demonstrate that contemporary Western democracies, such as the USA or Great Britain, have been afflicted by totalitarian features which bear resemblance to those envisioned by Orwell in *Nineteen Eighty-Four*.

The chapter proceeds in several parts: In the first, introductory section, I will discuss how *Nineteen Eighty-Four* has been understood in academic and popular culture. Drawing on critical literature and statements by Orwell himself, I will demonstrate that contrary to orthodox readings, the novel can be understood as a warning against any totalitarian system—independent of its political color. In the second part, I will highlight areas in which contemporary Western democracies mirror facets of the world described in *Nineteen Eighty-Four*. The essay utilizes a range of secondary source material.

INTRODUCTION: CHALLENGING ORTHODOX INTERPRETATIONS OF *NINETEEN EIGHTY-FOUR*

In orthodox Western intellectual culture, *Nineteen Eighty-Four* has been widely understood as a warning against the dangers of Stalinism and other features of 'real existing socialisms.' For instance, British writer David Aaronovitch (2013) argues that 'when *Nineteen Eighty-Four* was being conceptualised and then written, Orwell's overwhelming preoccupation was to warn against Stalinism and its onward march.' John Newsinger (2007: 124) also suggests that 'Stalinism was Orwell's most important concern from 1936 onwards ...' In fact, *Nineteen Eighty-Four* makes implicit references to features of Stalinist Russia. Having 'Communist' bureaucrats in mind, Polish dissident Czeslaw Milosz reflected in his 1953 classic *Captive Mind*:

> Those who know Orwell only by hearsay are amazed that a writer who never lived in Russia should have understood the functioning of the unusually constructed machine of which they are themselves a part (cited in Crick 2007: 148).

Milosz's remarks reflect, of course, on Orwell's genius as a political novelist. Because of its realism, it could be argued, *Nineteen Eighty-Four* has been used as an example to illustrate the dangers of Stalinism and other totalitarian systems based on political centralism. Yet significantly, *Nineteen Eighty-Four* does also allow for comparisons with totalitarianisms that might emerge in Western-style democracies. However, such analogies have been marginalized because the novel has been largely instrumentalized as a propaganda weapon by proponents of a 'free-enterprise' economic model. In this particular context, *Nineteen Eighty-Four* has been used to caution against societal developments that might be associated with 'socialism' but have nothing in common with Stalinism. This is conducted with the aim of strengthening corporate power at the expense of social democracy. As the late propaganda scholar Alex Carey (1995: 139) pointed out:

> Whatever Orwell's intentions, his work has been exploited so as to misdirect and confuse the public into looking in the wrong places for the 'brainwashing' instinctively felt by many ... in the name of free enterprise and anti-communism, a great number of [orthodox] social scientists, sponsored by corporations, are willingly engaged in advancing Orwell's thesis by way of a corporate-managed democracy.

In fact, Orwell did not write *Nineteen Eighty-Four* as a mere critique of 'socialist' developments. This was stated in a letter to Francis A. Henson of the United Automobile Workers, in 1949, seven months before his premature death:

> My recent novel is NOT intended as an attack on Socialism ... The scene of the book is laid in Britain in order to emphasize that the English-speaking races are not innately better than anyone else and that totalitarianism, *if not fought against*, could triumph anywhere (cited in Slater 2003: 240, emphasis in the original).

While being strongly opposed to Stalinism, Orwell was a democratic socialist and critical observer of societal developments in liberal Western democracies (see Mynick 2010). However, in the Cold War era when *Nineteen Eighty-Four* was published and also during later periods, the complexity of Orwell's political worldview tended to be ignored (see ibid.). Consequently, *Nineteen Eighty-Four* has been conflated with a critique of 'socialism.'

The novel can, of course, be understood as a warning against Stalinism and other forms of politically centralist totalitarianism. However, Orwell was critical of totalitarian tendencies in the Eastern *as well as* Western hemisphere. As Orwell had stated in the letter to Henson cited above: if a society such as the one described in *Nineteen Eighty-Four* was ever to be realized it could be anywhere. Orwell was not only concerned about Stalinism. Orwell also regarded the socio-political arrangements at the beginning of the Cold War as problematic. He rejected militarism as a policy tool as well as nuclear armament and was alarmed about intellectuals who supported the *status quo*. This became apparent when Orwell responded to early reviews published in major US magazines interpreting *Nineteen Eighty-Four* as 'anti-socialist' (Crick 2007: 153–154). In a written rectification, Orwell reflected on the prophetic potential of *Nineteen Eighty-Four*:

> I think that, allowing for the book being after all a parody, something like *Nineteen Eighty-Four could* happen. This is the direction in which the world is going at the present time, and the trend lies deep in the political, social and economic foundations of the contemporary world situation. Specifically the danger lies in the structure imposed on socialist and on Liberal capitalist communities by the necessity to prepare for total war with the USSR and the new weapons of which, of course, the atomic bomb is the most powerful and the most publicised. But danger lies also in the acceptance of a totalitarian outlook by intellectuals of all colours. The moral to be drawn from this dangerous nightmare situation is a simple one: *Don't let it happen. It depends on you* (cited in Crick 2007: 154, emphasis in the original).

This statement appears to further demonstrate that if *Nineteen Eighty-Four* was laid out as a prophecy, then Orwell had also Western democracies in mind as a breeding ground for totalitarianism. Orwell highlighted how 'the danger lies in the structure imposed on socialist and on Liberal capitalist communities by the necessity to prepare for total war with the USSR' (Orwell, cited in ibid.). While it is not clear to what particular structure Orwell referred to, it seems plausible to assume that he made a connection between deep political, social and economic forces on the one hand and societies' drive towards a state of war on the other. Accordingly, American/Canadian scholar Henry A. Giroux (2014) shed light on how Orwell's understanding of totalitarianism could be interpreted with a view on Western states:

> Central to George Orwell's nightmarish vision of a totalitarian society was a government so powerful that it not only dominated all of the major institutions in a society, but it also was quite adept at making invisible its inner workings of power. This is what some [commentators such as Peter Dale Scott (1993)] have called a shadow government, deep state, dual state or corporate state. In the deep state, politics becomes the domain of the ultra-wealthy, the powerful few who run powerful financial services, big corporations and the imperious elite of the defense industries and other components of the military-industrial complex.

Giroux regards the amalgam of corporate, financial, state and military power as the *structural* source of totalitarianism and suggests that such a view is in accord with Orwell's outlook. Richard Mynick (2010) provides a similar argument when writing that *Nineteen Eighty-Four*:

> ... considers the psycho-social machinery of unaccountable state power *in general*—regardless whether it originates from a ruling bureaucracy or from finance capital. It explores the general problem of maintaining social stability in a highly unequal society, which can be done only through some combination of repression, and controlling the population's consciousness (emphasis in the original).

Mynick adds the dimensions of mind control and repression as important elements by which the powerful exercise control over their host populations in highly unequal societies.

Considering these unorthodox interpretations of Orwell's views *vis-à-vis* totalitarianism, *Nineteen Eighty-Four* now appears to relate in particular to the societies we are currently living in. Accordingly, the following set of unorthodox themes[1] to be further explored in the light of Western democracies is fleshed out:

1) Deep structures: How wealth, inequality and corporate power undermine democracy.
2) Militarism: The state-corporate-military complex as the root cause of permanent war.
3) Coercion: Surveillance as a system of control.

DEEP STRUCTURES: HOW WEALTH, INEQUALITY AND CORPORATE POWER UNDERMINE DEMOCRACY

> But always ... there will be the intoxication of power, constantly increasing and constantly growing subtler.
>
> —GEORGE ORWELL, *NINETEEN EIGHTY-FOUR*

The totalitarian societal structure of Oceana as described in *Nineteen Eighty-Four* seems to be set in opposition to how contemporary liberal democracies are assumed to operate. In fact, Western-style democracy was constituted as a result of legal freedoms and formally operates on the basis of self-governing regulatory mechanisms. How Western democracies are run is supposed to be decided in accord with democratic principles and the will of the populace (see, for example, Alexander 1981).

More specifically, because contemporary democracies constitute representative systems, the governing sector is run by elected officials. Political decisions are formed by representatives during parliamentary debates and implemented by an executive body. Political officials are assumed to act in accord with the policy preferences of their constituency as expressed in opinion polls and via forms of direct action such as voting, demonstrating or lobbying. Citizens are supposed to be sufficiently informed by the mass media in order to evaluate the policies conducted on their behalf and to weigh their possible political choices—a process which can be described as public deliberation (see Page 1996). In a representative democracy, no societal group is assumed to hold unaccountable power over any other. How could there be any similarity between Western democracy and the society envisioned in *Nineteen Eighty-Four*?

The American sociologist William Domhoff (2012) has made a simple but succinct observation: 'Those who have the money—or more specifically, who own income-producing land and businesses—have the power.' According to this perspective, which is supported by a range of scholars, democracy has been undermined by wealth and power (see e.g., Balanyá et al. 2003; Dinan and Miller 2007; Domhoff 2002; Ferguson 1995; Kolko 1976; Miller and Dinan 2008). Wealth, it is argued, increases the ability to influence positively decision-making processes in democracies. For ordinary people who lack the disposal of monetary resources it is, on the other hand, difficult to influence politics. To understand better how wealth relates to power, it is important to discuss the distribution of monetary wealth in contemporary democracies.

As a matter of fact, wealth distribution has been highly uneven in Western democracies, and we can clearly identify different classes of people in relation to their monetary prosperity (see Domhoff 2013). If we look at individual countries, the following picture emerges: In the UK, the richest 10 per cent of the population have 31 per cent of all income. The poorest 20 per cent of the population have only 4 per cent of all income (see the Poverty Site 2015). Moreover, five UK families are wealthier than the bottom 20 per cent of the population combined (see Elgot 2014). Studies suggest that the 26,000 top earners in the UK receive more than £21,500 a month after tax whereas 6.7 million workers earn less than £800 a month (Dugan 2013). Oxfam warns that 20 per cent of the British population, 13 million people in total, currently live below the official poverty line

(Oxfam 2015b). In the USA, the top 1 per cent of households owned 35.4 per cent of all privately owned wealth in 2010. The next 19 per cent, the professional-managerial classes, owned 53.5 per cent, whereas the remaining 80 per cent, the working class, only owned 11 per cent of all household wealth (for the figures see Domhoff 2013). US Census Bureau data for 2013 suggest that in the USA, 45 million people lived at or below the poverty line, including 14.7 million children (Cook 2014).

A similar pattern emerges on a trans-Atlantic level: in major European and North-American democracies, the top 10 per cent of the population held between 42–71 per cent of all wealth in 2010 (see Domhoff 2013). A study published by Oxfam (2014a) found that if the current global trend of inequality persisted, then 'the combined wealth of the richest 1 per cent will overtake that of the other 99 per cent of people next year.' It continued: 'The richest 1 per cent have seen their share of global wealth increase from 44 per cent in 2009 to 48 per cent in 2014 and at this rate will be more than 50 per cent in 2016.'

Wealth is not only stratified on an individual/household level but also if economic entities are considered. Tracey Keys and Thomas W. Malnight (2012) document that corporations can constitute larger entities than entire economies. In fact, the authors argue that in 2009, of the world's 100 largest economic entities, 44 were corporations. The overall revenue of these corporations was US$6.4 trillion, which was about 11 per cent of global GDP (ibid.: 2). 'These combined revenues are larger than the combined economies of 155 countries, that is, all the countries in the world except the largest 40 in terms of GDP' (ibid.).

Incidentally, corporations are largely controlled by the wealthy as indicated by concentrations in stock ownership. For instance, in the USA, the top 20 per cent of the population in terms of wealth owned 91.6 per cent of all corporate stock ownership in 2010 whereas the bottom 80 per cent only owned 8.4 per cent of corporate stock (see Domhoff 2013).

Wealth and corporate stock ownership are crucial to exercise influence on governance via party donations, lobbying, policy planning networks, public relations, political advertisements and the formation of party programs. The political scientist Thomas Ferguson (1995: 36) thus argues that while political parties in liberal democracies need small amounts of money from many people 'most of their major endorsements, money, and media attention typically come as direct or indirect results of their ability to attract heavyweight investors.' This has the result that major political parties tend to represent the interests of the wealthy. As Ferguson (1995: 28) further points out:

> If it pays some other bloc of major investors to advertise and mobilise, these appeals can be vigorously contested, but … on all issues affecting the vital interests that major investors have in common, no party competition will take place … and if all major investors happen

to share an interest in ignoring issues vital to the electorate, such as social welfare, hours of work, or collective bargaining, so much the worse for the electorate.

A similar process is at work on the level of international governance. Noam Chomsky (2010) argues that heavyweight investors constitute a 'virtual senate' that is able to influence policy-making via measures such as 'capital flight, attacks on currency and other means.' Hence, Chomsky further stresses: 'In the contemporary world of state-capitalist nations, loss of sovereignty can lead to a diminution of democracy, and a decline in the ability of states to conduct social and economic policy on their own terms' (ibid.). As a general consequence, vital issues such as the distribution of wealth, the allocation of societal resources, or the foreign policy agenda are decided in accord with the overlapping interests of wealth, corporations and finance capital. Indeed, the extreme inequalities outlined above are maintained because the wealthy set the policy agenda.

It should be further noted that these are not mere theoretical positions. Polls in the UK demonstrate that public opinion on many domestic policy issues is 'far to the left of the mainstream pro-corporate parties' (Miller and Dinan 2010: 3). Similarly, Benjamin I. Page (1996: 118–119) has documented how US citizens significantly disagree with political officials, foreign policy elites and experts on a 'wide range of issues' including the use of force, economic/military aid, arms sales and trade agreements. Such 'elite-mass gaps' (ibid.: 118) have major implications for democracy because the preferences of large societal segments are not translated into policy if they are in disharmony with business elite interests. This is further evidenced in a recent empirical study by Martin Gilens and Benjamin I. Page who assessed how different societal groups in the USA saw their political preferences enacted (see BBC News 2014). The scholars concluded their study as follows:

> When a majority of citizens disagrees with economic elites and/or with organised interests, they generally lose. Moreover, because of the strong status quo bias built into the US political system, even when fairly large majorities of Americans favour policy change, they generally do not get it (ibid.).

While the USA formally comprises democratic institutions such as elections as well as freedom of speech and association, Gilens and Page's study suggests that 'America's claims to being a democratic society are seriously threatened' (ibid.).

In short, the kind of societies envisioned in *Nineteen Eighty-Four* appear to have come into being. Western democracies are afflicted by extreme wealth inequalities and poverty. Governance is conducted in agreement with the interests of the corporate-business elites and wealthy view. Power is subtly exercised by a deep state which represents the overarching interests of the business community—'The Party.'

MILITARISM: THE STATE-CORPORATE-MILITARY COMPLEX AS THE ROOT CAUSE OF PERMANENT WAR

WAR IS PEACE ...

—GEORGE ORWELL, *NINETEEN EIGHTY-FOUR*

The deep state outlined above has a military component. Public subsidies, disguised as 'defense' spending, have been crucial for the business sector.[2] Major technological inventions including airplanes, computers, or radars rest on public expenses. To provide just one example: the development of the internet goes back to state-military initiatives such as the founding of the Defense Advanced Research Projects Agency (DARPA) in 1958 as well as the funding and establishment of basic research to create computers with dialogue capabilities. According to Sascha Meinrath (New American Foundation), federal subsidy of the internet goes 'well into the hundreds of billions [of dollars] range' (cited in McChesney 2013: 101). The same applies to other technological sectors that heavily rely on 'defense' spending. As Nathan Newman writes 'the single overwhelming factor correlating with the rise of technology firms in any region is the level of defense spending' (cited in ibid.: 100)

While some of the technological innovations are important for popular use, the basic functions of subsidies are to uphold the superiority of the US economy and to produce military hardware. The existence of a state-sponsored war economy has, thus, two further implications. Firstly, at the heart of a heavily subsidized capitalist economy is an intersection comprising the state and the business sector—the deep state. To illustrate this further, we have to look back several decades: In his 1961 farewell address, US President Dwight D. Eisenhower warned of the 'military-industrial-complex' and its 'potential for the disastrous rise of misplaced power' that 'exists and will persist' in the form of a 'permanent arms industry of vast proportions' (cited in the *Independent* 2011).

Since the end of World War II, a massive war budget has been institutionalized as indicated by figures on military spending (see McChesney 2013: 159): For example, in 2001, annual US military spending was $312 million (see SIPRI 2011). In 2012, annual military spending had increased to about $1 trillion (see McChesney 2013: 159). The UK spends about £34 billion annually on 'defence' (see Defence Statistics 2013). These enormous sums are used to stimulate the high-tech and arms industries which are closely linked. Hence, Eisenhower's warning that converging interests of corporations, arms manufacturers, war-makers and politicians would disable democracy and lead society in a state of permanent war (see McChesney 2013: 158–159).

And this constitutes the second implication: it is to be expected that if industrial inventions are created under the umbrella of 'defense' spending, then military applicability will be incentivized. Indeed, by their very existence, the military-industrial complex and the vast military budget require the use of military hardware during foreign power projections. This is evidenced by the following data: since 1945, the USA and UK have deployed military forces virtually every year: the USA has used or threatened the use of force about 500 times between 1950 and 1991 (Keeble 1997: 16). The 1982 Falklands War was the 88th deployment of British troops since 1945 (in a total of 51 countries) (ibid.). Since the end of the Cold War, the USA and UK have been involved in major wars with Iraq (1991, 2003–present), the Former Republic of Yugoslavia (1995, 1999), Afghanistan (2001), and Libya (2011) among others.

The late Chalmers Johnson (2004) further highlighted how US military power has been translated through a worldwide web of military bases. In 2001, about 725 American military bases existed outside the United States while an unknown number of bases were unofficially operated or under construction (see Johnson 2004: 4). Johnson (ibid.: 4–5; 23) noted that this landscape resembled a 'military empire' and was a sign of 'militarism, the inescapable companion of imperialism' whereas US 'garrisons send a daily message that the United States prefers to deal with other nations through the use or threat of force rather than negotiations, commerce, or cultural interaction.'

The effects of US and UK militarism are well documented. The US intelligence agency, the CIA, had by 1991 been involved in 3,000 major and 10,000 minor operations, which, according to John Stockwell, were 'all illegal, and all designed to disrupt, destabilize, or modify the activities of other countries' (Stockwell 1991). William Blum highlights how 'the United States has attempted to overthrow more than 50 foreign governments, and to crush more than 30 populist-nationalist movements struggling against intolerable regimes' since the Second World War, thereby killing several million people (2006: 1–2). The most recent example constitutes the Iraq War of 2003, as a result of which a modern secular society has been destroyed with more than 600,000 civilians dead (for a discussion see Zollmann 2012). Moreover, the extremist terrorist group ISIS, which is currently making headlines taking over large swaths of Iraq and Syria, is an outcome of divide-and-rule policies enforced by Western powers on Iraq (see Zollmann 2014).

Throughout the 1970s, US aid has flown to repressive, human rights violating states in Latin America, Europe, Asia, Africa and the Middle East and, in many cases, US aid could be *'positively related to investment climate and inversely related to the maintenance of democratic order and human rights'* (Chomsky and Herman 1979: 44, emphasis in the original; see also Schoultz 1981: 155; 167).[3] Like the USA, Britain has financially supported oppressive regimes with horrendous human rights records in Asia, Africa, South America, Europe and the Middle East (Curtis 2003, 2004). According to Mark Curtis (2004), as a consequence of its military policies and support of allies 'Britain bears significant responsibility for around 10 million deaths since 1945' (ibid.: 2, 310–317).

To this extent, the militarization of the society and economy as envisaged in *Nineteen Eighty-Four* has come into being today. Furthermore, there is an important intellectual component. The state of permanent war has been justified by omission: since the Vietnam War (with the fall of Saigon in April 1975 to the Viet Cong), military action has largely been conducted in secrecy. Intellectual and media culture has remained silent as well (see Chomsky 1989; Keeble 1997; Zollmann 2012). Permanent war has been represented as a state of peace.

On the other hand, the 'quickie' wars in Latin America, the Balkans and the Middle East (as outlined above) as well as the vast apparatus of military spending had been framed with reference to the fight against 'communism.' Since the breakdown of the Soviet Union in 1990, Western military interventions against Islamist terrorists and 'rogue' adversaries have been largely justified on the basis of 'human rights' and 'humanitarianism' or disguised as 'peace keeping' or 'counterinsurgency' operations (see Keeble 1997; Hammond 2011; Zollmann 2012). But as we know today, the Soviet threat was overstated. Western documents reveal how the Soviet Union's supposed threats to launch an offensive war against the West were manufactured to uphold the war economy.[4] Similarly, the threat of Islamist-related terrorism has been manufactured, its root cause—Western foreign occupation of Muslim lands—is largely denied (for the root causes of Islamist-related terrorism see Pape 2006). Data by Europol suggest that between 2006 and 2009, Islamist-related terrorist incidents constituted less than 1 per cent of all terrorist incidents in the European Union (see Miller and Sabir 2012: 87–88).

The threat of communism and Islamist terrorism has been amplified by official fear-mongering—of the kind described in *Nineteen Eighty-Four*. As a consequence, the real aims of Western militarism have been overshadowed. Yet, a reading of the official documentary record strongly suggests that US/UK interventions have been conducted in tandem with the interests of the military-industrial complex and the wider business community which constitutes the deep state—'The Party.'[5]

COERCION: HOW SURVEILLANCE IS USED AS A SYSTEM OF CONTROL

> There was of course no way of knowing whether you were being watched at any given moment. How often, or on what system, the Thought Police plugged in on any individual wire was guesswork … But at any rate they could plug in your wire whenever they wanted to.
>
> —GEORGE ORWELL, *NINETEEN EIGHTY-FOUR*

In June 2013, whistleblower Edward Snowden, former contractor of the American National Security Agency (NSA), leaked classified documents whose partial publication by the press would lead to the so-called NSA scandal. The Snowden revelations exposed mass surveillance programs conducted by the NSA and the British intelligence organization, GCHQ (Government Communications Headquarters). Documents assessed by the *Guardian* indicate that as part of the PRISM program, the NSA has direct access to meta data, search histories, content of emails, file transfers and live chats stored by major digital companies such as Google, Facebook, Apple, Microsoft, or Skype. The revelation of the Tempora program, run by the GCHQ under headlines such as 'Mastering the internet' and 'Global telecoms exploitation,' suggests the agency's ability to tap and store data from the trans-Atlantic fibre-optic highway. The GCHQ potentially accesses international phone calls, emails, Facebook entries, log files/histories and other online information (for an overview see Greenwald 2014; MacAskill et al. 2013; *Guardian* 2013). Eli Pariser consequently argues that 'What was once an anonymous medium where anyone could be anyone ... is now a tool for soliciting and analyzing our personal data' (cited in McChesney 2013: 148). A team of *Guardian* journalists further contextualized the new surveillance system: 'For the 2 billion users of the world wide web, Tempora represents a window on to their everyday lives, sucking up every form of communication' (MacAskill et al. 2013). While the Snowdon files shed some light on the scope of surveillance, the journalists further stress: 'This is all being carried out without any form of public acknowledgement or debate' (ibid.).

The British Prime Minister David Cameron sought to justify surveillance as a policing tool applied to prevent terrorist and other criminal activities with these words: 'The ability to access information about communications and intercept the communications of dangerous individuals is essential to fight the threat from criminals and terrorists targeting the UK' (cited in *Huffington Post* 2014). But as discussed in the previous section, the Islamist terrorist threat has not only been overstated but also arises from Western foreign occupations. This begs the question as to whether surveillance might be applied for other means. For instance, the investigative journalist and NSA specialist James Bamford argues that 'the NSA has turned its surveillance apparatus on the US and its citizens' (cited in McChesney 2013: 161). Similarly, media scholar Christian Fuchs (2012: 43) describes how surveillance might be applied to intimidate the population:

> Surveillance by nation states and corporations aims at controlling the behavior of individuals and groups, i.e., they should be forced to behave or not behave in certain ways because they know that their appearance, movements, location, or ideas are or could be watched by surveillance systems.

According to this rationale, surveillance includes a coercive element that might be used to counter civil rights and society groups that work against the structures and policies of the deep state. This is further suggested by current domestic policies:

the US and UK governments have tightened their grip on home-grown dissidents. The most striking examples constitute the prosecution of lead editor of the whistleblowing site, Julian Assange, as well as the crackdown on other whistleblowers and their supporters. For example, the Obama administration has conducted legal actions against as many as eight people who have leaked or disseminated classified information. Jamie Tarabay (2013), who writes for *Al Jazeera America*, argues that the Obama administration 'has charged more Americans with violating the Espionage Act by leaking classified information than all previous administrations combined.' Similarly, in its first-ever published report on the USA, the Committee to Protect Journalists commented: 'The [Obama] administration's war on leaks and other efforts to control information are the most aggressive ... since the Nixon administration' (cited in Greenwald 2014: 214).

Does not all this suggest that the Big Brother, surveillance-dominated society described in *Nineteen Eighty-Four* is with us today? An overarching surveillance infrastructure has been used to spy on publics and intimidate political dissidents who deviate from the 'party' line. Whistleblowers, who actually provide a public service by shedding light on the machinations of the deep-state, face prosecution and criminal tribunals. These policies are carried out in order to uphold the current power structures, the inequality, the state of permanent war and the rule of the deep state—'The Party.'

CONCLUSION

This chapter provides a first approximation and more research is needed: The role of the deep state in preventing the institutionalization of effective climate change policies has to be interrogated. The implications of 'anti-terrorism' legislation and other domestic policies that infringe on democratic rights should be critically assessed. Furthermore, it is important to explore further the implications of the new surveillance apparatus and other mechanisms of thought and intellectual control in Western democracies. Western governments have been pursuing an extreme military agenda under the guise of liberal interventionism. NATO's aggressive expansion into Eastern Europe and the Middle Eastern hemisphere has evoked the possibility of a 'World War III scenario' in the not so distant future (Chossudovsky 2012).

In short, does not all this suggest that we are living in times that warrant a comparison with *Nineteen Eighty-Four*?

NOTES

1. Bernard Crick (2007: 147–148) also suggests that a closer reading of *Nineteen Eighty-Four* reveals several 'satiric themes' such as the division of the world, the dumbing down of the mass

media, power-hunger and totalitarianism, the service of intellectuals to power, the abuse of language and history and the emergence of a managerial culture that is constituted in capitalist as well as communist countries thus leading to a convergence of communism and capitalism.

2. For the following discussion on internet history and subsidies I mainly relied on McChesney (2013).

3. Lars Schoultz (1981: 153) investigated the relationship between the amount of aid the USA was providing to 23 Latin American countries in the mid-1970s and the amount of human rights violations conducted in the same countries. According to Schoultz (1981: 162): 'The correlations between relative (per capita) United States aid to Latin American countries and human rights violations by recipient governments are … as in the case of absolute aid levels, … uniformly positive. Thus, even when the remarkable diversity of population size among Latin American countries is considered, the findings suggest that the United States has directed its foreign assistance to governments which torture their citizens.' Perhaps a similar pattern could be identified in regard to US military bases. According to Catherine Lutz (2009) 'fully 38 per cent of those countries with US bases were cited in 2002 for their poor human rights record.'

4. In 1999, the *Guardian* reviewed declassified UK government documents from 1968. One document based on an analysis by the Foreign Office joint intelligence committee was summarized as follows: 'The Soviet Union had no intention of launching a military attack on the West at the height of the Cold War, British military and intelligence chiefs privately believed, in stark contrast to what Western politicians and military leaders were saying in public about the Soviet threat. The Soviet Union will not deliberately start general war or even limited war in Europe,' a briefing for the British chiefs of staff—marked "Top Secret, UK Eyes Only," and headed "The Threat: Soviet Aims and Intentions"—declared in June 1968.' This is not to suggest that the Soviet Union was an innocent power. Nonetheless, it is important to consider that Western planners were fully aware of the fact that the Soviet Union would have engaged in detente, a development which could have significantly relaxed the Cold War conflict but would have undermined the West's ability to subjugate the Third World and nurture the domestic military-industrial complexes via subsidies for the high-tech industries (cf. Chomsky 1989: 185). In the top secret National Security Council Report 68 (NSC 68) which was codified in 1950, US planners also shared evidence suggesting that they knew Soviet power did not match that of the USA but was limited to regional strength.

5. As Curtis (1995: 29–30), who looked at official government documents, argues: 'The primary threats to Anglo-American interests in the Third World have arisen from independent nationalist movements, from *within* states' (emphasis in the original). These movements commonly rejected traditional foreign control over their economic resources, the exploitation of these resources by Western business corporations, and the related impoverishment of the general population at the hands of a tiny, all-powerful ruling elite.

REFERENCES

Aaronovitch, David (2013) 1984: George Orwell's road to dystopia, *BBC News Magazine*, 8 February. Available online at http://www.bbc.co.uk/news/magazine-21337504, accessed on 28 January 2015.

Alexander, Jeffrey C. (1981) The mass news media in systemic, historical, and comparative perspective, Katz, Elihu and Szecskö, Tamás (eds) *Mass Media and Social Change*, London: Sage pp. 17–51.

Balanyá, Belén, Doherty, Ann, Hoedeman, Olivier, Ma'anit, Adam and Wesselius, Erik (2000) *Europe Inc.: Regional & Global Restructuring & the Rise of Corporate Power*, London: Pluto Press.

BBC News (2010) Study: US is an oligarchy, not a democracy, 17 April. Available online at http://www.bbc.co.uk/news/blogs-echochambers-27074746, accessed on 11 February 2015.

Blum, William (2006) *Rogue State: A Guide to the World's Only Superpower*, London: Zed Books Ltd, third edition.

Carey, Alex (1995) *Taking the Risk out of Democracy: Corporate Propaganda Versus Freedom and Liberty*, Urbana and Chicago, Ill.: University of Illinois Press.

Chomsky, Noam (1989) *Necessary Illusions*, London: Pluto Press.

Chomsky, Noam (2010) The high cost of neoliberalism, *New Statesman*, 28 June. Available online at http://www.newstatesman.com/south-america/2010/06/chomsky-democracy-latin, accessed on 11 February 2015.

Chomsky, Noam and Herman, Edward S. (1979) *The Washington Connection and Third World Fascism: The Political Economy of Human Rights: Volume I*, Nottingham: Spokesman.

Chossudovsky, Michel (2012) *Towards a World War III Scenario: The Dangers of Nuclear War*, Montréal, Québec: Global Research Publishers.

Cook, Lindsey (2014) Who are America's poor? *US News & World Report*, 18 September. Available online at http://www.usnews.com/news/blogs/data-mine/2014/09/18/census-bureau-data-sheds-light-on-americas-poor, accessed on 11 February 2015.

Crick, Bernard (2007) *Nineteen Eighty-Four*: Context and controversy, Rodden, John (ed.) *The Cambridge Companion to George Orwell*, Cambridge: Cambridge University Press pp. 146–159.

Curtis, Mark (1995) *The Ambiguities of Power: British Foreign Policy since 1945*, London: Zed Books.

Curtis, Mark (2003) *Web of Deceit: Britain's Real Role in the World*, London: Vintage.

Curtis, Mark (2004) *Unpeople: Britain's Secret Human Rights Abuses*, London: Vintage.

Defence Statistics (2013) *UK Defence Statistics Compendium 2013*, 21 November, London: Ministry of Defence. Available online at https://www.gov.uk/government/uploads/system/uploads/attachment_data/file/356873/UKDS_2013_Revised_Sept_2014.pdf, accessed on 21 February 2015.

Dinan, William and Miller, David, (eds) (2007) *Thinker, Faker, Spinner, Spy: Corporate PR and the Assault on Democracy*, London: Pluto Press.

Domhoff, William G. (2002) *Who Rules America: Power and Politics*, Boston: McGraw-Hill.

Domhoff, William (2012) The class-domination theory of power, February. Available online at http://www2.ucsc.edu/whorulesamerica/power/class_domination.html, accessed on 7 February 2015.

Domhoff, William (2013) Power in America: Wealth, income, and power, February. Available online at http://www2.ucsc.edu/whorulesamerica/power/wealth.html, accessed on 7 February 2015.

Dugan, Emily (2013) Income inequality is at highest level since the 1930s, says report, *Independent*, 3 March. Available online at http://www.independent.co.uk/news/business/news/income-inequality-is-at-highest-level-since-the-1930s-says-report-8518073.html, accessed on 8 February 2015.

Elgot, Jessica (2014) Income inequality soars with five UK families wealthier than bottom 20%, *Huffington Post*, 17 March. Available online at http://www.huffingtonpost.co.uk/2014/03/17/billionaires-uk-oxfam_n_4977201.html, accessed on 6 February 2015.

Ferguson, Thomas (1995) *Golden Rule: The Investment Theory of Party Competition and the Logic of Money-Driven Political Systems*, Chicago and London: University of Chicago Press.

Fuchs, Christian (2012) Critique of the political economy of Web 2.0 surveillance, Fuchs, Christian, Boersma, Kees, Albrechtslund, Anders and Sandoval, Marisol (eds) *Internet and Surveillance: The Challenges of Web 2.0 and Social Media*, London: Routledge pp. 31–70.

Giroux, Henry A. (2014) Beyond Orwellian nightmares and neoliberal authoritarianism, *Truthout*, 15 October. Available online at http://www.truth-out.org/news/item/26817-henry-a-giroux-beyond-orwellian-nightmares-and-neoliberal-authoritarianism#startOfPageId26817, accessed on 3 February 2015.

Greenwald, Glenn (2014) *No Place to Hide: Edward Snowden, the NSA and the Surveillance State*, London: Hamish Hamilton.

Guardian (2013) The NSA files. Available online at http://www.theguardian.com/world/the-nsa-files, accessed on 20 February 2015.

Hammond, Philip (2011) *Framing post-Cold War Conflicts: Media and International Intervention*, Manchester: Manchester University Press.

Huffington Post (2014) David Cameron says phones and email surveillance 'is essential,' as new bill is announced, 10 July. Available online at http://www.huffingtonpost.co.uk/2014/07/10/david-cameron-snoopers-charter_n_5573147.html, accessed on 16 January 2015.

Independent (2011) Ike was right all along: The danger of the military-industrial complex, 17 January. Available online at http://www.independent.co.uk/news/world/americas/ike-was-right-all-along-the-danger-of-the-militaryindustrial-complex-2186133.html, accessed on 5 February 2015. See also http://www.eisenhower.archives.gov/research/online_documents/farewell_address.html, accessed on 22 February 2015.

Johnson, Chalmers (2004) *The Sorrows of Empire: Militarism, Secrecy, and the End of the Republic*, London: Verso.

Keeble, Richard (1997) *Secret State, Silent Press: New Militarism, the Gulf and the Modern Image of Warfare*, Luton: John Libbey Media.

Keys, Tracey and Malnight, Thomas W. (2012) *Corporate Clout: The Influence of the World's Largest Economic Entities*, London: Strategy Dynamics Global Limited. Available online at http://www.globaltrends.com/images/stories/corporate%20clout%20the%20worlds%20100%20largest%20economic%20entities.pdf, accessed on 20 February 2015.

Kolko, Gabriel (1976) *Main Currents in Modern American History*, New York: Harper & Row.

Lutz, Catherine (2009) Introduction: Bases, Empire, and Global Response. In: Lutz, Catherine (ed.) The Bases of Empire: The Global Struggle against U.S. Military Posts, London: Pluto Press, pp. 1–44.

MacAskill, Ewen, Borger, Julian, Hopkins, Nick, Davies, Nick and Ball, James (2013) GCHQ taps fibre-optic cables for secret access to world's communications, *Guardian*. Available online at http://www.theguardian.com/uk/2013/jun/21/gchq-cables-secret-world-communications-nsa, accessed on 20 February 2015.

McChesney, Robert W. (2013) Digital Disconnect: How Capitalism is Turning the Internet Against Democracy. New York: New Press.

Miller, David and Dinan, William (2008) *A Century of Spin: How Public Relations Became the Cutting Edge of Corporate Power*, London: Pluto Press.

Miller, David and Dinan, William (2010) Introduction, Klaehn, Jeffery (ed.) *The Political Economy of Media and Power*, New York: Peter Lang pp. 1–5.

Miller, David and Sabir, Rizwaan (2012) Propaganda and terrorism, Freedman, Des and Thussu, Daya Kishan, (eds) *Media & Terrorism: Global Perspectives*, London: Sage pp. 77–94.

Mynick, Richard (2010) A comment: Revisiting George Orwell's *Nineteen Eighty-Four* in 2010, *World Socialist Website*, 12 June. Available online at http://www.wsws.org/en/articles/2010/06/1984-j12.html, accessed on 28 January 2015.

Newsinger, John (2007) Orwell, Anti-semitism and the Holocaust, Rodden, John (ed.) *The Cambridge Companion to George Orwell*, Cambridge: Cambridge University Press pp. 112–125.

Oxfam (2015a) Richest 1% will own more than all the rest by 2016, 19 January. Available online at http://www.oxfam.org/en/pressroom/pressreleases/2015-01-19/richest-1-will-own-more-all-rest-2016, accessed on 7 February 2015.

Oxfam (2015b) Poverty in the UK. Available online at http://policy-practice.oxfam.org.uk/our-work/poverty-in-the-uk, accessed on 7 February 2015.

Page, Benjamin I. (1996) *Who Deliberates? Mass Media in Modern Democracy*, Chicago: The University of Chicago Press.

Pape, Robert A. (2006) *Dying to Win: The Strategic Logic of Suicide Terrorism*, Random House, New York.

Poverty Site (2015) Income inequalities. Available online at http://www.poverty.org.uk/09/index.shtml, accessed on 6 February 2015.

Schoultz, Lars (1981) US foreign policy and human rights violations in Latin America: A comparative analysis of foreign aid distributions. *Comparative Politics*, Vol. 13, No. 2 (January) pp. 149–170.

Scott, Peter Dale (1993) *Deep Politics and the Death of JFK*, Berkeley and Los Angeles: University of California Press. See also http://www.peterdalescott.net/B-IV.html, accessed on 22 February 2015.

SIPRI (Stockholm International Peace Research Institute) (2011) The SIPRI military expenditure database. Available online at http://milexdata.sipri.org/, accessed on 7 February 2015.

Slater, Ian (2003) *Orwell: The Road to Airstrip One*, Montréal, Quebec: McGill-Queen's University Press, second edition.

Stockwell, John (1991) *The Praetorian Guard: The US Role in the New World Order*, Cambridge, MA: South End Press.

Tarabay, Jamie (2013) Obama and Leakers: Who Are the Eight Charged Under the Espionage Act? *Al jazeera America*, 5 December. Available online at http://america.aljazeera.com/articles/2013/12/5/obama-and-leakerswhoaretheeightchargedunderespionageact.html, accessed on 20 February 2015.

Zollmann, Florian (2012) *Manufacturing Wars? A Comparative Analysis of US, UK and German Corporate Press Coverage of the US Occupation of Iraq*, PhD dissertation, Lincoln: University of Lincoln.

Zollmann, Florian (2014) State-ending: A brief history of the destruction of Iraq, *teleSUR*, 21 July. Available online at http://www.telesurtv.net/english/opinion/State-Ending-a-Brief-History-of-the-Destruction-of-Iraq-20140722-0024.html, accessed on 21 February 2015.

CHAPTER THREE

A Portrait OF THE Artist AS A Collector

Tracing Orwell's Collecting Project from Burma to Big Brother

HENK VYNCKIER

INTRODUCTION

The cultural practice of collecting has attracted a lot of attention in recent decades. As the Canadian novelist and one-time collector of vintage watches, William Gibson, commented in 1999:

> The idea of the collectible is everywhere today, and sometimes strikes me as some desperate instinctive reconfiguring of the postindustrial flow, some basic mammalian response to the bewildering flood of sheer stuff we produce. But the main driving force in the tidying of the world's attic, the drying up of random, 'innocent' sources of rarities, is information technology. We are mapping literally everything, from the human genome to Jaeger two-register chronographs, and our search engines grind increasingly fine.

Gibson's statement, while offering a valuable reflection on the ways in which consumer capitalism and information technology are fueling a collecting frenzy in contemporary culture, should not obscure the fact that collecting and related practices such as stocktaking, cataloguing, and archiving originated in the ancient civilizations of the Middle East and the Mediterranean Basin, as well as China, and other early civilizations. In fact, if we are to believe one critical study of the subject, namely John Elsner and Roger Cardinal's *The Cultures of Collecting* (1994), collecting can be traced back to the mythical beginnings of humanity: 'Noah was the first collector. Adam had given names to the animals, but it fell to Noah to collect them ... And Noah, perhaps alone of all collectors, achieved the complete set' (ibid.: 1). They further reflect that: 'In the myth of Noah as ur-collector resonate all the themes of collecting itself: desire and nostalgia, saving and loss, the urge to erect a permanent and complete system against the destructiveness of time' (ibid.).

Notwithstanding this caveat regarding the extreme antiquity of collecting, Gibson's comments remain useful and inspire the central thesis of this chapter. My aim is to investigate 'the idea of the collectible' in George Orwell by examining the biographical evidence regarding his collecting interests and reviewing some of his major writings in light of these interests. Orwell, indeed, deserves consideration in discussions about this important aspect of modern culture, just as he remains central to many other debates about contemporary society. Hence the title of this edited collection: *George Orwell Now*! Not only do many of his novels—from *A Clergyman's Daughter* (1935) to *Nineteen Eighty-Four* (1949)—begin with images of various clocks, alarm bells, or other indicators of the destructiveness of time, he also had, as he commented in his seminal essay 'Why I Write' (1946), a passion for 'solid objects and scraps of useless information' (*Complete Works* 18: 320). The precise meaning of this phrase has become much clearer since the publication of half a dozen major biographies and Peter Davison's edition of *The Complete Works*, and we now know that he was an eclectic collector whose interests ranged from books, political pamphlets, and comic postcards to candle-holders, Victorian commemorative mugs, and other objects which he collected for their 'curiosity value ... rather than for their convenience or beauty' (Crick 1980: 346). Moreover, the same year he wrote 'Why I Write,' he analyzed his collecting interests critically and humorously in a 1946 essay, published in the London *Evening Standard*, entitled 'Just Junk – But Who Can Resist It?' (*Complete Works* 18: 19) and three years later demonstrated his expertise as a collector in his great last novel *Nineteen Eighty-Four*. The latter's protagonist, Winston Smith, I argue, is a belated urban collector and *flâneur* who is stranded in an age of collectivism and endeavors to construct a private sphere with the help of beautiful objects from the past. My chapter, therefore, documents Orwell's collecting interests as they developed over the course of his life and examines how these private passions gradually seeped into his writings and helped him formulate a consistent literary and political agenda. In sum, whereas James Joyce offered *A Portrait of the Artist as a Young Man* (1916), I intend to sketch *A Portrait of the Artist as a Collector*.

ORWELL'S OLD CURIOSITY SHOP

Bernard Crick, Orwell's first biographer, records an anecdote from the mid-thirties which represents a useful starting point for a portrait of Orwell the collector. In February–March 1936, Orwell visited the North of England to conduct research for a book on conditions in the depressed industrial districts commissioned by his publisher Victor Gollancz. The project resulted in a serious journalistic reportage,

The Road to Wigan Pier, which Gollancz published in the following year as a book choice of the newly-founded Left Book Club. As Crick reports, Orwell spent several days in Liverpool and was shown around the docks and urban slum areas by members of the Independent Labour Party and a communist seaman turned docker. Much of what he saw left little doubt as to the harsh realities of life in working class Liverpool, and Orwell appears to have observed everything attentively. Crick notes that he witnessed two hundred and fifty hungry and ragged men waiting for work while a company agent offered jobs to fifty men only; he saw the police patrolling the docks after a fight; and he was much impressed by the sight of some slums being cleared. At one point, and this is where this fact-finding expedition in industrial England becomes less straightforward, Orwell also asked his hosts to stop 'at several antique-cum-junk shops … and he bought two brass candlesticks and a ship in a bottle.' Moreover, to explain his behavior to his surprised hosts, he then told them that 'he was thinking of trying to set up a small antique shop in a cottage or shop he was about to rent down in Hertfordshire' (Crick 1980: 186).

Readers who know Orwell mainly as the author of *Animal Farm* (1945) and *Nineteen Eighty-Four* (1949) may be surprised, just like his hosts in Liverpool in 1936, and wonder what this talk about setting up an antique shop was about. Indeed, looking back at this scene from a twenty-first century point of view, the idea that Orwell, whom many believe to be the greatest political writer of the twentieth century, at one time thought about going into the antique business and spending his days among candlesticks and ships in bottles seems perplexing and comical. One wonders, therefore, if he was joking and perhaps echoing a storyline from Charles Dickens, one of his favorite writers, whose *The Old Curiosity Shop* (of 1841) contains a memorable description of an antique store and its quaint proprietor:

> The place through which he made his way at leisure was one of those receptacles for old and curious things which seem to crouch in odd corners of this town and to hide their musty treasures from the public eye in jealousy and distrust … The haggard aspect of the little old man was wonderfully suited to the place; he might have groped among old churches and tombs and deserted houses and gathered all the spoils with his own hands. There was nothing in the whole collection but was in keeping with himself, nothing that looked older or more worn than he (ibid.: 5).

Is this what Orwell was proposing for his future? That he would open an Old Curiosity Shop in an 'odd corner' of the country and become a groper among old churches and deserted houses like Dickens's protagonist? It is difficult to imagine him doing so, but he did soon move into a cottage in Hertfordshire which dated back to the 16th century and was known as 'The Stores' as it had formerly been the location of the village grocery store. He also did open a shop, though not an antique shop, rather the same sort of village grocery store which his cottage had hosted before (Bowker 2003: 185). Even before that, during his employment in a second-hand bookstore in London, he occasionally went out to buy books from private houses on behalf of his employer, which, says Crick, indicates that 'he must have shown some aptitude in the trade beyond a love of books' (op. cit.: 161). It is equally true that, as he confessed in 'Just Junk—but Who Can Resist It?,' he continued to visit 'antique cum junk stores' and included an interesting store of this type in *Nineteen Eighteen-Four*.

Thus, though there never was to be an Orwell's Old Curiosity Shop, this snapshot of Orwell from the mid-thirties is fascinating as we see two Orwellian selves temporarily collide with one another: the up-and-coming leftist writer and the antiques collector. The manifest purpose of Orwell's visit to Liverpool, as of the entire two-month journey, was to research working class life and everything about *The Road to Wigan Pier* (1937) suggests that he was very serious about this undertaking. Readers of the book will remember its stark vision of a desolate north of England world of coal mines, slag heaps, foundries, filthy lodging houses, and dilapidated workers' slums and conclude how far Orwell had come as a writer since early non-fiction writings such as 'The Spike' (1931), 'Hop Picking' (1931), 'Clink' (1932), and *Down and Out in Paris and London* (1933). In one of the most striking passages of the book, he describes how he went down a coal mine in order to experience personally what colliers went through day after day and, though totally unfit for moving about in the low tunnels given that he was a very tall man and had a weak chest, he spent hours crawling back and forth to the coal face. Indeed, as his biographer Gordon Bowker claims, his two months in the North of England, together with the subsequent journey to Spain in December 1936 and participation in the civil war on the Republican side, were true journeys of discovery that shaped the author's personal and political values for the rest of his life (Bowker 2003: 180–200). It is evident, therefore, that as an emerging author Orwell was hard at work during these years forging his literary-political program and, while his socialist politics were still rather undefined, he was clearly affiliated with progressive literary journals and publishers such as the *Adelphi* and Victor Gollancz (ibid.: 177). At the same time, it is also irrefutable that as a private individual he was fond of a cultural practice which celebrates nostalgia, childhood, domesticity, and the pleasures of acquisition and ownership, i.e., the sort of cultural baggage which could be understood as conflicting with his public persona and political agenda.

The Liverpool city tour, moreover, was not the only time during the *Wigan Pier* journey that we see Orwell give free reign to his collecting interests. In the so-called *Road to Wigan Pier Diary*, which remained unpublished at the time, but was included in Vol. 10 of the *Complete Works*, another anecdote is found which offers proof of the pleasure which Orwell took in the collecting enterprise. In his entry for 2 February 1936, the third day of his journey, he records staying in a small hotel and having the following conversation with the hotel warden:

> In the morning long talk with the warden who keeps poultry and collects glass and pewter. He told me how in France in 1918, on the heels of the retreating Germans, he looted some priceless glass which was discovered and looted in turn by his divisional general. Also showed me some nice pieces of pewter and some very curious Japanese pictures, showing clear traces of European influence, looted by his father in some naval expedition about 1860 (*Complete Works* 10: 419).

That neither this conversation regarding dubious collecting strategies such as looting in war zones, nor the anecdote about the 'antique-cum-junk stores' in Liverpool made it into *The Road to Wigan Pier* indicates the selectiveness and self-censoring which Orwell engaged in when sorting through his experiences. Readers of *Keep the Aspidistra Flying* (1936), Orwell's third novel which was published just before *The Road to Wigan Pier*, will not be surprised by his silence on the subject as the protagonist, a second-hand bookstore employee like Orwell, makes no secret of his contempt for the book collectors who frequent the store and for his second employer, a repulsive rare book dealer by the name of Cheeseman. In sum, though collecting and antiquarianism were clearly of interest to Orwell, he does not seem to have been able or willing to acknowledge these interests in his writing at this stage of his career and he did not give them a place of honor in his literary program till a decade later when his reputation had been solidified by *Animal Farm*, and he finally addressed the subject openly in 'Just Junk—but Who Can Resist It?'

In her study *On Longing: Narratives of the Miniature, the Gigantic, the Souvenir, the Collection* (1993), Susan Stewart offers a perceptive analysis of the economy of collecting, which may yield clues to Orwell's ambiguous attitude in relation to his own collecting interests. Noting that the original title of Honoré de Balzac's great novel about a collector *Cousin Pons* (1847) was *The Parasite*, Stewart observes that the collector's hunt for curios, souvenirs, knick-knacks, and other collectible objects in flea-markets and junk stores is a kind of a false labor which points out 'the ironic nostalgia of the collector's economic system' (1993: 159). The collector, namely, creates a 'smaller economy' which 'although dependent upon and, a mirroring of, the larger economy of surplus value ... is self-sufficient and self-generating with regard to its meanings and principles of exchange' (ibid.). Orwell similarly seems to have practiced two modes of labor during his travels. As a writer, he devoted himself to criticizing 'the larger economy of surplus value,' i.e., capitalism, and he was beginning to be very good at this. His contemporary Edith Sitwell, for instance, compared *The Road to Wigan Pier* favorably to Friedrich Engels's *The Condition of the Working Class in England* (1887) which had sketched an unforgettable portrait of the industrial hells of the mid-nineteenth century (Meyers 2000: 137). Yet, there were also times when he would set aside politics and literature and trot off to junk stores and flea-markets in search of curiosities. It is not impossible, however, that even at this early stage there may have been political overtones to Orwell's actions as a collector. As John Windsor, another critic of collecting, commented, collections are 'identity parades' and 'collections of high art, especially in battered country houses, declare: "I am rich and have a well-developed taste." Quirky collections of kitsch and ephemera say "Look how quirky but clever I am"' (1994: 64). This, then, may have been a case of the quirky and clever Orwell asserting his individuality in the face of a political activity such as this visit to the down-and-outs of Liverpool that might otherwise have had a whiff of ideological conformity about it.

THE LITERATURE OF COLLECTING

Whatever his rationale for bypassing the collecting episodes in *The Road to Wigan Pier*, Orwell may have been right to be careful on the subject at this time when his larger political vision was still being formulated and his collecting interests may have seemed half-baked to outsiders. Collectors by and large did not have a very good reputation in the contemporary literature and were generally suspected of having a *petit bourgeois* outlook unbecoming truth-seeking intellectuals. In 1947, for example, Orwell's French contemporary Jean-Paul Sartre mocked French middle class collectors as follows:

> The postal-clerk, the blacksmith, the engineer, the departmental treasurer, all have their nocturnal and solitary *fêtes*. Consuming passions and wild conflagrations dwell deeply within them … we were to learn to recognize in stamp and coin collecting all the nostalgia for the beyond, all the Baudelairean dissatisfaction. For I ask you, why would one spend one's time and money acquiring medallions, were it not that one was past caring for the friendship of men and the love of women and power? And what is more gratuitous than a stamp collection? Not everybody can be a Leonardo or a Michelangelo, but those useless stamps pasted on the pink pages of an album are a touching homage to all the nine muses; it is the very essence of destructive consumption (1950: 148).

Stewart's pairing of labor/false labor is here paralleled with another pairing: namely, transgressive artistic expression and sham avant-garde self-love, whereby petty government officials who come home from work and pore over stamp albums or fondle antique coins take on the airs of a Baudelaire writing an ode to his mistress.

The situation was no different in England, at least as far as the literary representation of collectors was concerned.[1] Legendary eighteenth-century aristocratic collectors such as Horace Walpole (1717–1797) and William Beckford (1760–1844) made vital contributions to the literature of their time and Walter Scott (1771–1832), himself a formidable collector of Scottish antiquities, celebrated antiquarianism as an alternative form of historiography in his bestselling novel

The Antiquary, of 1816. The tide turned, however, during the course of the nineteenth century and Dickens's *The Old Curiosity Shop*, mentioned earlier as a possible influence on Orwell, is a cautionary tale about misguided antiquarianism. His protagonist Trent, namely, falls victim to a gambling habit and is forced to borrow money from a scheming moneylender, thus setting in motion a chain of events that results in the closure of his shop and eventual death. Dickens, therefore, draws an analogy between the trade in antiques on the one hand and gambling on the other hand, and criticizes Trent and his ilk for their lack of good sense and dependence on Lady Luck.

Orwell, no doubt, would have been familiar with classic turn-of-the-century fiction about collectors, including Oscar Wilde's *The Picture of Dorian Gray* (1891), Joseph Conrad's *Lord Jim* (1900), Arthur Conan Doyle's *The Hound of the Baskervilles* (1901), and H. G. Wells's *Tono-Bungay* (1909), all of which show collectors in an unfavorable light. The protagonist of *The Picture of Dorian Gray*, for instance, is the most extravagant collector in nineteenth-century English literature, but his spectacular collections, richly detailed in Chapter 11 of the novel, can never fully erase the haunting memory of his portrait and in the long run a violent and ignominious death awaits him. As for the wealthy European merchant and butterfly collector Stein in Conrad's *Lord Jim*, his story sheds light on the connection between empire building and collecting projects as he acquired the most prized specimen in his collection barely minutes after he shot some natives who had tried to ambush him in the jungle. Another famous butterfly collector appears in *The Hound of the Baskervilles* in the person of Stapleton, an embittered member of the Baskerville clan; pretending to be a retired schoolteacher who has taken up butterfly collecting and amateur archaeology, he seeks to destroy the legitimate heirs of the Baskerville estate, but in the end is no match for Sherlock Holmes. *Tono-Bungay*, by H. G. Wells, an author whose writings Orwell knew very well and repeatedly discussed, features a very different collector: namely, an English businessman who admires the French Emperor Napoleon and collects Napoleonic artifacts. The 'Tono-Bungay' mentioned in the title is a patent medicine of doubtful efficacy developed by the businessman and promoted by his talented nephew. In spite of the latter's determined efforts, the Tono-Bungay empire ultimately collapses, and the disgraced entrepreneur escapes to France, the homeland of his hero but, contracting pneumonia during the journey, he falls ill and dies an inglorious death in a village in the French countryside.

No significant improvements would be visible in the literary lot of collectors in the second half of the twentieth century. John Fowles's debut novel *The Collector* (1963), for example, is a dark fable about class relations in post-World War II England and features a butterfly collector from a working class background who abducts an art school student and keeps her locked up in the hope that she will fall in love with him and accept her confinement. The scheme miscarries horribly and the young woman dies. And Bruce Chatwin's *Utz* (1988), about a collector of Meissen porcelain in the socialist Czechoslovakia of the Cold War era, raises fundamental questions about the personal and political values of collectors. At first sight, the protagonist's attachment to his valuable collection of porcelain figurines marks him out as a stubborn individualist and political non-conformist. Yet, when it appears that he is able to travel to Switzerland to sell pieces from his collection, the suspicion arises that he is an agent acting on behalf of the Czechoslovak government to acquire hard currencies from the West.[1]

THE JACKDAW INSIDE ALL OF US

Collectors, as the above survey indicates, have not been viewed very favorably by many canonical writers, and it is interesting to consider why that this did not deter Orwell from becoming a collector and exploring collecting as a literary theme in his work. As is typical for many collectors, family history seems to have been an important factor. Orwell's real family name was Blair, and the Blairs, who had a heraldic crest and a case of family silver, had been a prominent family with aristocratic connections dating back to the 17th century, but their fortunes had declined gradually throughout the Victorian age. Bowker calls attention to Orwell's inheritance in Chapter 1 of his biography, and notes that Orwell was 'keenly aware of his family ancestry – the procession of ghostly forebears' whose names were 'inscribed in the family Bible inherited from his father' (Bowker 2003: 4). He also inherited an oil painting of Lady Mary Blair, a mid-18th century aristocratic ancestor, and 'a set of leather-bound volumes once owned by his great uncle, Captain Horatio Blair, to which he became sentimentally attached' (ibid.). So here was a first source of collectible objects, his ancestral heritage.

In addition, his father served in the Indian colonial service for decades and his mother had artistic interests, and this meant that, as a relative commented, the family home was full of all sorts of objects such as embroidered stools, bags, cushions, pin cushions, interesting mahogany or ivory boxes full of sequins, wooden needle-cases, amber beads, small boxes from India and Burma, and so forth. All of which, the relative added, was 'fascinating for children' (Crick 1980: 13). Orwell would recreate this family atmosphere in extract 3 from 'The Autobiography of John Flory,' which Peter Davison dates back to 1926–1930, and ranks among Orwell's earliest attempts to create fiction (*Complete Works* 10: 97). In this fragment, the narrator recollects his father's library with its many books, Indian furniture, tiger skins, old photographs, Asian weapons, and assorted 'rubbish' such as 'empty cartridge cases, bad rupees, or dried up peacock feathers, and recalls the time that he spent there leafing through books, or listening to his father's stories' (ibid.). Orwell included a similar Anglo-Indian family setting in his 1939 novel

Coming Up for Air, when the protagonist describes his wife's parental home and notes how, in addition to being full of carved teak furniture, brass trays, and yellow photographs of chaps in sun-helmets: 'It smelt perpetually of Trichinopoly cigars, and it was so full of spears, blow-pipes, brass ornaments and the heads of wild animals that you could hardly move about in it' (*Complete Works* 7: 139). As is evident from *Coming Up for Air*, Orwell would sometimes mock the Anglo-Indian context which shaped him as a child, but this same context, with its theatrical assemblages of colonial trophies and cross-cultural artifacts, was clearly another source of collectibles.

As a child he began to collect butterflies, birds' eggs, picture books, and so forth, and gradually acquired, as he said himself, 'the sort of mind that takes pleasure in dates, lists, catalogues, concrete details, descriptions of processes, junk-shop windows, and back numbers of Exchange and Mart.' ('Charles Reade' 1940; *Complete Works* 12: 232). Even during his five years of service as a colonial police-man in Burma from 1922 to 1927 we see flashes of the collecting instinct as he surrounded himself by a small menagerie of animals, including goats, ducks, and geese (Rodden 2012: 73). Another aspect of Orwell which, indeed, remained constant throughout his life was his love of nature, and when he lived in the country, he would conscientiously record the number of eggs, cups of goat milk, and other produce which he gathered in. Whether in the city or the country, Orwell could never resist the pleasures of accumulation and stocktaking and in an essay on *Foul Play*, a desert island story by the late Victorian adventure novelist Charles Reade, he observed: 'A list of the objects in a shipwrecked man's possession is probably the surest winner in fiction, surer even than a trial scene' (*Complete Works* 12: 233).

Following his return to England, he began to collect boys' weeklies, political pamphlets, seaside postcards, detective fiction, and other literary and printed materials, as well as beer tankards, Victorian trinkets, glass paperweights, and all sorts of other curiosities. To be sure, as noted above, there were times when he criticized collecting and collectors, and we see this not only in *Keep the Aspidistra Flying*, but also the essay 'Bookshop Memories,' which was published the same year and was similarly inspired by his employment in a second-hand bookshop. As Crick comments, however, the time which Orwell spent in this employment was productive and 'fortified Orwell's interest in popular culture' (Crick 1980: 160). Orwell, moreover, continued to frequent such stores all his life. Crick notes, for example, that in 1945–1946, while living in London, Orwell spent much time 'browsing in second-hand bookshops, indeed second-hand shops of all kinds' (ibid.: 348).

Perhaps the strongest formulation of his collecting interests is the essay 'Just Junk—but Who Can Resist It?' from 1946. The appeal of such junk shops, he suggests, is to 'the jackdaw inside all of us, the instinct that makes a child hoard copper nails, clock springs, and glass marbles out of lemonade bottles' (*Complete*

Works 18: 19). He also catalogues some of the objects which are worth looking for in the junk shops of London: Victorian brooches and lockets, papier maché snuffboxes with pictures painted on the lid, muzzle-loading pistols made around 1830, ships in bottles, musical boxes, Jubilee mugs, glass paperweights with pictures at the bottom or pieces of coral enclosed in the glass, scrap books, scrap screens, French sword-bayonets, and many other curiosities. The most striking passage occurs towards the end of the essay, however, when he concludes with a story about a particularly rubbishy shop in London which he has known for years even though it sold nothing which he would ever be tempted to buy and, at the same time, admits, 'it would be all but impossible for me to pass that way without crossing the street to have a good look' (ibid.). This, clearly, is the mark of the true collector who goes by instinct rather than intellect.

It is noteworthy that all of the typical Orwellian themes under discussion—writing, collecting, and listing—are touched on in one key sentence in 'Why I Write' when he says: 'So long as I remain alive and well I shall continue to feel strongly about prose style, to love the surface of the earth, and to take a pleasure in solid objects and scraps of useless information' (*Complete Works* 18: 319). Thus, Orwell's love of objects was but one dimension of a sort of personal archaeology of 'ingrained likes and dislikes' (ibid.) which he never relinquished. Meanwhile, as he admitted, that archaeology of attitudes, while enabling him to invest his writing with a certain aesthetic quality, did not always line up very well with his political objectives.

Orwell's collecting practices over time, nevertheless, began to inspire his writing and resulted in such classic essays as 'Boys' Weeklies' (1940), 'The Art of Donald McGill' (1941), about the graphic artist famous for his saucy seaside postcards, and his introduction to Volume 1 of *British Pamphleteers*, edited by Reginald Reynolds (1948). William E. Cain sums up the position of many critics when he calls 'Boys' Weeklies' 'a pioneering foray in cultural studies' (2007: 78) and the same can be said for 'The Art of Donald McGill,' an essay based on Orwell's collection of mildly obscene seaside postcards. As Jeffrey Meyers observed, Orwell 'took comic postcards seriously, and explored the meaning and purpose of the genre' (Meyers 2000: 268). As for *British Pamphleteers*, Orwell's collection of pamphlets was extensive, numbering close to 2,000 items, and his introduction to the volume was described by its editor Reynolds as 'characteristic and provocative' (ibid.: 182). In all of these instances, therefore, Orwell's writing profited from life-long research and collecting interests, and it is evident that over time Orwell's collecting practice moved beyond the sort of awkward expeditions he undertook in Liverpool. The false labor of those junk shop expeditions undermined the literary and political project he was undertaking at that time, but the essays on boys' weeklies, comic postcards, junk shops, pamphlets, crime fiction, etc. of later years indicate that he was developing an identity as a collector which underpinned his writing program and political views.

ORWELL COLLECTOR: THE PHOTOGRAPHIC EVIDENCE

More facts could be gathered jackdaw-like from the published record, but it is interesting to note finally how any number of photographs of Orwell tell the same story and show him living and working amidst the collectible objects which inhabit the pages of his fiction and essays. I briefly comment on four well-known photographs. The first is Dennis Collings's snapshot of Montague House in Southwold where his parents lived from 1932 to 1939. To the right of the fairly impressive Montague House, which Orwell frequently visited over the years, we see a smaller building, the business premises of Rush and Winyard, well-known Southwold estate agents. The presence of such a business next door to his parents' residence must have been of interest to him as estate agents appraise, catalogue, and auction real estate, furniture, works of art, jewelry, and other valuables and are to the high street what curiosity shops are to the odd corners of the city.[2]

The next three photographs are by Vernon Richards and capture Orwell at home in his flat in Islington in 1946. The first shows Orwell standing upright against a wall, unsheathing a Burmese sword. The second is the well-known photograph of Orwell at his typewriter, in front of rows of bookshelves, with the books neatly grouped according to their various colors and sizes. The third is the photograph of Orwell seated on a chair with the infant, Richard, on his knees; behind him the antique painting of Lady Blair and a scrap screen of the kind described in the 'Just Junk' essay.[3] All these photographs show an Orwell who reminds us of the younger Orwell in the antique cum junk stores in Liverpool in 1936, i.e., a man who defines himself in relation to objects and shows himself in his 'little kingdom' amidst cherished trophies. These trophies, then, in their turn help to frame their owner in the various roles he wished to be remembered for: the old Asia hand and connoisseur of foreign cultures; the writer and man of many books; and the family man with ancient lineages and a taste for Victorian home furnishings and decorative objects.

THE COLLECTOR COLLECTED

This view of Orwell as someone who developed a coherent articulation of his collecting interests and made them serviceable to his literary agenda is supported by his famous last novel, *Nineteen Eighty-Four*, published in 1949. As in the anecdote about Orwell in Liverpool in 1936, the story begins with a commercial transaction in a junk-shop in a proletarian neighborhood. Winston Smith, while exploring an unfamiliar part of town, sees a book in the window of a little junk-shop and is 'stricken immediately by an overwhelming desire to possess it' (*Complete Works* 9: 8). He buys the book without further ado and commences the journey home knowing that what he carries with him is 'a compromising possession' (ibid.). During later inspections of the 'thick, quarto-sized blank book with a red back and a marbled cover' in his bare apartment, so different from that of his creator, he notices how special this book is: 'It was a particularly beautiful book. Its smooth creamy paper, a little yellowed by age, was of a kind that had not been manufactured for at least forty years past. He could guess, however, that the book was much older than that' (ibid.). Orwell, for all his sneering at bibliophiles in *Keep the Aspidistra Flying*, applies the correct book collector's terminology when he uses words such as quarto, red back, marbled cover, and creamy paper to describe the material characteristics and condition of the book. Bibliophiles call books which are old, beautiful and still in excellent condition 'collectible' books, and they highly prize such books for inclusion in their collections. Smith's book, though not a printed book, rather a blank keepsake diary, is such a well-preserved and authentic collectible book.

In Big Brother's Oceania, however, efforts to indulge in subjective musings and reconnect with an earlier, pre-revolutionary age are referred to with the Newspeak concept 'ownlife' and constitute a serious crime. What then could have driven a Party member and government employee such as Smith to transgress in this manner? Winston Smith's job in the Ministry of Truth is to rewrite newspaper articles in order to maintain the illusion that the Party's vision of history has always been accurate. Yet, he never gives up believing in truth, yearns for his long-lost mother and younger sister, dreams of a Golden Country beyond the reach of the Party, and hates rather than loves Big Brother. Such is the man who wanders around proletarian sections of town like some kind of urban *flâneur* and brings home compromising possessions. An old Latin saying holds that things which please will be repeated—*bis repetita placent*—and the restless Smith soon pays a second visit to the junk-shop. This time he is attracted to an antique glass paperweight with a bit of red coral embedded in its core and, struck by its beauty and 'the air it seemed to possess of belonging to an age quite different from the present one' (ibid.: 99) he purchases the paperweight. He also listens to the proprietor's musings that the trade in antiques is dying out as there are no customers anymore and no stock either and finally examines some furniture and an old steel engraving in a bedroom upstairs. The entire experience is such that he resolves to make future visits to this fascinating shop in order to buy more 'scraps of beautiful rubbish' (ibid.: 104), thereby indicating the continuation of an open-ended collecting project and Smith's ongoing personal and political awakening.

Peter Davison comments in a footnote to the 'Just Junk' essay that Charrington's shop, with its picture frames, penknives, broken watches, nuts and bolts, lacquered snuff-boxes, agate brooches, and other odds and ends, clearly reflects Orwell's familiarity with the London junk shop scene (*Complete Works* 18: 19). Expanding on this, I would say that Orwell's extensive knowledge of collecting, junk shops, second-hand bookstores, print culture, and other aspects of material culture thoroughly informs all of Parts I and II of *Nineteen Eighty-Four*. Winston Smith has the collector's keen awareness of the destructiveness of time and endeavors to salvage whatever remnants of the old civilization are still available to him. This old civilization, though thoroughly ransacked and difficult to reconstruct from the scattered artifacts, oral history sources, and topographical vistas he encounters, seems to beckon the wandering hero upon a journey of self-discovery and political awakening and he eagerly responds to the call. Yet, as Samuel Johnson, another famous London collector and dictionary compiler, warned: 'In the purchase of old books, let me recommend to you to examine with great caution whether they are perfect' (Carter and Barker 2004: 69). Smith, however, is unable to do so and lacks the necessary caution. He has many longings, but insufficient expertise, and does not see that Charrington, the junk store proprietor, is really a member of the Thought Police, the antique shop a police trap, and the beautiful old book a lady's keepsake, which has been made available by the Party as a medium for Smith to incriminate himself. It was once a precious and antique implement for collecting one's thoughts; now it is but another device of political control similar to the telescreen.

A similar irony exists in the excitement with which Smith receives *The Theory and Practice of Oligarchical Collectivism* by Emmanuel Goldstein, the traitor whose book has now become the source of inspiration for a shadowy organization of dissidents known as the Brotherhood. It is: 'A heavy black volume, amateurishly bound, with no name or title on the cover. The print also looked slightly irregular. The pages were worn at the edges, and fell apart easily, as though the book had passed through many hands' (*Complete Works* 18: 191). In the language of book collecting such a book would be described as 'a poor copy' or 'a reading copy,' meaning that its poor production values and deteriorated condition from having passed through many hands would prevent any serious book collector from ever buying it, that is unless he is desperate to obtain a copy and no better copies can be found. And, of course, that's what this particular book is all about. Though it may not be beautiful like the antiquarian lady's keepsake, its amateurish manufacture and worn pages are the guise necessary to convince Smith of its authenticity as a forbidden book from the underground.

In conclusion, throughout Parts I and II of *Nineteen Eighty-Four*, Smith turns to collectible objects and other scraps of the past in order to, as Walter Benjamin stated in his classic essay 'Unpacking My Library: A Talk on Book Collecting,' 'renew the old world' (1988: 61). It is a great enterprise and the methods he uses are the opportunistic, low-tech tactics of the collector in a struggle with the strategically mobilized forces of the Party. The authenticity of his awakening is real, and the effort is heroic, but unfortunately, Smith overlooks the innate tendency of the collecting project to strip objects of their historical essence. As Susan Stewart states: 'The collection replaces history with classification, with order beyond the realm of temporality. In the collection, time is not something to be restored to an origin; rather, all time is made simultaneous or synchronous within the collection's world' (1993: 150). This analysis of the culture of collecting matches the Party's slogan: 'Who controls the past, controls the future: who controls the present controls the past' (*Complete Works* 18: 37). Smith, in other words, cannot hope to wrest away control over his own life from the Party by means of precarious collecting projects, the more so since the agents of the Party are finely attuned to such projects, having conducted many of them themselves, but to destroy, not preserve the past. In sum, in the bleak world of *Nineteen Eighty-Four*, it the collectivist, not the collector, who triumphs.

POSTSCRIPT: THE FARMER JONES MUSEUM OF HISTORY

One final passage, and this one from an unexpected source, namely, *Animal Farm*, may be referenced to conclude my central argument regarding Orwell's rich relevance to the study of the characteristic modern subjects of collecting and material culture. In a scene near the beginning of *Animal Farm*, the victorious animals, having chased Farmer Jones from the farm, inspect the farmhouse and are overwhelmed by what they see:

> They tiptoed from room to room, afraid to speak above a whisper and gazing with a kind of awe at the unbelievable luxury, at the beds with their feather mattresses, the looking glasses, the horsehair sofa, the Brussels carpet, the lithograph of Queen Victoria over the drawing-room mantelpiece (*Complete Works* 8: 14).

While readers may smile at the notion that the conventional furnishings of an English farm house signify 'unbelievable luxury,' they will also be reminded of similar visits to the palaces of fallen dictators which litter the pages of modern history, from the boudoirs of Marie Antoinette (1755–1793) to the palace of President Victor Yanukovych (1950–) of Ukraine, toppled in February 2014.[4] During the course of their tour the animals discover that Mollie, the mare, has stayed behind to admire herself in Mrs. Jones's mirror, and they also find some hams hanging in the kitchen, which they take out for burial, and a barrel of beer, which Boxer the horse demolishes with a kick of his hoof. Incidents such as these make clear the haunted nature of the farmhouse and: 'A unanimous resolution was passed on the spot that the farmhouse should be preserved as a museum. All were agreed that no animal must ever live there' (ibid.). Such is the animals' noble intention, to remember the corruptions of human civilization and preserve the farmhouse as a history museum. As readers of *Animal Farm* know, however, Comrade Napoleon and his pig brothers are not the sort to be bound by resolutions and soon take up residence in the museum. 'All animals are equal, but some are more equal than others.' Ultimately, therefore, no political statecraft nor historical agency is achieved by the founding of the museum, but the episode, nevertheless, shows that in Orwell's fictional universe even farm animals have a keen curatorial instinct and understand the politics of the collection. We may, therefore, add one more lesson to the many lessons taught by Orwell's delightful animal fable: beware those who give up their collections, for they shall be enslaved.

NOTES

1. On collecting and collectors in English literature, see Kelly Eileen Battles's doctoral dissertation *The Antiquarian Impulse: History, Affect, and Material Culture in Eighteenth and Nineteenth Cent. British Culture* (English, Michigan State University, 2008), Richard Wendorf's *The Literature of Collecting and Other Essays* (Boston: Oak Knoll Press, 2008), and Paul Goetsch's book chapter 'Uncanny Collectors and Collections in Late Victorian Fiction' in Elmar Schenkel and Stefan Welz (eds) *Magical Objects: Things and Beyond* (Berlin: Galda + Wilch Verlag, 2007) pp. 67–89. Janell Watson's *Literature and Material Culture from Balzac to Proust: The Collection and Consumption of Curiosities* (Cambridge: Cambridge University Press, 2000) is an excellent study of collectors in French literature.
2. For Collings's photograph, see Miriam Gross (ed.) *The World of George Orwell* (New York: Simon and Schuster, 1971) illustration 34 ('The house at Southwold where Orwell's parents lived'), or Crick, 'Montague House, Southwold, where the Blairs lived from 1932 to 1939,' between pages 130 and 131, 1980.
3. The three photographs by Vernon Richards are included in *George Orwell at Home (And Among the Anarchists)* (London: Freedom Press, 1998), with a cropped version of the photo of Orwell and Richard in front of the scrap screen and painting of Lady Blair also featured on the front cover. They can also be viewed in Miriam Gross: illustrations 20 ('George Orwell with a native sword, a souvenir of his Burmese days'), 69 ('Fatherhood'), and 72 ('The writer at work'). The 'Fatherhood' photograph, though, is a variant which offers a particularly good view of the scrap screen, but only reproduces the lower part of the Lady Blair painting. Crick also has Orwell 'Typing in his flat in Islington, winter 1945' (between 290 and 291) and 'Orwell with Richard, Islington, winter 1945' (between 258 and 259); the latter is another version of the same domestic scene with perhaps the most memorable image of the infant Richard, but in this take the scrap screen is almost entirely blocked by a chair.
4. See Patrick Kingsley 'When rebels toured the palace: How does Ukraine's presidential compound measure up?' *Guardian*. Available online at http://www.theguardian.com/world/2014/feb/24/rebels-toured-palace-ukraine-presidential-compound-viktor-yanukovych, accessed on 15 January 2015.

REFERENCES

Benjamin, Walter (1968) *Illuminations: Essays and Reflections*, trans. by Zohn, Harry, New York: Schocken Books.

Bowker, Gordon (2003) *George Orwell*, London: Little, Brown.

Cain, William E. (2007) Orwell's essays as a literary experience, Rodden, John (ed.) *The Cambridge Companion to George Orwell*, Cambridge: Cambridge University Press pp. 76–86.

Carter, John and Barker, Nicolas (2004) *ABC for Book Collectors*, New Castle, Delaware: Oak Knoll Press.

Crick, Bernard (1980) *George Orwell: A Life*, London: Secker and Warburg.

Dickens, Charles (1841) *The Old Curiosity Shop*: *The Works of Charles Dickens, Vol. 8*, New York: Books Inc.

Elsner, John, and Cardinal, Roger (eds) (1994) *The Cultures of Collecting*, London: Reaktion Books.

Gibson, William (1999) My obsession, *Wired*, 7 January. Available online at http://archive.wired.com/wired/archive/7.01/ebay.html, accessed on 20 Jan. 2011.

Gross, Miriam (ed.) (1971) *The World of George Orwell*, New York: Simon and Schuster.

Meyers, Jeffrey (2000) *Orwell: Wintry Conscience of a Generation*, New York: Norton.

Orwell, George (1986–1987 and 1998) *The Complete Works*, Davison, Peter (ed.) London: Secker and Warburg, 20 volumes.

Richards, Vernon (1998) *Orwell at Home (And Among the Anarchists): Essays and Photographs*, London: Freedom Press.

Rodden, John (ed.) (2007) *The Cambridge Companion to George Orwell*, Cambridge: Cambridge University Press.

Rodden, John (ed.) (2012) *The Cambridge Introduction to George Orwell*, Cambridge: Cambridge University Press.

Sartre, Jean-Paul (1950) The situation of the writer in 1947, '*What Is Literature?' and Other Essays*, London: Methuen & Co. pp. 141–238.

Stewart, Susan (1993) *On Longing: Narratives of the Miniature, the Gigantic, the Souvenir, the Collection*, Durham: Duke University Press.

Windsor, John (1994) Identity parades, Elsner, John, and Cardinal, Roger (eds) *The Cultures of Collecting*, London: Reaktion Books pp. 49–67.

CHAPTER FOUR

Little Nephews

Big Brother's Literary Offspring

ADAM STOCK

No doubt you've heard of the old lady who went to see *Hamlet* acted, and came away saying: 'I didn't care for it. There are too many quotations in it.' Well it's rather the same with Samuel Butler and certain other thinkers.

—GEORGE ORWELL (1998A: 172)

INTRODUCTION: FULL OF QUOTATIONS

Orwell's assessment of Samuel Butler's continuing cultural influence could easily be applied to his own journalism and novels, and especially *Nineteen Eighty-Four* (1989 [1949]).[1] Yet the very term 'Orwellian' has become the sort of cliché that Orwell himself railed against in essays such as 'Politics and the English Language' (1998a: 429). For Christopher Hitchens, 'to describe a state of affairs as "Orwellian" is to imply crushing tyranny and fear and conformism' (2002: 5), suggesting the term is a metonym for the full power of Oceania in *Nineteen Eighty-Four*.[2] Insofar as these themes recur in many dystopian fictions, however, to choose the term 'Orwellian' is implicitly to treat *Nineteen Eighty-Four* as a synecdoche for the whole genre. This includes texts such as Yevgeny Zamyatin's *We* (1972 [1921]), which Orwell openly acknowledged he had drawn upon, as well as the dozens of 'Orwellian' dystopian fictions that have followed over the subsequent years. Here, I argue that in such fictions Orwell exerts an influence in narrative terms as well as themes. In other words, to call a novel 'Orwellian' is to make a claim about its narrative, not just thematic concerns.

This is an important point to note because, in popular parlance, the term 'Orwellian' often serves merely to denote any perceived tyranny or dishonesty. Indeed, if 'Godwin's Law' states that 'as an online debate increases in length, it becomes inevitable that someone will eventually compare someone or something to Adolf Hitler or the Nazis' (OED Online, 2 November 2014), I would like to posit Stock's Addendum, *viz.* that as an online debate increases in length 'Godwin's Law' has a direct, positive correlation with the probability of someone invoking the terms 'Orwell,' 'Orwellian,' '*Nineteen Eighty-Four*' or 'Big Brother,' and with much the same effects. The rhetorical maneuvers mapped by 'Godwin's Law' and 'Stock's Addendum' share similar dangers: like the invocation of the horrors of the crimes of Nazism, drawing an analogy between a particular form of fictional world-making and political reality risks being read as mere hyperbole. Nevertheless, the widespread use of the term 'Orwellian' demonstrates that many readers continue to have extraordinarily affective reactions to *Nineteen Eighty-Four*.

Perhaps because the novel engenders fear and terror so effectively, critical responses to the novel have tended to dwell on it primarily as a political text rather than as a literary achievement. One early US review, for example, stated that 'as a narrative it has tension and actuality to a terrifying degree; still it will not do to judge it primarily as a literary work of art' (Rahv 1949: 743). *Nineteen Eighty-Four* is, indeed, an expressly political work; it engages with and positions itself within the utopian-dystopian tradition as a novel of political ideas, the 'basic thrust' of which is 'toward better understanding of the dialectic between Self and Society' (Malmgreen 1991: 17). Moreover, (and notwithstanding the issue of authorial intentionality) Orwell himself famously declared:

> When I sit down to write a book, I do not say to myself: 'I am going to produce a work of art.' I write it because there is some lie I want to expose, some fact to which I want to draw attention, and my initial concern is to get a hearing (1998b: 319).

The words which immediately follow are less-often quoted: 'I could not do the work of writing a book, or even a long magazine article, if it were not also an aesthetic experience' (ibid.). Approaches centered on the political content of *Nineteen Eighty-Four* have been valuable and productive for literary scholarship and journalism, but here I turn instead to Orwell's treatment of temporality and its role in the narrative structure of the novel. I aim to re-cast the term 'Orwellian' as relating not only to a description of tyranny, lies and fear, but a particular narrative means of explaining individual experience of the modern world.

Leaving aside the Newspeak Appendix, to which I will return below, *Nineteen Eighty-Four* follows the traditional Victorian three-part novel structure. This is a significant authorial decision that sets it apart from Orwell's other novels.[3] In what follows I show how Orwell employs narrative devices to explore and create new understandings of the world with which other novelists have subsequently entered into dialogue. Following the structure of *Nineteen Eighty-Four*, I split this discussion into three parts and an appendix, each tracking a section of Orwell's novel in conjunction with more recent fictions that I argue are 'Orwellian' for reasons that both engage with and go beyond the thematic. First, however, I turn to the question of subjective experience which lies at the heart of the Orwellian narrative.

THE EVERYDAY IN AIRSTRIP ONE

Phillip Wegner argues that Orwell owed a deep literary debt to the naturalism of George Gissing, and may have 'had Gissing's work in mind when developing his vision of Oceania' (2002: 189). Quoting Karl Mannheim's definition of 'conservative utopias' in which 'the presentness and immediacy of the past becomes an actual experience' (see Wegner 2002: 194), Wegner contends that:

> These nostalgically longed for past utopias … are likewise located on the textual horizons— think of Winston Smith's childhood, his golden country, the sanctuary above Mr. Charrington's shop, and the glass paperweight containing the Indian Ocean coral—while the naturalist vision remains the dominant note in the text (2003: 173).

Yet such images, and especially the glass paperweight, should be seen within the context not only of a potentially politically troubling nostalgia, but also within the everyday concerns of the immediate aftermath of World War II which, as Waugh concurs, Orwell 'captured vividly' (2010: 39). For Freedman, the concern with detail is symptomatic of the novel's 'loose-jointed, empiricist, Wellsian naturalism' (1984: 601). However, I argue that this recording of the everyday is more deeply indebted to Orwell's engagement with literary modernisms. As Antonis Balasopoulos argues of the latter:

> Literary modernism legitimates itself as a 'making strange' of the otherwise all-too-transparent, self-trivializing experience of the everyday, as the means toward a profound recognition that invests everyday life, for all its cesspools of boredom or distracted ennui, with a transcendental potential: Proust's time regained, the vast formal and stylistic ambition of *Ulysses* as aesthetic compensation for the transcendence the novel's actual content everywhere negates (2014: 281).

In *Nineteen Eighty-Four*, it is precisely Winston's ability to invest his inner life with 'transcendental potential' by making-strange his experiences of the everyday that so troubles the Oceania regime. As the at times awkward forays into metaphysics show, at the heart of the power struggle in *Nineteen Eighty-Four* is a battle over Winston's subjectivity, not his immortal soul (see Stock 2013: 117).[4] Indeed, for Smyer, the novel 'is to a great extent a psychodrama within a single mind' in which 'the whole narrative—the settings, characters, institutions, and events—is an objectification of Winston's inner self' (1979: 143). Like modernism itself, Orwell's naturalist text does not mark a significant shift away from the concern with the everyday for which Virginia Woolf satirized Edwardian novelists in *Mr. Bennett and Mrs. Brown* (Woolf 2008 [1924]), but rather a growing self-reflexivity with regards to the epistemological act of representation in artistic expression.

Ray Bradbury's *Fahrenheit 451* (1957) has a more conservative appeal to the undifferentiated past than Orwell's epistemological concerns with representation. When the protagonist Montag takes his illicit copy of the *Bible* to an ex-English professor called (significantly) Faber, the latter tells him that it has 'quality,' which he defines as 'texture':

> This book has *pores*. It has features. This book can go under the microscope. You'd find life under the glass, streaming past in infinite profusion. The more pores, the more truthfully recorded details of life per square inch you can get on a sheet of paper, the more 'literary' you are. That's *my* definition, anyway. *Telling detail.* Fresh detail ... now do you see why books are hated and feared? They show the pores in the face of life (ibid.: 83, emphasis in the original).

At the level of surface (that is to say, a level concerned with surface as distinct from a superficial 'surface level'), books as material objects are here described in terms reminiscent of the sensuously creamy and skin-like paper of Winston's diary. Books, Bradbury's character insinuates, are capable of a life-process corresponding to breathing or osmosis whereby they can both draw in and ooze out this *life detail*. The very purpose of books is concerned with microscopic 'detail,' and implicitly an ability to challenge official narratives precisely through their recording of seemingly trivial matters. Montag imagines the pages of a book burning 'delicately like the petals of a flower' (ibid.: 77): a beautiful, delicate and, in some way, ephemeral thing, in contrast to the permanence of the ideas they may contain.

The magnifying power of books gives their subjects a living depth that both freezes them in time and opens them up to a form of magnified gaze (reading), which is analogous to the empirical observations of the laboratory. Faber's description of a book (here the *Bible*) seems to mirror the symbolic life-form of the coral suspended and magnified inside the glass paperweight which Winston buys from Mr. Charrington in *Nineteen Eighty-Four* ('how small it always was!' Winston thinks to himself—and *of* himself—when he is arrested and the paperweight is smashed before his eyes by the Thought Police) (1989: 232). Faber's questionable description of 'quality,' therefore, points to an important intersection between metafiction and literary naturalism. Here books are rated in terms of 'truthfully recorded detail,' a definition that is seemingly meant to cover fiction and non-fiction alike. The *Bible* is chosen as a sacred text with didactic purpose whose truth is not to be found in its direct representation of contemporary reality but rather its transcendental message. Its materiality as banned artifact is conflated with the potential of its context as a vehicle for self-reflexivity. The *Bible*'s value lies not in connecting Faber to a lost past, but as a means of understanding the world through a self-reflexive understanding of his own life in narrative terms, much as Winston does when he sees the true size of the piece of coral.

This valuing of a religious textual artifact as an aesthetic experience of self-reflexive narrative understanding similarly occurs in the Orwellian narrative of James McTeigue's film *V for Vendetta* (2006), based on the classic Alan Moore graphic novel of the same name. In a secret cellar in his London townhouse, the TV star and secret opponent of the country's totalitarian regime, Gordon Deitrich (Stephen Fry), shows the heroine Evey (Natalie Portman) a collection of illegal artworks and documents, including his copy of the *Qu'ran*:

Evey:	What is that?
Deitrich:	It's a copy of the Qur'an. Fourteenth century.
Evey:	Are you Muslim?
Deitrich:	No, I'm in television.
Evey:	But why would you keep it?
Deitrich:	I don't have to be Muslim to find the images beautiful, or its poetry moving.

To reinforce the point that the value of the *Qu'ran* to Deitrich lies in its literary merit as a means for self-reflection rather than its literal revelatory message or didactic content, it is immediately contrasted with a shot of Deitrich's collection of gay erotica on the opposite wall. Like V, Deitrich has been 'wearing a mask' for a long time he says. The *Qu'ran* as text connects the essentially Kantian understanding of individual subjective aesthetic experience with political pluralism, but as an artifact within a glass case it resembles nothing so much as the Indian Ocean coral in *Nineteen Eighty-Four*—something with 'texture' that is precious and ephemeral. To Philip Wegner,

> Winston Smith's description of what makes the glass *objet d'art* a 'beautiful thing,' a process of aestheticization that erases its more mundane instrumental functions, recalls the Kantian definition of the aesthetic object as that which possesses 'purposiveness without purpose' … the aesthetic in *Nineteen Eighty-Four* operates … as a form of *nostalgia* (2002: 206–207, emphasis in original).

Similarly, what Deitrich ultimately values in the *Qu'ran* is his ability to curate it within his own private museum collection as an exotic cultural artifact. Placed within a glass case, the book becomes a relic not from the fourteenth century, but from the colonialist museum of the late-nineteenth to early twentieth centuries; exactly the same period as Winston Smith's paperweight.

PART I

The complex attitude toward temporality, which the emphasis on the material presentness of historical artifacts such as Winston's paperweight introduces, can be traced in the narrative structure of *Nineteen Eighty-Four* from its opening pages. In Part I of the novel, the passage of time in Winston's story world is detailed extensively. Winston's first diary entry is dated 4 April 1984, and chapters 1–5 *could* conceivably all take place within 24 hours of story world time. The only other date mentioned in the novel is Sunday 2 May when Winston and Julia meet in the countryside in Part II (123), and counting back from here Part I must end around 15 April. The amount of story world time compressed into each chapter varies from thirty minutes to around four hours. Within each chapter, however, Orwell introduces important additional information through the extensive employment of *analepses*, which are essentially flashbacks, or as Genette describes them, 'any evocation after the fact of an event that took place earlier than the point in the story where we are at any given moment' (1980: 40). Genette splits analepses into *internal* (within the time frame of the story) and *external* (anterior to the time frame of the story—for instance in a character's childhood).

Chapter	Length in story world time	Event(s)	Most notable analepses
One	35 minutes	Commences diary	Two Minutes Hate
Two	35 minutes	Fixes sink, dedicates diary 'to the future or to the past ...'	O'Brien's appearance in a dream seven years previously
Three	45 minutes	Dreams, wakes, performs 'physical jerks'	Reminiscences: Winston's childhood, his mother, the murky origins of Big Brother
Four	4 hours–4.5 hours	Work	Comrade Withers' story
Five	1 hour 10 minutes	Lunch in the canteen	Syme: Prisoners hanging. Parsons: his children's activities. Winston: Julia following him.
Six	?	Diary writing	Katherine (Winston's wife); visit to prostitute
Seven	?	Diary writing	Prole argument over saucepans; Jones, Aaronson and Rutherford.
Eight	c. 4 hours	Drinking in the prole pub, visit to Mr. Charrington's shop	Old man's reminiscences

Fig 1. Story world time and analepses in Part I of *Nineteen Eighty-Four*.

As Figure 1 shows, Part I is concerned with the everyday structurally as well as thematically. From the invocation of clocks striking 'thirteen' in the opening sentence, the narrator introduces the 'strange newness' or *novum* (Suvin 1972: 373) 'by which the work is shown to exist in a different world than that of the reader'. This is done in a deliberately incidental style, in which this 'thirteen' is notable because it is integrated into the everyday, detailed narration.

This concentration of story time alongside ever-longer external analepses suggests the influence of the sort of modernist techniques developed by Joyce, Woolf and others. Orwell's choice of a third person omniscient narrator here enables him to take the sort of tour of his fictional society around which most literary utopias traditionally were built, but rather than the explanation for its formation being revealed through dialogue as in, say, H. G. Wells's *A Modern Utopia* (2005 [1905]) or Edward Bellamy's *Looking Backward: 2000–1887* (2007 [1888]) here it is accomplished through free indirect discourse: the subject alone with his thoughts, revealing his increasing sense of alienation. This introduces a complex temporality. As we move through the series of events that form the novel's plot, the reader is constantly thrown between different time frames both relating to Winston's own life (his childhood, the photograph of the three 'traitors' and so on) and to wider historical periods—particularly the recent past and postwar present in which Orwell wrote.

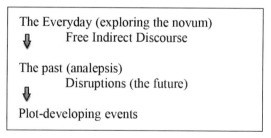

Fig 2. The structure of Part I of *Nineteen Eighty-Four.*

In the 1970s, feminist writers of utopian and dystopian fiction led a trend toward increasingly complex temporality. Reacting in part against the patriarchy of *Nineteen Eighty-Four* (see Stock 2012), their fictions included greater ambiguity between the positive and negative aspects of their imagined other worlds. Marge Piercy's *Woman on the Edge of Time* (1979 [1976]), for example, uses time travel to explore mental illness and liminal psychic spaces. In an authoritarian realist present, the protagonist Connie is kept prisoner in a public mental hospital, where she has visions of a utopian future. *Nineteen Eighty-Four* begins in the dystopian story world and travels through memory to the past and back via free indirect discourse. *Woman on the Edge of Time* begins with the bad place of a more recognizable 1970s present and flows back and forth to a future critical *eu-topia* (good place) via the more self-referentially postmodernist device of vision quests.

In the opening chapter, the protagonist Connie's niece, Dolly, arrives at her apartment, pursued by her pimp Geraldo, who is forcing her to undergo a backstreet abortion. When Connie attacks Geraldo, he beats her unconscious. The scene is closely described with the boiling of a kettle serving to anchor its temporal length. With the complicity of her own brother, Luis, Geraldo then has Connie committed to a mental hospital. Once tranquilizers administered against her will begin to take effect, the linear experience of time becomes less certain for Connie: 'The doctor asked her only her name and the date. First she said it was the fourteenth and then she changed it to the fifteenth, thinking it must be after midnight. She had no idea how long she had been unconscious' (ibid.: 19). Connie grasps for clues as to the time. Entering the day ward, 'she caught sight of a clock on the way in and she knew it was eleven in the morning' (ibid.: 21). But barely has the narrator described the other patients in the room (as seen by Connie) when it is lunchtime. As I will explore below, much like Winston's treatment in Part III of *Nineteen Eighty-Four*, part of the power of the institution is to control how Connie experiences time: 'Wednesday and Thursday went by like long, long freight trains and finally Friday came' (ibid.: 30). The opening chapters of *Woman on the Edge of Time* share with *Nineteen Eighty-Four* a concern with the expansion of a relatively short period of story time (around a week) through analepses. Hence Chapter Two extends the timeframe of Piercy's novel by looping back to the week preceding that of the opening chapter.

However, there are immediate and important differences in the way the two novels approach the key question of subjectivity and everyday experience from their first pages. For example, while Winston Smith has fantasies of committing terrible violence there is also something cowardly and cowering about him. In contrast, Connie is characterized as a fighter and a survivor, and she attacks Geraldo the pimp despite being outnumbered three-to-one by his hoodlums. But we learn from her interview with a social worker in Chapter Two that she also has a history of violence and that she previously lived on the proceeds of petty crime until the death of her partner drove her to drink and neglect of her daughter Angelina, who was eventually taken away from her for adoption after she hit her. Whereas the 'blowtorch' of Winston's hate is quickly forgotten in the narrative of *Nineteen Eighty-Four* (only re-surfacing when O'Brien asks him in Part II if he is prepared to throw acid in a child's face to further the cause of the Brotherhood), in the secure hospitals in which Connie is successively imprisoned, a capacity for violence is valued by the protagonist as a means for the survival of the integrity of the self.

PART II

The plot of Part II of *Nineteen Eighty-four* is structured around the twin poles of the consummation of the romantic tryst between Winston and Julia and their reading of the forbidden book, *The Theory and Practice of Oligarchical Collectivism*. Both the love story and the forbidden book have their precedents in texts such as Katherine Burdekin's *Swastika Night* (1985 [1937]). Orwell does, however, use these elements in a distinctive way.

Time passes more rapidly and disjointedly in Part II than in Part I, with numerous gaps between the chapters. Commencing four days after Part I finishes, the first chapter charts nine full days. After the 2 May rendezvous in Chapter 2, the following chapter references a market-place meeting on 6 May ('four evenings hence' (133)) and one other meeting during May to have sex in the ruins of a church. In chapter 4 we learn that 'four, five, six–seven times they met during the month of June' above Mr. Charrington's junkshop (Orwell 1989: 157). After this period O'Brien makes contact with Winston. Some days later he and Julia go to O'Brien's apartment and Hate Week commences soon afterward. The pair are arrested shortly after Hate Week ends. In the surviving earlier draft of the novel, Mr. Charrington says to Winston as he enters the shop for the last time, 'it's a try-ing month, is August' (Orwell, 1984: 195 [sheet 184]). But in the published novel, no such conversation appears, and the timescale of events could just as reasonably suggest mid-July 1984 as the arrest date. Whereas Part I covers a period of less than two weeks, Part II covers the events of roughly eleven to fifteen weeks.

The narrative style in Part II is generally more naturalistic, with literary experi-mentation centering on the 34-page extract from Goldstein's book (which O'Brien later claims to have written), *The Theory and Practice of Oligarchical Collectivism*. Winston reads the first paragraph of Chapter 1 in bed, when the frame narrator interrupts to inform us that 'Winston stopped reading, chiefly to appreciate that he *was* reading, in comfort and safety' (ibid.: 192). He then skips to Chapter 3 (ibid.: 193–208), before Julia's arrival again interrupts him. Both during their first encounter in the woods and here in the bedroom, carnal knowledge engenders or precipitates political knowledge. Returning to the book after they have been in bed for half an hour, Winston again starts at Chapter 1, this time reading aloud to Julia (ibid.: 209–226). The repetition of an entire paragraph serves to emphasize the importance of the tripartite split between 'High', 'Middle' and 'Low' social groups which Goldstein/O'Brien posit form the historical consistent organizing principle of societies. But it is noticeable that once again after reading it Winston stops, this time to check that Julia is still awake. Given Julia's general lack of interest in the book, we can assume that her comment 'Go on. It's marvellous' (ibid.: 210) is ironic and, indeed, she soon falls asleep.

Although Goldstein's text is located in specific temporal relation to the nar-rated events of the novel, the re-ordering of this text combined with the intru-sion of its different narrative voice (i.e., that of 'Goldstein' as supposed author) disrupts how we experience time in the story world. Indeed, on more than one occasion Orwell reminds us of the effectively paratextual status of the extracts by interrupting the 'reading' to remind us of the bedroom location in which the text is being read.

Cory Doctorow's Young Adult (YA) novel *Little Brother* (2008) chooses a more intimate first person narrative style to engage its audience with the lived experience of adolescent protagonist Marcus Yallow as he struggles to grow up in a world turned upside down by the authoritarianism and surveillance of the post-9/11 state. As with the first person narration of Zamyatin's *We*, the reader therefore shares the protagonist's partial and fragmented knowledge of events as they unfold. Unlike *We*, however, as a YA fiction *Little Brother* is heavily didactic. Having a teenage narrator enables Doctorow to explain the mathematical principles of security technology, the US constitution and other complex documents in a manner intended to be comprehensible without being patronizing. With little by way of a novum beyond a perfectly plausible terrorist attack, the plot owes more to the political thriller than to dystopian fiction. Notwithstanding this, in the linguistic register Doctorow's title references *Nineteen Eighty-Four*, as does Marcus Yallow's online identity at the start of the novel, W1n5t0n. In this regard, the novel follows Hitchens's understanding of the term 'Orwellian.'

Interestingly, *Little Brother* follows Jack London's strategy in an important regard concerning the protagonist's love interest:[5] Angela Carvelli is one of the few people Yallow can trust throughout the novel, even when they temporarily fall out. Indeed, the presentation of this romance marks Doctorow's critical engagement with gender relations in *Nineteen Eighty-Four*. In opposition to Orwell, all of the strong characters in *Little Brother* are women, from Marcus's torturer Carrie Johnston to his British mother Lillian, the journalist Barbara Stratford and his girlfriend Angela. As with *Nineteen Eighty-Four*, Ange is both a love interest and a partner in crime. In common with Julia, Ange has a highly developed sexuality, and is 'as much of a horn-dog' as Marcus (Doctorow 2008: 210). Indeed, like Julia it is often Ange who initiates sexual contact. Thus, despite Doctorow's critical distance from Orwell, one limitation of the use of a first person narrator is that sexuality is only explored through a presentation of heterosexual normative male desire—much as it is in *Nineteen Eighty-Four*.

But while Carvelli and Julia share a careful intelligence and justified paranoia, which helps them to flout rules, unlike Julia, Carvelli is as much of a political activist as Yallow. In *Nineteen Eighty-Four*, Julia fulfills Winston's fantasy of pre-war working class domestic prosperity by creating a domestic space above Mr. Charrington's shop filled with black market goods. Her motherly ability to source such material is, like her multiple past sexual partners, clearly something that excites Winston. She performs a 'transformation' by wearing make-up that makes her 'above all, far more feminine,' and a scent of synthetic violets which links her to the prostitute Winston describes visiting in Part I. Julia finds the party's deliberate falsifications of history, such as their claim to have invented the airplane, 'totally uninteresting' (Orwell 1989: 161). Winston is only half-joking when he says that she is 'only a rebel from the waist downwards' (ibid.: 163).

Marcus already has a strong mother figure and Ange fulfills a rather different role of co-conspirator. She is a rebellious hacker who avidly engages with the XNet online community that Marcus establishes to oppose Federal Government oppression. It is her idea to hold an anonymous online press conference through a computer game. In an especially didactic manoeuver, much to Marcus's own surprise they put off having sex in order to participate in this press conference. Marcus has given up the moniker 'W1n5t0n' by this point in favor of the pseudonym 'M1k3y.' When Marcus gets tired of participating in the press conference he tells us that he handed 'the keyboard to Ange and let her be M1k3y for a while. It didn't really feel like M1k3y and me were the same person anymore anyway' (Doctorow 2008: 230). Like Goldstein, M1k3y has become an iconic symbol of resistance and vilification that has little to do with a real-life identity: M1k3y is a networked identity, a set of political ideas. He expresses the shared thoughts and feelings of an activist network, encouraging others to speak for the movement and reposting and linking to their blogs and citizen journalism. The downside is that precisely because of his anonymity 'M1k3y' can be used by anyone, a point driven home when Marcus is sent a video of his torturer Johnston boasting about her successful infiltration of Xnet:

> Our people in the Xnet have built up a lot of influence. The Manchurian Bloggers are running as many as fifty blogs each, flooding the chat channels, linking to each other, mostly just taking the party line set by this M1k3y. But they've already shown that they can provoke radical action, even when M1k3y is putting the brakes on (ibid.: 272).

The Department for Homeland Security (DHS) are taking the M1k3y, if the pun may be excused. If the Goldstein/O'Brien text introduces an idea that even documents claiming to resist hegemonic power structures can be faked, then the DHS in *Little Brother* demonstrates that as online identities are merely textual, their creators can only ever claim limited ownership. A key message of Doctorow's text is that if the online world is democratizing and a potential means of holding those in power to account, it is also a potential means for those in power to marshal and manufacture dissent simply to increase their own power and tyranny.

PART III

With the exception of two final short scenes, Part III of *Nineteen Eighty-Four* takes place entirely within the Ministry of Love. If Part I records time obsessively to the minute, mirroring Winston's growing alienation from Oceania, then a key means by which O'Brien attacks Winston's sense of autonomous subjecthood in Part III is by denying him the means to measure time. Within the blank walls of

Miniluv, the narrator gives the reader little information as to how long Winston's incarceration lasts, a point the protagonist first notices when with a growing feeling of hunger he realizes that 'it might be twenty-four hours since he had eaten, it might be thirty-six' (Orwell 1989: 237). There is a direct path from this sense of helplessness to the terror of Room 101.

Before O'Brien comes to Winston he encounters a succession of cellmates, including the poet Ampleforth, the 'skull-faced' man and the 'chinless' man, Parsons, and the prole woman who, with vomit-smelling breath, tells Winston: 'I could be your mother.' Each of the visitors teaches Winston something about the lot of a prisoner in the Ministry of Love, and all of them in their different ways plunge him deeper into despair, loneliness and isolation. In narrative terms, these characters build tension through revealing information to Winston (and the implied reader) such as the existence of the terrible Room 101. They also serve to show how Winston is caught up in a vast state apparatus that is big enough to concern itself with a lowly desk clerk such as himself in a personal manner.

These scenes anchor the fantastic and even absurdist conversations between Winston and O'Brien that follow in a more believable experience of incarceration. They show that it requires more than brute force and O'Brien's superior intellect to break Winston Smith. As O'Brien himself puts it: 'There are three stages in your re-integration ... there is learning, there is understanding, and there is acceptance' (ibid.: 273). The dialogue that ensues between the protagonist and his social superior is characteristically but not distinctively Orwellian. Such scenes can be found in numerous older dystopias including those of Aldous Huxley (in *Brave New World*, of 1932) and Zamyatin. Indeed, these sorts of set piece conversations can be easily traced at least as far as Dostoyevsky's *The Brothers Karamazov* (of 1889) (see Kumar 1987: 122, 338). For other authors, Orwell's text is only one among many models for this technique. In the highly metafictional conversation between the eponymous hero and 'the Author' in Alasdair Gray's *Lanark* (1981), a footnote states that this type of dialogue:

> ... is mainly a device to let a self-educated Scot (to whom the 'dominie' is the highest form of social life) tell the world what he thinks of it: three books by disappointed socialists which appeared after the second world war [sic] and centred upon what I will call dialogue under threat: *Darkness at Noon* by Arthur Koestler [1940], *1984* by George Orwell, and *Barbary Shore* by Norman Mailer [1951] (2011: n. 6, 489).

In a similar vein, David Mitchell's acclaimed novel *Cloud Atlas* (2004), which tells six interlinking stories spanning lives from the 1700s to the far future, styles one of these six stories on the model Gray terms 'dialogue under threat.' Mitchell frames the story 'An Orison of Sonmi-451' as the interview of a prisoner called Sonmi by an oral historian called 'the Archivist' in far-future Seoul before her execution. Sonmi is a genetically modified clone who has escaped from slavery as a server in a fast food restaurant, nine storeys below ground in a shopping mall. While the story's title references Ray Bradbury's *Fahrenheit 451*, it is made clear that *Nineteen Eighty-Four* is one among several source texts for the structure through direct reference to Orwell alongside Huxley in the text.

Cloud Atlas as a whole is concerned with the intertwining history, global development and future of story telling in the novel form, with special regard to genre fiction. In the story of Sonmi-451, Mitchell patches together features drawn from a whole host of other dystopias. Sonmi is an autodidact who teaches herself about world history from a portable electronic device, a little like Winston teaches himself from Goldstein's book and John Savage in *Brave New World* teaches himself about culture through a battered copy of Shakespeare's *Complete Works*. Likewise, and in common with *Nineteen Eighty-Four*, *Brave New World*, *We*, John Wyndham's *The Chrysalids* (1958 [1955]), Suzanne Collins's *The Hunger Games* (2011 [2008]), and any number of other dystopias, the most important historical event between the authorial present and the future time in which the narrative is a terrible (atomic) war, here called 'the Skirmish.' Yet as is common in dystopian fiction, many of the details of this war are withheld from the reader. Indeed, as with so many other dystopias, books (and films) from the past are censored in Sonmi's time. The university library from which she downloads books to her handheld device refuses many requests, but Sonmi tells her interviewer: 'I succeeded with two Optimists translated from the Late English, Orwell and Huxley; and Washington's *Satires on Democracy*' (Mitchell 2004: 220). No such work by that stalwart democratic republican George Washington exists. But Orwell and Huxley are not commonly regarded as optimists either (though there are slivers of hope in their dystopian novels): this is a signal that these works have been doctored or amended in 'translation' from what is now (presumably) a dead language: 'Who controls the present controls the past,' as O'Brien would have it. At the end of Sonmi's story, she reveals that she has understood all along that she has been a pawn used by the 'corprocracy,' an actor in an elaborate game. But as with Doctorow's *Little Brother*, she subverts the story that those in power want to project about the revolutionary inhumanity of clones by use of electronic communication. By co-operating with her 'judases' (ibid.: 364) Sonmi is able to guarantee the 'billionfold' reproduction of her catechisms about the rights of 'fabricants.' She ends by issuing a warning: 'To Corprocracy, to Unanimity, to the Ministry of Testaments, to the Juche and to the Chairman, I quote Seneca's warning to Nero: "No matter how many of us you kill, you will never kill your successor"' (ibid.: 365).

NEWSPEAK APPENDIX

Sonmi's story is only one of six in the *Cloud Atlas* narrative. The (chronologically) subsequent story leaves the reader in no doubt that the world powers Sonmi describes are overthrown and the knowledge of how to create cloned humans has been lost. By way of contrast, *Nineteen Eighty-Four*'s ending is ambiguous. Readers are forced to choose between seeing Winston's final defeat and expression of love for Big Brother as a cry of despair, or else reading the Newspeak Appendix as a historical document from some point external to the main narrative, implying that Oceania is later defeated. Orwell himself never explicitly indicated whether the end of the novel expresses hope or pessimism.

One likely source for the idea of an appendix is Jack London's *The Iron Heel* (1908), which is written as a first-hand account of the struggle of Avis Everhard, a female member of the underground resistance that fights the 'Oligarchy' or 'Iron Heel.' Throughout the novel footnotes supposedly written by a scholar some 400 years after the narrative events of the story describe the fall of a regime which from the start we are told the main characters do not live to see. This narrative framing resembles Margaret Atwood's description of Orwell's ending:

> The essay on Newspeak is written in standard English, in the third person, and in the past tense, which can only mean that the regime has fallen, and that language and individuality have survived. For whoever has written the essay on Newspeak, the world of *Nineteen Eighty-Four* is over (2003).

The appendix at the end of Atwood's own novel *The Handmaid's Tale* (1985) is the transcript of a keynote speech at the 'Twelfth Symposium on Glideadean Studies, held as part of the International Historical Association Convention ... June 25, 2195' (2009: 311). The future-set dystopian world of Gilead is itself othered into the historical past, a move which Atwood herself (2003) has subsequently stated is indebted to Orwell's Newspeak Appendix. Atwood's novel, therefore, ends with a sense of hopeful closure, while refusing to outline the precise mechanisms by which the downfall occurs, as 'the past is a great darkness, and filled with echoes' (ibid.: 324).

Marge Piercy's *Woman on the Edge of Time* (1979 [1976]) contains a more pessimistic Orwellian ending. In the climax Connie is taken from Rockover, the public mental hospital where she is held, to participate in a mind-control experiment using electronic brain implants in a research hospital. The penultimate chapter ends with Connie poisoning the doctors' coffee in order to escape this operation, justifying her act as part of her war to prevent an even more dystopian future she has seen in a vision. The final chapter consists entirely of selected medical notes that undermine the reliability of Connie's perspective. The book ends: 'There were one hundred thirteen more pages. They all followed Connie back to Rockover' (ibid.: 381), suggesting that she is apprehended and defeated. Although it is written in a different style, discourse and format to the rest of the novel it is surely significant that this final chapter, which foregrounds the fantastic nature of the preceding story, is integrated into the narrative arc and not an appendix. While the shift in perspective unsettles our understanding and empathies, *Woman on the Edge of Time* remains temporally self-contained, ending at a defined point and in a sharply critical vein.

More recently, however, there has been a pronounced tendency toward unambiguously positive and even cathartic endings in dystopian fiction, shedding the influence of *Nineteen Eighty-Four*'s ambiguity. This tendency has a positive correlation with strong growth in the number and popularity of dystopias written for the Young Adult market. As Basu, Broad and Hintz argue, cathartic endings in such works presume that:

> … adolescents should be idealists, offering a gratifying view of adolescent readers as budding political activists—a portrayal that flatters adolescents and reassures adults that they are more than apathetic youth. However, the easily digestible prescriptions suggested by many of these novels may allow young readers to avoid probing the nuances, ambiguities, and complexities of social ills and concerns too deeply (2013: 5).

At the very moment that speculative fiction set in radically alternative story worlds has become a dominant force in mainstream entertainment, such speculations have become ever more conservative or narrowly reformist at base. These novels carry a message that certain universal values and support for the *status quo* can help communities to bind together for the common good, no matter how radically estranged the circumstances. As Couzelis puts it: 'Some narratives risk making the future look so bad that young readers are grateful for their contemporary society as is' (2013: 133).

CONCLUSIONS: ORWELL'S 'LITTLE NEPHEWS' ARE TROUBLESOME TEARAWAYS

Since the end of the Cold War, dystopias have become big business. In the 1980s and 1990s, 'the consolidation of global entertainment industries had a significant influence on the kind of SF produced' (Bould and Vint 2011: 165). For dystopian fiction too, since this period the potential for the re-presentations of the same story world across different media including film, TV, novels, comics and video games, has influenced the type of narratives produced. The instantly recognizable Hollywood happy ending, which restores familiar patterns of power, is noticeable even in many of the more progressive texts. Thus Katherine Broad notes that Suzanne Collins's *The Hunger Games* has been celebrated for its portrayal of a 'tough-minded' female hero, Katniss Everdeen, who proves that 'girls can do anything boys can do, including strategize, make demands, and even hunt and kill.' However, Broad continues, 'a closer reading suggests that her character also imparts a very different message, one that tells girls the importance of growing up to find satisfaction in heterosexual love and the nuclear family' (2013: 117–118). If in *Nineteen Eighty-Four* Winston and Julia's rebellion rotates around their private romantic love, in *Hunger Games* it is ultimately in romantic love and not in the widespread social change which Katniss and her fellow revolutionaries bring about that the novels provide narrative closure.

Similarly, Doctorow's *Little Brother* contains a radical liberal edge in its didactic efforts to educate the reader about state surveillance, constitutional powers and the potentially liberating uses of technology. But Marcus Yallow's opposition to the US government is based upon his understanding of the liberal social contract theory of the Founding Fathers. The novel ends with the overthrow of the Department of Homeland Security and a return to constitutional government respecting the US constitution as a hallowed document guaranteeing individual rights.

Orwell's 'Little Nephews' are troublesome tearaways who have ruthlessly criticized and torn apart both the content and structure of *Nineteen Eighty-Four* even as they have borrowed and appropriated from it. The most perceptive and acute of his followers have engaged with the novel not only as a presentation of ideas or as a means of invoking an atmosphere of fear and tyranny, but as a work concerned with the alienating experience of modernity. By this means the novel continues to exert a powerful effect on readers and remains invaluable to contemporary novelists.

NOTES

1. In her valuable and highly critical discussion of *Nineteen Eighty-Four*, Daphne Patai contends: 'The main contribution of *Nineteen Eighty-Four* to modern culture probably resides in the catchy names, such as Newspeak and doublethink that Orwell invented for familiar phenomena' (1984: 257). Patai does not dwell on these aspects, however, although she suggests: 'In the future … interest in Orwell will focus not on his work but on the phenomenon of his fame and what it reveals about our own civilization' (ibid.: x). In addition to such well-known examples of neologisms from *Nineteen Eighty-Four*, according to the *OED* Orwell is responsible for 'Cold War.' He was also an early adopter (though not the inventor) of 'totalitarianism'.

2. More polemically, Hitchens asserts a second meaning: 'to describe a piece of writing as "Orwellian" is to recognize that human resistance to these terrors is unquenchable' (2002: 5). This relies on a specific sympathetic reading of both Orwell's final novel and his wider oeuvre for which Hitchens does not provide evidence.

3. *Burmese Days* (1934) is split into 25 numbered chapters, *A Clergyman's Daughter* (1935) is split into five 'chapters' (each with several numbered sections), *Coming Up for Air* (1940) is split into four parts, and the children's-novel length *Animal Farm* (1945) is split into 10 chapters.

4. Wegner (2002) argues that this is a question of individual autonomy, and (drawing on Mannheim) that Orwell produces a 'conservative utopia' (pp. 192–197).

5. For a definition of Prucher, Jeff (ed.) (2006) Novum, *The Oxford Dictionary of Science Fiction*, Oxford: Oxford University Press. Available online at http://www.oxfordreference.com/view/10.1093/acref/9780195305678.001.0001/acref-9780195305678-e-421, accessed on 4 January 2015

6. Both Orwell and Zamyatin may have drawn on Jack London's *The Iron Heel* (1908) in placing a star-crossed romance at the heart of their narratives. But as Parrinder points out, it is never certain what the personal feelings and motives are of either I–330 in *We* or Julia in *Nineteen Eighty-Four* (2010: 170), a situation quite unlike London's Avis and Ernest Everhard.

REFERENCES

Atwood, Margaret (2003) Orwell and me, *Guardian*, 16 June. Available online at http://www.theguardian.com/books/2003/jun/16/georgeorwell.artsfeatures, accessed on 7 January 2015.

Atwood, Margaret (2009) *The Handmaid's Tale*, London: Bloomsbury.

Balasopoulos, Antonis (2014) Factories, utopias, decoration and upholstery, *Utopian Studies*, Vol. 25, No. 2, pp. 268–298.

Basu, Balaka, Broad, Katherine R. and Hintz, Carrie (2013) Introduction, Basu, Balaka, Broad, Katherine R. and Hintz, Carrie (eds) *Contemporary Dystopian Fiction for Young Adults: Brave New Teenagers*, New York: Routledge pp. 1–15.

Bellamy, Edward (2007 [1888]) *Looking Backward, 2000–1887*, Oxford: Oxford University Press.

Bould, Mark and Vint, Sheryll (2011) *The Routledge Concise History of Science Fiction*, Abingdon: Routledge.

Bradbury, Ray (1957) *Fahrenheit 451*, London: Corgi.

Broad, Katherine R. (2013) The dandelion in the spring, Basu, Balaka, Broad, Katherine R. and Hintz, Carrie (eds) *Contemporary Dystopian Fiction for Young Adults: Brave New Teenagers*. New York: Routledge pp. 117–130.

Burdekin, Katherine (1937) *Swastika Night*, London: Victor Gollancz.

Collins, Suzanne (2008) *The Hunger Games*, New York: Scholastic.

Couzelis, Mary J. (2013) The future is pale: Race in contemporary young adult dystopian novels, Basu, Balaka, Broad, Katherine R. and Hintz, Carrie (eds) *Contemporary Dystopian Fiction for Young Adults: Brave New Teenagers*, New York: Routledge pp. 131–144.

Doctorow, Cory (2008) *Little Brother*, London: Harper Voyager.

Dostoyevsky, Fyodor (2003 [1880]) *The Brothers Karamazov*, trans. McDuff, David, London: Penguin.

Freedman, Carl (1984) The antinomies of *Nineteen Eighty-Four*, *Modern Fiction Studies*, Vol. 30, No. 4, pp. 601–620.

Genette, Gérard (1980) *Narrative Discourse: An Essay in Method*, trans. Lewin, Jane E., Ithaca: Cornell University Press.

Gray, Alasdair (2011 [1981]) *Lanark*, Edinburgh: Canongate.

Hitchens, Christopher (2002) *Orwell's Victory*, London: Penguin.

Huxley, Aldous (2005 [1932]) *Brave New World* and *Brave New World Revisited*, New York: Harper Perennial.

Kumar, Krishan (1987) *Utopia and Anti-Utopia in Modern Times*, Oxford: Basil Blackwell.

London, Jack (1908) *The Iron Heel*, London: Macmillan.

Malmgreen, Carl D. (1991) *Worlds Apart: Narratology of Science Fiction*, Bloomington: Indiana University Press.

McTeigue, James (dir.) (2005) *V For Vendetta*, Warner Brothers: USA.

Mitchell, David (2004) *Cloud Atlas*, London: Hodder and Stoughton.

Orwell, George (1984) *Nineteen Eighty-Four: The Facsimile of the Extant Manuscript*, Davison, Peter H. (ed) London: Secker & Warburg.

Orwell, George (1989) *Nineteen Eighty-Four*, Davison, Peter H. (ed.) London: Penguin.

Orwell, George (1998a) *The Complete Works*, Vol. 17: *I Belong to the Left: 1945*, Davison, Peter H. (ed.) London: Secker & Warburg.

Orwell, George (1998b) *The Complete Works*, Vol. 18: *Smothered Under Journalism 1946*, Davison, Peter H. (ed.) London: Secker & Warburg.

Parrinder, Patrick (2010) Utopia and Romance, Claeys, Gregory (ed.) *The Cambridge Companion to Utopian Literature*, Cambridge: Cambridge University Press.

Patai, Daphne (1984) *The Orwell Mystique: A Study in Male Ideology*, Amherst: University of Massachusetts Press.

Piercy, Marge (1979 [1976]) *Woman on the Edge of Time*, London: The Women's Press.

Rahv, Philip (1949). The unfuture of Utopia, *Partisan Review*, Vol. 16, No. 7, pp. 743–749.

Smyer, Richard I. (1979) *Primal Dream and Primal Crime: Orwell's Development as a Psychological Novelist*, Columbia and London: University of Missouri Press.

Stock, Adam (2012) Of pigs and men: The politics of nature in the fiction of George Orwell, Keeble, Richard Lance (ed.) *Orwell Today*, Bury St. Edmunds: Abramis pp. 38–53.

Stock, Adam (2013) Dystopia as post-Enlightenment critique in George Orwell's *Nineteen Eighty-Four*, Vieira, Fátima (ed.) *Dystopia(n) Matters: On the Page, on Screen, on Stage*, Newcastle-upon-Tyne: Cambridge Scholars Press pp. 115–129.

Suvin, Darko (1972) On the poetics of the science fiction genre, *College English*, Vol. 34, No. 3, pp. 372–382.

Waugh, Patricia (2010) The historical context of post-war British literature, Cockin, Katherine and Morrison, Jago (eds) *The Post-War British Literature Handbook*, London: Continuum pp. 35–37.

Wegner, Phillip E. (2002) *Imaginary Communities: Utopia, The Nation and the Spatial Histories of Modernity*, Berkeley: University of California Press.

Wegner, Phillip E. (2003) Where the prospective horizon is omitted: Naturalism and dystopia in *Fight Club* and *Ghost Dog*, Baccolini, Raffaella and Moylan, Tom (eds) *Dark Horizons: Science Fiction and the Dystopian Imagination*, New York: Routledge pp. 167–185.

Wells, H. G. (2005 [1905]) *A Modern Utopia*, Claeys, Greg and Parrinder, Patrick (eds.) London: Penguin.

Woolf, Virginia (2008 [1924]) Mr. Bennett and Mrs. Brown, *Selected Essays*, David Bradshaw (ed.) Oxford: Oxford World Classics pp. 32–36.

Wyndham, John (1958 [1955]) *The Chrysalids*, London: Penguin.

Zamyatin, Yevgeny (1972 [1921]) *We*, trans. Ginsburg, Mirra. New York: Harper Collins.

Orwell, THE Literary Canon—AND Further Explorations

CHAPTER FIVE

In Defence OF Bernard Crick

PAUL ANDERSON

George Orwell's politics have always been contentious. In his lifetime, he was a notable intellectual contrarian whose antipathy to received wisdom of all kinds made him admirers and enemies across the political spectrum—and since his death in 1950 the argument about where he stood politically has been vigorous. It shows no sign of ending soon. Of course, the polemics ebb and flow according to events in the real world and publishers' schedules, and there has been little in the past quarter-century to match the vituperation of the Cold War battle for Orwell.[1] Apart from a few notable peaks of invective—the last of them in 2003, the centenary of his birth, the one before that in 2000, the 50th anniversary of his death—the struggle for Orwell's legacy has recently been subdued.

Yet even today, people from all over the political spectrum *still* want to appropriate the mantle of Orwell—from Trotskyists and anarchists on the far left who embrace the anti-Stalinist revolutionary socialism of *Homage to Catalonia* (1938) to conservatives who revere him as a 'Tory anarchist' and consider *Nineteen Eighty-Four* (1949) as the ultimate warning against any kind of collectivism.[2] On the other side, there are those who find different things with which to fault Orwell—leftists who see him as an establishment Cold War informer or a defeatist, feminists who question his attitudes to women, and so on.[3] And that is before you take into account the vast interpretative literature by writers without any obvious partisan political preferences and the dozens of authors engaging with particular aspects of Orwell's politics, from the theory of geopolitics to surveillance.[4]

This one will run and run, and so it should. Orwell was a complex and in many ways contradictory writer who drew on a vast range of personal experience and reading, constantly developing his ideas. He did this, moreover, not primarily by issuing political manifestos but by way of fiction and cultural criticism, much of it designed as satire or polemic to provoke real or imagined critics and enemies and thus notably open to multiple interpretations. For all Orwell's famous clarity and simplicity of style, much of his writing is deeply politically ambiguous. If it is clear that *Animal Farm* is an allegory for the Bolshevik revolution and its aftermath that is unequivocally anti-Stalinist, it is by no means obvious what its lessons are. That all revolutions are doomed? That Trotsky was right, or that the anarchists were, about 1917?

Much the same can be said of *Nineteen Eighty-Four*: the novel is unmistakably a satire on key characteristics of world politics in the 1930s and 1940s, notably the seeming permanence of war and the emergence of totalitarian states that rule by propaganda, surveillance and terror, with Stalin's Russia as the exemplar. But to what extent was it intended as predictive? How far does it pick up on trends Orwell perceived in 1940s Labour Britain or in the United States? It is impossible to give definitive answers to such questions. Even Orwell's apparently straight-forward political journalism of the 1940s leaves a lot hanging. He is, for example, explicit in his denunciation of leftist fellow-travellers and crypto-communists in Labour's ranks. Whether he saw them as genuine potential contenders for political power is Britain, however, anything but evident.

Nevertheless, my contention is that the best description of Orwell's mature politics is still that given by the late Bernard Crick more than 30 years ago: that Orwell was 'a pretty typical *Tribune* socialist.'[5] Orwell was a regular contributor to *Tribune*, the Labour left weekly, from 1940; was the paper's literary editor from 1943 to 1945; and from 1943 to 1947 (with a couple of gaps) contributed a column, mostly under the title 'As I Please,' that occupied the most prominent spot in the paper and is to this day the model of how to write opinion journalism for many practitioners of the craft (Anderson 2006). From 1947 until his death in 1950 he remained sympathetic towards the paper (though not uncritically) and engaged with his friends on the staff. Some writers—most notably the brilliant and charming Polish exile journalist Leopold Labedz in a rumbustious piece in *Encounter* in 1984—have tried to dissociate Orwell from *Tribune* by showing that he was at odds with the paper's editorial line more often than not. But he wasn't: for the last years of his life Orwell was as much a member of the *Tribune* club as anyone could be (Labedz 1984).[6]

TRIBUNE SOCIALISM

But what is *Tribune* socialism? When Orwell wrote for the paper, *Tribune* was—as today—the organ of the democratic left in the Labour Party, independent of the party leadership but unswerving in its support of Labour at election time. But it had not always occupied this political space. It had been founded by the left-wing MPs Stafford Cripps, Aneurin Bevan and others in 1937—bankrolled by Cripps and to a lesser extent by the Labour MP George Strauss—as the weekly organ of a quixotic attempt to create a 'united front' against fascism, war and the National government, the Unity Campaign. The campaign involved Cripps's Labour-affiliated Socialist League, the Communist Party of Great Britain and the Independent Labour Party, and it lasted a few weeks before it foundered in the face of the hostility of the Labour Party establishment, which expelled the Socialist League. What remained of it disintegrated within months after the CPGB and ILP fell out irrevocably over Spain and Stalin's show trials (see Pimlott 1977). *Tribune* survived the debacle with the help of Cripps's cash and the support of Victor Gollancz's Left Book Club. But it continued to flog the dead horse of Communist-Labour unity, adopting the Communist Party policy in favor of a 'popular front' of Labour, communists and 'bourgeois' anti-fascists—a platform that resulted in Cripps and Bevan being expelled from the Labour Party—and wholly uncritical of the Soviet Union.

It was not until 1939–1940, in the wake of the Nazi-Soviet pact and the out-break of war in Europe, that it shook off the CP's baleful influence. By spring 1940, with Cripps off the scene, Strauss in charge of the purse-strings and Bevan as political director, it had broken definitively with the Moscow line—rather tar-dily for Orwell, who claimed (diplomatically, in a piece he wrote for its tenth anniversary), to have been only vaguely aware of its existence before then. And ever since its break with the CP it has been where the democratic Labour left has argued and sometimes fought its campaigns.

Of course, many aspects of *Tribune*'s politics have changed over time, and it is difficult to find consistency in its approach in some crucial areas—most impor-tantly here the Cold War and Soviet communism, on which right to the end in 1989 it was always a battleground between optimists who hoped for the best from every new Soviet bloc leader and pessimists who despaired that the Soviet model would bury all hope for democratic socialism. On this, Labedz's 1984 polemic in *Encounter* hits some targets (Labedz 1984).[7] But there are two counters to Labedz: first, that he misunderstands *Tribune*'s political culture; and secondly that he does not understand the politics of the late 1940s.

For all its wavering, there is an underlying consistency to *Tribune*. Since 1940, the paper has always been a voice for common ownership of the means of pro-duction, distribution and exchange, egalitarianism, anti-colonialism, free elections, support for the Labour Party—and for a culture of libertarian freedom of expres-sion. It has never published only Labour loyalist writers, and has always been open to the non-Labour left—particularly to anarchists, pacifists and Trotskyists but also sometimes to communists and, latterly, the Greens—as well as to all sorts of single-issue campaigner. Labedz fails to grasp that, except for its first three years, *Tribune* has always been pluralist.

Labedz makes a particular meal of the 1940s, when Orwell wrote for it. The paper was broadly anti-communist throughout that period, viscerally so after 1947—and Labedz does not realize this. Yes, during the war, it was all-out for Allied victory just like every newspaper in Britain, supporting the heroic efforts of the Red Army on the Eastern front. Yes, in 1946–1947—with Bevan in government and the paper's editorial direction under his protégé Michael Foot—*Tribune* briefly argued for Britain and Europe to form an independent bloc, aligned with neither the US nor the Soviet Union—a position radically at odds with the Labour government but also with the communists (see Crossman, Foot and Mikardo 1947).

Tribune's enthusiasm for non-alignment was, however, fleeting: it collapsed in the face of the hostility of the Labour leadership and of the Soviet suppression of democratic socialist parties and independent trade unions in Eastern Europe. *Tribune* embraced the West. From the summer of 1947 the only key question on which the Foot *Tribune* disagreed with Ernest Bevin, the foreign secretary, was Palestine, on which the paper took a Zionist line. The paper condemned unequivocally the Soviet crushing of democracy in Hungary (1947) and Czechoslovakia (1948) and the Soviet blockade of West Berlin (1948–1949); and it enthusiastically supported the creation of NATO as an anti-Soviet military alliance in 1947–1948.

LABOUR LIBERTARIANISM

Orwell's politics cannot be reduced to '*Tribune* socialism'—or vice versa. He and *Tribune* disagreed, notably on its position on the Cold War in 1946–1947 and Zionism. He took a harder line than *Tribune* on Soviet fellow-travellers in Labour's ranks, particularly the MP Konni Zilliacus.[8] But these were niggling differences. For the last decade of his life, Orwell was a free-thinking but hardly atypical Labour libertarian leftist, and to situate him otherwise—as John Newsinger (1999) and Robert Colls (2013) both do in their different ways, Newsinger by exaggerating Orwell's dissidence from Labour, Colls by playing it down—is a mistake. When he wrote, in 'Why I Write'—published in the small magazine *Gangrel* in 1946 and read by next to nobody at the time—that 'every line of serious work that I have written since 1936 has been written, directly or indirectly, against totalitarianism and for democratic socialism, as I understand it,' he was telling the truth (Orwell 1946a). And 'democratic socialism' as he understood it was neither, at least from 1941–1942, a revolutionary creed nor a matter of accepting that, as Herbert Morrison is supposed to have put it, 'socialism is what a Labour government does.'

Orwell's journey to *Tribune* socialism was not straightforward. Born in India, the son of a colonial official, in 1903, Eric Blair was educated at a southern England prep school and Eton, then took a job in the imperial Indian police force. There is no indication that the young Blair had much interest in politics until he decided to become a writer, dropped out of the police and adopted the pen-name George Orwell. What made him do what he did is an intriguing question, but unless a new cache of letters is discovered in some Southwold attic that provides new evidence we shall be in the land of guesswork here forever.

It is, nevertheless, incontestable that the Orwell of *Down and Out in Paris and London* (1933), *Burmese Days* (1934) and *A Clergyman's Daughter* (1935) was a young man raging against the complacency of the English middle classes about poverty and imperialism. It is also incontrovertible that he was increasingly influenced in his politics by the Independent Labour Party *milieu* of the small-circulation review *Adelphi*, owned by John Middleton Murry and co-edited by Richard Rees and Max Plowman, although he was still working out exactly where he stood.[9]

But was Orwell being serious in the early 1930s when he told his *Adelphi* ILP friends—Rees (1961: 122) and Jack Common (see Coppard and Crick 1984: 142)—that he was a 'Tory anarchist'? In a recent article in *Political Studies*, Peter Wilkin tries to show that he was, and that he remained a 'Tory anarchist' for the rest of his life—though Wilkin says that 'this does not represent a theoretical framework; it is not an ideological response to social change,' which rather spoils his case (Wilkin 2013). He goes on: 'On the contrary, Tory anarchism is a stance, usually driven by artistic or literary ambitions, and a practice that reflects a certain temper that is in significant part a reaction to profound changes in Britain's place in the world system' (ibid.), in particular the decline of empire. For Wilkin, 'Tory anarchism' is moral and cultural conservatism based on disdain for modern fads that undermine or underestimate the inherent common decency of the British working class, on pessimism and empiricism, on patriotism, with a penchant for satire and contrarianism.

This is a theme worth exploring, not least because there is a grand tradition from Jonathan Swift (1667–1745) to the London-based satirical magazine, *Private Eye*, of just such an attitude to life, but there are real problems with it too. Wilkin's parameters are drawn too widely: who is *not* a 'Tory anarchist' on this definition apart from the desiccated calculating machines of Fabian socialism, orthodox communism, free-market economics, university quality assurance administrations—and the whole of the professional political class that has grown up over the past 40 years addicted to opinion polling?

As Wilkin almost admits, you can be a Tory anarchist in these terms and at the same time a revolutionary socialist or a Labour Party cabinet minister—or a crusty voter for an anti-immigration party in the saloon bar. On Wilkin's definition, Aneurin Bevan and Michael Foot were Tory anarchists and so was Karl Marx. The problem is the catch-all notion of 'cultural and moral conservatism.' Ambiguity about 'progress' is the norm among thinking people in any advanced capitalist society—and was felt by Orwell in the 1930s and 1940s. If Orwell was a 'cultural and moral conservative' who regretted much that had been lost, appreciated warm beer, and was intolerant of the cant of the day, he was also a bohemian rebel *against* moral conservativism and a critical enthusiast for the modern in culture.

Orwell dropped out from respectability when he left the Indian police and for the rest of his life lived unconventionally, avoiding the trap of a traditional career, travelling to Spain to fight for his vision of communism, escaping London for crazy experiments in subsistence in rural Hertfordshire and later Jura, hanging out with poets in wartime Fitzrovia, perhaps even having extramarital sex. For all his dislike of the poet, W. H. Auden, and his circle and his antipathy to the elitism of much high modernism—and for all his enthusiasm for Jonathan Swift, Charles Dickens and George Gissing—he was as engaged as anyone with the serious modernist and experimental literature of the first half of the 20th century (Joseph Conrad, D. H. Lawrence, T. S. Eliot, James Joyce, Henry Miller and so on), and his fiction was influenced both by high modernism and by the anti-elitist reaction to it of the 1930s. He was also an enthusiast for contemporary popular culture, ahead of his time in taking seriously pulp fiction, sport, mass holiday resorts, boys' weeklies and a lot else besides. He reviewed films (Tulloch 2012) as they became part of everyday life, and he worked as an international radio broadcaster in the early 1940s when radio was newer than the internet is today. He was a man as at ease with his times as he was uneasy.

Which is not to say that anarchism did not play a role in Orwell's intellectual life. He was sympathetic to the anarcho-syndicalist CNT in Spain in the 1930s—'As far as my purely personal preferences went I would have liked to join the anarchists,' he writes in *Homage to Catalonia* (1938)—and he was friendly with many anarchist contemporaries from the late 1930s until his death.[10] But these anarchists, in Britain as in Spain, were revolutionary libertarian socialists—and they hated the Tories or anyone like them. In Spain, they killed them.

THE WRETCHED OF THE EARTH

Enough, though, of 'Tory anarchists.' It is clear from Orwell's earliest published work that he identified with the left—though by no means uncritically or unambiguously. And I would say, with the benefit of hindsight, that his engagement with the wretched of the earth (the exploited poor of the colonies and the casual and itinerant laborers of the imperialist homelands, Marx's lumpen proletariat) was remarkable. It indicates a commitment that was different in crucial respects from that of many other leftist writers of his time, whose interest was much more focused on the respectable working class.

If he had died in 1935, however, Orwell would have been forgotten or at best a minor cult figure for left-wing enthusiasts for reportage and modernist-influenced realist fiction, one of several writers who, touched by Marxism and far-left ethical socialism, tried to tell how capitalism and imperialism exploited the proletariat and the peasant masses in the colonies. What changed that, what made Orwell different, were two things: his experience researching *The Road to Wigan Pier*, where he first confronted (albeit tentatively) the idea that a lot of the left was at best useless and that some of it represented a threat to working-class interests and, most importantly, Spain.

The Road to Wigan Pier was Orwell's first big-selling book, a major success for Victor Gollancz's Left Book Club despite Gollancz's unease about some of Orwell's criticisms of the left.[11] And, as John Newsinger has made very clear, Spain was a crucial watershed in Orwell's politics (Newsinger 1999: Chapter 3). He went out believing that all socialists should get together and fight fascism, a standard position whatever his quirks—and returned convinced by his experience that the Soviet Union and its communist clients were not just unreliable allies but enemies of the revolutionary socialist and anti-fascist cause. He started off despairing at the anarchists' and radical leftists' lack of serious military organization—while he admired the social revolution that was taking place in Catalonia, he considered leaving the POUM militia with which he had joined up as an ILP sympathizer (though not actually a member) for the communist-controlled International Brigades. He ended up in horror at the communists' suppression of the revolution (from which he escaped by the skin of his teeth). *Homage to Catalonia*, rejected by Gollancz for telling awkward truths, was the result.[12]

All the same, Orwell was in the middle and late 1930s a fairly orthodox ILPer—which means that he was a revolutionary socialist attracted by Trotskyism and by an anarchism that was anything but Tory. He even joined the ILP after returning from Spain. He was against British rearmament to counter Nazi Germany (which would give the British bourgeoisie the means to attack the workers) and still a sceptical supporter of an international alliance between Britain and the Soviet Union against Hitler despite his Spanish experience. But his affiliation with the ILP lasted only until the Hitler-Stalin pact of summer 1939. His account of the breach is too good to be true—he claimed to have had a dream on the eve of the pact in which war came and he realized that his only option was to fight for Britain—but the breach was certainly for real (Orwell 1940a). Like quite a few others on the far left, he was disgusted by the Soviet betrayal and appalled by the ILP's official position of pacifism once war began, though he remained personally friendly with many former ILP comrades.

THE 1940S: ORWELL'S THREE DISTINCT PHASES

What, though, of the 1940s? I think there are three phases: 1939–1941, 1941–1947 and 1947–1950. The first was when Orwell settled accounts with the 1930s left, in particular the Communist Party. Even if you take sceptically his account of how his eyes were opened by the Hitler-Stalin pact, there is no doubt that the event propelled him into a radical change of political position: the pact was another watershed, almost as important as Spain. From 1939–1940, he was a socialist patriot, a supporter of the war effort – and someone who saw the war as a means of effecting revolutionary socialist change in Britain, seeing the Home Guard as a nascent revolutionary militia. He was not alone in this. His friend Tosco Fyvel took a similar point of view; so did Tom Wintringham, Aneurin Bevan and Francis Williams. This patriotic revolutionary left did not sweep all before it in 1940–1941, but Orwell's contributions to Gollancz's collection of essays against the Hitler-Stalin pact, *Betrayal of the Left*, undoubtedly caught something of a mood (Orwell 1941). This is when Orwell started to write for *Tribune* under the editorship of Raymond Postgate, though the relationship cooled a little after Postgate attacked Orwell's contributions to *Betrayal of the Left*. Soon after this Aneurin Bevan fired Postgate and appointed himself as *Tribune* editor, though actually the work was done by Jon Kimche, a former ILPer who had worked with Orwell in a Hampstead bookshop in the 1930s (see Anderson 2006: 1–56).[13]

The second phase was from some time in 1941, when Orwell's sense of the revolutionary possibilities in Britain waned, until the beginning of the Cold War. I don't think there was a particular turning point, rather a series of events. The anti-Soviet temper of the left weakened after Hitler's invasion of the Soviet Union; and Orwell secured a job at the BBC, working as a propagandist for its India service. He gave that up in November 1943 to join *Tribune* as literary editor, however, and for the next 18 months, while writing *Animal Farm*, he was employed by the paper, leaving it briefly in spring 1945 to work as a war correspondent for the *Observer* and *Manchester Evening News*, returning to its pages in the autumn of the same year as a freelance columnist, a role he continued until spring 1947. Orwell's contributions to *Tribune*, notably the 'As I Please' columns, generally steered clear of mainstream politics, but he wrote plenty on British politics both for other publications in the UK (the *Observer*, the *Manchester Evening News* and various little magazines) and in his 'London Letters' for *Partisan Review* in the US, and his sympathies are very clear.[14] He was engaged in a string of arguments with former Trotskyist, pacifist and anarchist friends and was growing closer and closer to the mainstream Labour left. He was an admirer of Bevan (as well as a colleague),[15] and in 1945 he actively campaigned for Labour in the run-up to the party's extraordinary landslide.

Of course, Orwell continued to be influenced by all sorts of things outside the narrow confines of the British left. He was a voracious consumer of small magazines and pamphlets, and it is clear he took very seriously the pessimistic visions of recently Trotskyist American writers such as James Burnham and Dwight Macdonald, the right-libertarian polemics of Friedrich von Hayek and a lot more besides. Burnham is particularly important: The Book in *Nineteen Eighty-Four*,

The Theory and Practice of Oligarchical Collectivism by Emmanuel Goldstein, draws heavily on Burnham's *The Managerial Revolution*, which Orwell wrote about in a column in *Tribune* in early 1944 (Orwell 1944) and returned to in 1946 (very critically) in one of his greatest political essays, 'Second Thoughts on James Burnham,' published in Humphrey Slater's *Polemic* (Orwell 1946b). But he was by no means alone on the Labour left at the time in taking Burnham seriously—it is notable that 'Second Thoughts ...' was republished as a pamphlet by the Socialist Book Centre, a small left-wing bookshop on the Strand near *Tribune's* London office that published several pamphlets by the paper's writers—and there is no evidence at all that Burnham's book caused Orwell to rethink his commitment to democratic socialism. Unlike Burnham, who became a mainstay of the American Cold War right, Orwell never embraced conservative defeatism.

Phase three, 1947–50 is where it starts to get much more difficult, for two reasons. First, Orwell was from 1946–1947 increasingly detached from orthodox political engagement. He stopped writing his column for *Tribune* in May 1947 to finish *Nineteen Eighty-Four*, and although there were still occasional journalistic contributions to other periodicals, they were fitful. He was ill, and spent most of his time when not in sanitoriums in splendid isolation in Jura, a remote island off the Scottish coast. Secondly, there was much greater ambiguity to his political interventions. This was partly because the most important of them, *Nineteen Eighty-Four*, was a great work of satire that was and remains open to infinite interpretations, but it was also because Orwell, like everyone else at the time, was faced with a massively changed world in which old certainties had been destroyed by nearly six years of total war and the emergence of an armed stand-off between capitalist West and communist East. In Britain, Labour was engaging in implementation of a socialist program of nationalization and creation of a welfare state—which had been almost unthinkable before 1939. It was doing so, moreover, technocratically and joylessly, in conditions of extreme austerity and in the face of an effective collapse of Britain's role as a world power. Meanwhile, both the US and the Soviet Union were on the march: the US as the only country until 1949 with the atom bomb, the only major economy that had done well out of the war, with global military commitments; the Soviet Union as the new master of east-central Europe, and from 1949 the second power with the atom bomb and the apparent hegemon in China. These were world-historical events, and Orwell was trying to make sense of them. He got some things right and some things wrong.

How Orwell called the early years of the Cold War is, of course, what all the arguments are really about today. Did he sell out his principles? Or was he the greatest sage of the era? Or maybe both or neither?

The Cold War ended 25 years ago, but it still casts a shadow over contemporary geopolitics and intellectual life. Our understandings of its early years are mediated through almost 70 years of hindsight, and hardly anyone who was a participant in the politics of the time is still alive. It is very hard to get to grips with what it was actually like to live through the late 1940s, and easy to forget that at any time in history no one knows what is going to happen next. When Orwell died, in January 1950, the Soviet bomb was four months old, the People's Republic of China three months old. Alger Hiss had yet to be convicted of espionage; Klaus Fuchs and the Rosenbergs were yet to be arrested. A statement of the obvious, perhaps, but it matters because Orwell died before the democratic left consensus in support of the West in the Cold War came into question except from communists.

Until 1951—when it looked as if the Americans might be prepared to escalate the Korean War into an all-out global nuclear conflict—there was little dissent from the Cold War in the West from the non-communist left. Orwell was certainly one of the most consistent and effective anti-communist voices on the left, but apart from a brief period in 1946–1947, when he poured scorn on the Labour left's short-lived proposals for a 'third way' foreign policy, there was very little to separate him from what *Tribune* was saying about the immediate need to resist Soviet expansionism in eastern Europe and support the creation of a transatlantic anti-communist alliance. It is true that he had a much more pessimistic—and realistic—view than most of what was wrong with Soviet communism (it wasn't enough to hope for a replacement of Stalin and democratic elections), but the biggest difference he had with his friends on the paper was over their support for the creation of the state of Israel, which he saw as colonialism of a new kind. There was no point at which Orwell dissociated himself from *Tribune*: he remained a reader and supporter of the paper, as far as anyone knows, until his death.[16]

ORWELL'S LIST

None of this is to overlook the much-discussed question of the list of Soviet-sympathetic writers and artists Orwell handed over in 1949 to Celia Kirwan, a friend to whom he had once proposed marriage. She had asked his advice on who should and who should not be asked to write by the Foreign Office propaganda unit for which she worked, the newly established Information Research Department.[17] This has been a bone of contention for almost 20 years, and the canard that it was a blacklist has now entered popular mythology (see Norton-Taylor and Milne 1996). What actually happened was rather more mundane. With his friend Richard Rees, Orwell in the 1940s compiled a notebook listing people prominent in literary and political circles, mainly in Britain and the US, who they thought might be 'crypto-communists' (secret members of the Communist Party) or 'fellow-travellers' (non-members of the CP who publicly defended Stalin's Russia). There were—are—135 names in this notebook, and most were published in a volume of Peter Davison's edition of Orwell's *Collected Works* in the 1990s. There are four important factual points here:

- This was a speculative list two friends put together for their own amusement. It was not intended for wider circulation, let alone publication.
- Although some of the names in the notebook have notes appended that identify them as probable covert CP members or even Soviet agents, far more are defined as merely naïve, dishonest, sentimental or silly in their attitudes to the Soviet Union and the CP.
- Orwell and Rees were largely accurate in their assessments. Nearly everyone in the notebook had expressed gushing admiration for Stalinist Russia or participated in CP-run campaigns.
- The list in the notebook was *not* the list Orwell gave to Kirwan. The IRD list contained only 'about 35' names, according to Orwell, and a definitive version is yet to be published.

Of course, the facts are not what are really at stake. The big questions are first whether Orwell was right to compile his notebook for his own purposes, and secondly whether he was right to hand over the shorter list to the IRD. On the first, can anyone object to a political journalist keeping tabs on his or her subjects' political affiliations and backgrounds? Every political journalist does it, and should do it. Unless you know, say, that the chair of campaign A is a member of the central committee of a Stalinist micro-party, or that the leader of trade union B is affiliated to a Trotskyist groupuscule, or that the columnist for respectable broadsheet C was once a lobbyist for Slobodan Milosevic, or that the Tory MP for D has repeatedly taken freebie holidays in Northern Cyprus you miss important stories.

Handing over the shorter list to the IRD is more controversial, but did it amount to more than an error of judgement? The purpose of the list was to advise the Foreign Office about whom not to hire to write articles, pamphlets and books for a new outfit that had been set up by the Labour government to counter Soviet propaganda abroad with arguments for democratic socialism. Now, it is perfectly possible to argue that the IRD should never have been set up on the grounds that a democracy should have no recourse to propaganda—and there is no doubt that in later years its role in spreading rumor and disinformation was reprehensible (Lashmar and Oliver 1998). But in 1949, the idea of the IRD did not seem at all shady. There was good reason to fear Stalin's intentions in Europe. The Soviet Union had ruthlessly suppressed nascent democracies in Hungary and Czechoslovakia, imposing pliant puppet dictatorships and imprisoning democratic socialists. West Berlin was under Soviet military blockade, and it seemed to many that Stalin was preparing for all-out war. Orwell was by no means alone on the left in thinking a British socialist propaganda effort justified. If there is a case against

Orwell's action, it is that he did not know to what use his list would be put by the state. That was certainly a risk, but in the circumstances of the time it was an understandable one to take for a *Tribune* socialist.

CONCLUSION

So, to sum up: Bernard Crick is right. Orwell was for the last decade of his life a *Tribune* socialist, and there is little to suggest that he was having second thoughts even on his deathbed. But what does it matter today? Well, in some ways not a lot. The Orwell who advocated a planned economy and pored over Trotskyist and anarchist polemics against Stalinism and supported the Attlee government is in some respects a figure of historical interest who does not speak to our time, however much we admire his style, or his contrarianism or certain other aspects of his political engagements.

The democratic socialism for which Orwell stood is now a marginal current in British politics, at least as it is portrayed in the media—and it would take an extraordinary leap of faith to consider it likely in the near future to be adopted explicitly by the Labour Party leadership, which is still beholden, as it has been for 20 years or more, to broadly neoliberal economics and a concern for the interests of big business and 'aspirational' middle-class voters. But it's not far off the common sense of the Labour Party on the ground or, indeed, of much of the British public—and there have been signs that Labour's neoliberalism is cracking. I am not holding out great hopes, but the prospect of Labour fighting elections on a platform that would have been recognized by Orwell and by Crick as democratic socialist is better now than it has been for more than 20 years.

NOTES

1. For the Cold War battle for Orwell, see John Rodden's *The Politics of Literary Reputation: The Making and Claiming of 'St George' Orwell* (1989) and the same author's *Every Intellectual's Big Brother: George Orwell's Literary Siblings* (2006). For Cold War conservative and liberal attempts to appropriate Orwell, see the work of Lionel Trilling (1952); Russell Kirk (1956); Norman Podhoretz (1983); and Leopold Labedz (1984). Cold War critiques of Orwell from the left came first of all from out-and-out Stalinists, but there were subsequently several from writers associated with the New Left in the 1950s and 1960s—the most important Isaac Deutscher (1955); E. P. Thompson (1960); and Raymond Williams (1970). The theme was given another outing in Christopher Norris (ed.) (1984) which includes Beatrix Campbell's 'Orwell—Paterfamilias or Big Brother.' 1984 also saw Campbell's *Wigan Pier Revisited* and Daphne Patai, *The Orwell Mystique: A Study in Male Ideology*. For the pro-Orwell left during the Cold War, see the contributions of the American former-Trotskyist critic Irving Howe

(1950 and 1956), the Canadian poet and critic George Woodcock (1967); Peter Sedgwick (1969) and, most convincingly, Bernard Crick (1980).

2. The most convincing writer on Orwell from the far left of late is John Newsinger (see 1999, 2014). The late Christopher Hitchens's polemical defence of Orwell (2002) takes much the same position as Newsinger on Orwell's politics—Orwell 'was essentially right' about 'the three great subjects of the 20th century … imperialism, fascism and Stalinism'—but its critical reception was mediated through left hostility to his support for George Bush's response to 9/11. For contemporary right claims to the mantle of St. George, see Mount (2010) and Wilkin (2013).

3. The leftist anti-Orwell trope was advanced by Scott Lucas (2003 and 2004). For the feminist critique see Császár (2010).

4. The two heavyweight biographies published to mark the centenary of Orwell's birth were Gordon Bowker (2003) and D. J. Taylor (2003), though neither supplanting Crick. Since 2003, the only full-length biographies are John Rodden and John Rossi (2012) and Robert Colls (2013). Rodden's invaluable works also include *The Cambridge Companion to George Orwell* (2007) and *Critical Insights: George Orwell* (2012).

5. *Tribune*, 6 January 1984.

6. See also Mark Jenkins (1979); and Jonathan Schneer (1988).

7. Labedz is largely right about the paper's often uncritical approach to Soviet foreign policy in the 1970s and its lukewarm welcome for Solidarnosc in Poland in 1980–1981, but he has little to say about its late-1950s and early-1960s optimism about the prospects for Soviet socialism. For the history of the Labour left and Soviet communism, see Anderson and Davey (2014).

8. Orwell's hostility to Zilliacus, then MP for Gateshead, who had the Labour whip withdrawn for his pro-Soviet activities and statements in 1949, is outlined in his polemic (see Orwell 1947b). The article was never sent.

9. Newsinger's *Orwell's Politics* is particularly good on the influence of the *Adelphi*. For the ILP, see Dowse (1966) and Cohen (2007).

10. The Confederación Nacional del Trabajo was the anarcho-syndicalist trade union in Spain that organized most of the Catalan working class in the 1930s. Among Orwell's anarchist friends in Britain were Herbert Read, George Woodcock, Vernon Richards and Marie-Louise Berneri. Orwell was vice-chairman of the Freedom Defence Committee (with Read as chairman) initially set up to defend Richards and others who had been prosecuted in early 1945 for distributing anarchist literature deemed by the authorities to incite disaffection among British troops. He came to the anarchists' defence again in *Tribune* in his essay 'Freedom of the Park' (Orwell 1945).

11. Gollancz famously appended a preface to the book distancing himself from it.

12. The Partido Obrero de Unificación Marxista was an anti-Stalinist revolutionary socialist party of the 1930s, influenced by Trotskyism but by no means Trotskyist, with a power-base among the Catalan working class, particularly in Barcelona, in a working alliance with the anarcho-syndicalist CNT. It was affiliated with the Independent Labour Party in Britain, and Orwell joined one of its militias on arrival in Spain. The POUM was suppressed by the communists in May 1937, an event detailed in *Homage to Catalonia* (see Bowker 2003: 201–227).

13. Postgate's review of Orwell appeared in *Tribune* on 14 March 1941.

14. *Partisan Review* was founded by William Phillips and Philip Rahv as an orthodox communist literary magazine in 1934, but relaunched by them as anti-Stalinist (broadly Trotskyist but with non-Trotskyist contributors) in 1937 after they split with the communists over Spain and Stalin's show trials. Orwell wrote a quarterly London letter for *Partisan Review* from 1941 to 1945 and occasional pieces after that.

15. See Orwell's profile of Bevan, *Observer*, 14 October 1945.

16. For Orwell's thoughts on *Tribune* after he ceased writing for it, see two articles published in America: 'Britain's left-wing press,' *Progressive*, June 1948, and 'The Labour government after three years', *Commentary*, October 1948.

17. The Information Research Department was set up in 1948 as a Foreign Office 'white propaganda' operation to brief diplomats, politicians and journalists with factual material on conditions in the Soviet bloc and Soviet foreign policy, to circulate publications broadly sympathetic to British foreign policy against Moscow's denunciations and to publish its own books and pamphlets: according to Christopher Mayhew, the junior minister whose idea it was, its purpose though not its existence was kept quiet to avoid criticism from the Labour left, and the initial idea was that it would take an explicitly social democratic political line. The FO stopped it doing any such thing, and it became a shady unaccountable 'black' propaganda outfit processing intelligence material on anything to do with communism, domestic and international, that was fed to 'reliable' journalists and politicians. It was shut down by the Labour government in 1977. See Mayhew (1998) and Lashmar and Oliver (1998).

REFERENCES

Anderson, Paul (ed.) (2006) *Orwell in* Tribune: *'As I Please' and Other Writings 1943–47*, London: Politico's/Methuen.

Anderson, Paul and Davey, Kevin (2014) *Moscow Gold? The Soviet Union and the British Left*, Ipswich: Aaaargh! Press.

Bowker, Gordon (2003) *George Orwell*, London: Little, Brown.

Campbell, Beatrix (1984a) Orwell—Paterfamilias or Big Brother, Norris, Christopher (ed.) *Inside the Myth*, London: Lawrence and Wishart pp. 127–132.

Campbell, Beatrix (1984b) *Wigan Pier Revisited*, London: Virago.

Cohen, Gidon (2007) *Failure of a Dream: The Independent Labour Party from Disaffiliation to World War II*, London: I. B. Tauris.

Colls, Robert (2013) *George Orwell: English Rebel*, Oxford: Oxford University Press.

Coppard, Audrey and Crick, Bernard (eds) (1984) *Orwell Remembered*, London: Ariel.

Crick, Bernard (1980) *George Orwell: A Life*, London: Allen Lane.

Crossman, Richard, Foot, Michael, and Mikardo, Ian (1947) *Keep Left*, London: New Statesman.

Császár, Ivett (2010) Orwell and women's issues—A Shadow over the Champion of Decency, *Eger Journal of English Studies*, Vol. 10, pp. 39–56. Available online at http://anglisztika.ektf.hu/new/content/tudomany/ejes/ejesdokumentumok/2010/Csaszar_2010.pdf, accessed on 11 March 2015.

Deutscher, Isaac (1955) *1984*: The mysticism of cruelty, *Heretics and Renegades and Other Essays*. London: Hamish Hamilton. Available online at https://www.marxists.org/archive/deutscher/1955/1984.htm, accessed on 11 March 2015.

Dowse, R. E. (1966) *Left in the Centre: The Independent Labour Party 1893–1940*, London: Longman.

Hitchens, Christopher (2002) *Orwell's Victory*, London: Penguin.

Howe, Irving (1950) Utopia reversed, *New International*, November.

Howe, Irving (1956) Orwell: History as nightmare, *American Scholar*, Spring.

Jenkins, Mark (1979) *Bevanism: Labour's High Tide*, Nottingham: Spokesman.

Kirk, Russell (1956) *Beyond the Dreams of Avarice*, Chicago: Henry Regnery.

Labedz, Leopold (1984) Will George Orwell survive 1984? *Encounter*, June and July–August.

Lashmar, Paul and Oliver, James (1998) *Britain's Secret Propaganda War*, Stroud: Sutton.

Lucas, Scott (2003) *Orwell: Life and Times*, London: Haas.

Lucas, Scott (2004) *The Betrayal of Dissent: Beyond Orwell, Hitchens and the New American Century*, London: Pluto.

Mayhew, Christopher (1998) *A Cold War Witness*, London: I. B. Tauris.

Mount, Ferdinand (2011) Orwell and the oligarchs, *Political Quarterly*, Vol. 82, No. 2, pp. 154–155. Available online at http://theorwellprize.co.uk/events/orwell-lecture-2010-ferdinand-mount/, accessed on 28 March 2015.

Newsinger, John (1999) *Orwell's Politics*, Basingstoke: Macmillan.

Newsinger, John (2014) Defusing Orwell, *International Socialism*, Summer. Available online at http://www.isj.org.uk/www.isj.org.uk/index080e.html?id=987&issue=143, accessed on 28 March 2015.

Norris, Christopher (ed.) (1984) *Inside the Myth: Orwell: Views from the Left*. London: Lawrence and Wishart.

Norton-Taylor, Richard and Milne, Seamus (1996) Orwell offered writers' blacklist to anti-Soviet propaganda unit, *Guardian*, 11 July.

Orwell, George (1940a) My country right or left, London: *Folios of New Writing*, autumn.

Orwell, George (1940b) The Home Guard and you, London: *Tribune*, 20 December.

Orwell, George (1941) Freedom and democracy and Patriots and revolutionaries, Gollancz, Victor (ed.) *Betrayal of the Left*, London: Gollancz.

Orwell, George (1944) As I Please, London: *Tribune*, 14 January.

Orwell, George (1945) Freedom of the park, *Tribune*, 7 December.

Orwell, George (1946a) Why I Write, *Gangrel*, June.

Orwell, George (1946b) Second thoughts on James Burnham, *Polemic*, May.

Orwell, George (1947a) As I Please, *Tribune*, 31 January.

Orwell, George (1947b) In defence of Comrade Zilliacus, unpublished until collected in Orwell, Sonia and Angus, Ian (eds) (1970) *The Collected Essays, Journalism and Letters*, Vol. 4, pp. 227–229.

Patai, Daphne (1984) *The Orwell Mystique: A Study in Male Ideology*, Amherst: University of Massachusetts Press.

Pimlott, Ben (1977) *Labour and the Left in the 1930s*, Cambridge: Cambridge University Press.

Podhoretz, Norman (1983) If Orwell were alive today, *Harper's*, No. 266, pp. 30–37.

Rees, Richard (1961) *George Orwell: Fugitive from the Camp of Victory*, London: Secker and Warburg.

Rodden, John (1989) *The Politics of Literary Reputation: The Making and Claiming of 'St George' Orwell*, Oxford: Oxford University Press.

Rodden, John (2006) *Every Intellectual's Big Brother: George Orwell's Literary Siblings*, Austin: University of Texas Press.

Rodden, John (ed.) (2007) *The Cambridge Companion to George Orwell*, Cambridge: Cambridge University Press.

Rodden, John (ed.) (2012) *Critical Insights: George Orwell*, Ipswich, Massachusetts: Salem Press.

Rodden, John and Rossi, John (2007) *The Cambridge Introduction to George Orwell*, Cambridge: Cambridge University Press.

Schneer, Jonathan (1988) *Labour's Conscience: The Labour Left 1945–51*, London: Unwin Hyman.

Sedgwick, Peter (1969) George Orwell: International Socialist? *International Socialism*, June–July pp. 28–34. Available online at www.marxists.org/archive/sedgwick/1969/xx/orwell.htm, accessed on 11 March 2015.

Taylor, D. J. (2003) *Orwell: The Life*, London: Chatto and Windus.

Thompson, E. P. (1960) Outside the whale, Thompson, E. P. (ed.) *Out of Apathy*, London: New Left Books pp. 158–165.

Trilling, Lionel (1952) George Orwell and the politics of truth, *Commentary*, March pp. 218–227.

Tulloch, John (2012) Sceptic in the palace of dreams: Orwell as film reviewer, Keeble, Richard Lance (ed.) *Orwell Today*, Bury St. Edmunds: Abramis pp. 79–101.

Wilkin, Peter (2013) George Orwell: The English dissident as a Tory anarchist, *Political Studies*, Vol. 61, No. 1, pp. 215–230.

Williams, Raymond (1970) *Orwell*, London: Fontana.

Woodcock, George (1967) *The Crystal Spirit: A Study of George Orwell*, London: Jonathan Cape.

CHAPTER SIX

Trust THE Teller AND NOT THE Tale

Reflections on Orwell's Hidden Rhetoric of Truthfulness in the London Section of *Down and Out in Paris and London*

LUKE SEABER

The title of Orwell's first book, much parodied and much reinvented, is in fact misleading and a form of sleight of hand.[1] It (banally enough) suggests that it deals with the experience of being down and out in two cities, and that such differences as one may expect to find in these experiences will lie in what differs between the French capital and the English. This is not the case. Orwell's experiences in Paris are methodologically quite distinct from those in London.

This can be seen emblematically in the use of the two cities' names in the title, even though only one of them is the *sole* site of his (assumed) poverty in the country in question. Orwell is certainly down and out in Paris, but it would be more precise, although undoubtedly less euphonious to speak of 'London and sur-rounding areas.' In France, Orwell remains within the city; in England, he travels from casual ward to casual ward. This is not just a reflection of the fact that Orwell investigated more than one type of poverty, and that the casual ward system nec-essarily implied a wandering status that was absent from the hand-to-mouth but nonetheless working world of *plongeurs* and others in Paris. Living and working in a place on the one hand, and living the wandering life of the homeless on the other are two quite different methodologies in what will here be called incognito social investigation.[2] By this is meant the collection of information on a social group considered 'lower' by an observer from a 'higher' group *when the observer endeavors to pass for a member of the group under observation.* There are various types and sub-types of this phenomenon, but the one that concerns us here is the oldest, that which began in 1866 with James Greenwood's 'A Night in a Workhouse.'[3]

I wish here to examine just one section of *Down and Out in Paris and London*, that concerning 'London,' a section that (unlike the Paris one) belongs firmly in the classic English tradition of the Greenwoodian incognito social investigation text. Although the case may be made that Orwell's account is in many respects the swan song of the form that Greenwood had invented some seventy years earlier, it will not be examined here in that light. Rather, we shall look at it *vis-à-vis* the question of how within an ostensibly documentary, yet certainly partially fictionalized, form Orwell was able to suggest to his readers that what they were reading was reasonably pure non-fiction. In this sense, London has far more to offer us than Paris.

EARLY EXPERIENCES OF 'THE POOR': ELOQUENT ABSENCES IN *DOWN AND OUT IN PARIS AND LONDON*

George Orwell had his first experience as a down-and-out long before he was George Orwell; he was still Eric Blair when in August 1920 he wrote to his Eton friend Steven Runciman about his 'first adventure as an amateur tramp' (Orwell 2000a: 76).[4] This was not social investigation of any type; Blair was not showing a precocious interest in the poor that can be followed until it reaches its realization in the publication of *Down and Out in Paris and London*. As he says, like most tramps, he was driven to it (Orwell 2000a: 76). Blair was travelling down to Polperro in Cornwall on holiday; a failed attempt to change train compartments at Seaton Junction led to his arriving too late at Plymouth to catch a train to Looe that night, and he thus found himself faced with having to choose whether to sleep at the YMCA and not eat or eat something but sleep rough. He chose the latter alternative, profiting from the fact that he was wearing his Eton Officers' Training Corps uniform and thus taken by passers-by to be a demobbed soldier; he slept in a field corner whilst worrying about the possibilities of being arrested, and notwithstanding the cold and discomfort in the end managed to oversleep and miss the first train out. His conclusion, ironically enough, was: 'I am very proud of this adventure, *but I would not repeat it*' (Orwell 2000a: 77; italics mine). Reading too much significance into this episode would be anachronistic—Orwell himself never mentions this experience when discussing his forays amongst the poor, whether as a first spark kindling his interest in such things or merely as a curious coincidence.

However, this very reticence is not without meaning, I feel. *Down and Out in Paris and London* is presented not as an experiment but as an account of experiences lived through chance; the most cursory knowledge of Orwell's correspondence and biography, though, shows that this is false (at least for 'London'): Orwell set out quite deliberately to hunt for new experiences—hop-picking, rough-sleeping, imprisonment, lodging houses, workhouses. Reference, even knowing, ironic, reference, to this previous event would have given rise to various problems. Any reference would surely only have been worth including if the coincidence of such an incident happening to one who would later write a whole book putatively based around such experiences were highlighted, but this would have meant a more explicit admission of Orwell's privileged background than can be found at any point in his 1933 book.

Equally, although there are various possible psychological interpretations of Orwell's relationship with the poor that draw on incidents in his childhood, no attempt is made to link such episodes with what happens in *Down and Out in Paris and London*. For example, later in the 1930s Orwell would go on to record in *The Road to Wigan Pier* that:

> Before that age [six] my chief heroes had generally been working-class people … I remember the farm hands on a farm in Cornwall who used to let me ride on the drill when they were sowing turnips … and the plumber up the road with whose children I used to go out birds-nesting. But it was not long before I was forbidden to play with the plumber's children; they were 'common' and I was told to keep away from them (Orwell 1997b: 117).

The important thing here is not whether such vignettes are 'true,' but the fact that Orwell decided not to include them in his first book. Whereas the second part of *The Road to Wigan Pier* (from which this comes) is an avowedly contrastive reflection on its author's part, ruminating on what he had learnt about class as he had gone through life, and therefore necessitating very explicit admission of his original class status, *Down and Out in Paris in London* never truly grapples with this question.

THE FICTIONALIZATION OF THE NARRATIVE STRUCTURE IN *DOWN AND OUT IN PARIS AND LONDON*

Orwell's book, it should be repeated, is not presented as incognito social investigation, and any attempts at seeking motivation would of course have run up against the quite false narrative framework of poverty experienced through necessity that Orwell sets up for the English section.

Orwell's text is strongly fictionalized, and this in terms of the genre of incognito social investigation texts is extremely interesting as well as rather rare. The London section of Orwell's book is undoubtedly the most famous text in the Greenwood tradition, but it also departs significantly from that tradition in this central point. Orwell does not wish to appear a brave explorer of unknown realms and social depths: he wishes, rather, to be taken for one plunged *volente nolente* unprepared into a life of poverty. This leads to a rather interesting situation. Let us take the completely fictional moment when Orwell finds himself back in England and, having just learnt from 'B.' that he has to wait a month before his promised employment materializes, faces the prospect of being a pauper. This is worth quoting at length:

> There was a month to wait, and I had exactly nineteen and sixpence in hand. The news had taken my breath away. For a long time I could not make my mind up what to do. I loafed the day in the streets, and at night, not having the slightest notion of how to get a cheap bed in London, I went to a 'family' hotel, where the charge was seven and sixpence. After paying the bill I had ten and twopence in hand. By the morning I had made my plans. Sooner or later I should have to go to B. for more money, but it seemed hardly decent to do so yet, and in the meantime I must exist in some hole-and-corner way. Past experience set me against pawning my best suit. I would leave all my things at the station cloakroom, except my second-best suit, which I could exchange for some cheap clothes and perhaps a pound. If I was going to live a month on thirty shillings I must have bad clothes—indeed, the worse the better. Whether thirty shillings could be made to last a month I had no idea, not knowing London as I knew Paris. Perhaps I could beg, or sell bootlaces, and I remembered articles I had read in the Sunday papers about beggars who have two thousand pounds sewn into their trousers. It was, at any rate, notoriously impossible to starve in London, so there was nothing to be anxious about (Orwell 1997a: 128–129).

Whereas previous incognito social explorers had made much of their expertise regarding the tramp's life, Orwell here is making himself seem far *less* expert than was in fact the case. He is falsely naïve, falsely ignorant. He was fully aware of how to get a cheap bed in London; indeed, he is here making himself out to be not only less knowledgeable than he was, but also less knowledgeable than was likely: the existence of lodging houses for those not yet reduced to casual wards, Salvation Army shelters or Embankment sleeping was common knowledge, as was the existence of the Rowton Houses, created by Lord Rowton at the end of the nineteenth century to provide working men with a better option for accommodation than that provided by the common lodging houses.[5]

It would perhaps be useful here to distinguish between Orwell, author of *Down and Out in Paris and London*, and 'Orwell,' its narrator. The former was far more knowledgeable than the latter, but the narrator too was not without *some* expertise: he knew better than to pawn his best suit. Why may the narrator here in a scene aimed at presenting him as an innocent abroad in London in many respects be allowed this one flash of pre-existing wisdom regarding poverty? The answer, I suspect, lies in the book's two-part structure. The pseudo-documentary nature of the text means that, structured as it is, when we read the above passage not only does the assumed ignorance of how to deal with poverty in London prepare us for the presentation of the adventures of 'Orwell' that are to come, but the nod to his knowledge about not pawning his best suit, an awareness that can only have come from his Paris experiences, also reinforces, I would suggest, the 'veracity' of the French section of the book. This little detail of not pawning the best suit is in some ways the true link between the 'Paris' and 'London' sections: it underscores both his ignorance of London poverty and hard-earned knowledge of its Parisian equivalent—and in doing so subliminally suggests to the reader that the end result of the narrator's experiences will be a gain in awareness; the detail of not pawning the suit adumbrates the final chapter and the 'one or two things I have definitely learned by being hard up' (Orwell 1997a: 215–216). Of course, both terms in Orwell's implied before-and-after scheme are false. He was not that ignorant; nor was the knowledge that he had gained in Paris quite so hard-won as this aside (as well, obviously, as the whole of the book's first section) suggested.

The strange situation whereby Orwell sought to make his text, the importance of which lay in his being a middle-class observer of poverty and not in his being simply middle class and poor, deny that it in any way appertained to the text tradition initiated by Greenwood is something that still commands our attention. The question that it leads us to is this: what can be said in relation to the *two* stories being told by *Down and Out in Paris and London*—the fictionalized one contained within its narrative and the historical one contained not only within the text but also within a whole host of extra-textual material regarding Orwell?

A FACE IN THE CROWD: TYPICALIZING INDIVIDUALIZATION AS A RHETORICAL TACTIC

Our focus here will be above all on a technique that I believe Orwell uses to muddle questions of his true nature as an observer, a technique I shall call, at risk of stating an oxymoron, 'typicalizing individualization.' This is the seemingly paradoxical situation whereby individualizing oneself makes one seem more typical of a group. It is, in fact, no paradox, but almost a truism. If one only wishes to suggest that one can pass for belonging to a group, then it is, indeed, enough to take on all that group's attributes, to the point of stereotypicality. However, if one wishes to suggest—rarer thing—that one *is* part of a group, then it is better to present oneself as individually as possible. Self-individualization, in this sense, suggests that one belongs to a group despite those characteristics that one has that are not (stereo)typical thereof. This is of course more realistic, for the truly typical is, in fact, untypical: however rare a public-school-educated tramp interested in making notes on slang may be, he is more likely to be accepted as a 'real' tramp than someone who is absolutely typical—and yet is able to write up his experiences and have them published. The narrator's story in *Down and Out in Paris in London* may be accepted as true *because* he is not a 'typical' tramp rather than in spite of this fact. I shall argue that Orwell consciously drew attention to the fact of his typicalizing atypicality in order to increase the authority of what he says.

A good starting point for an example of what I consider typicalizing individualization, and more generally the uneasy relationship between Orwell's desire for fact-finding and his role-play, comes when he meets a crowd on Tower Hill assembled to listen to the preaching of two Mormons. The combined heckles of an atheist and someone denouncing the Mormons for their presumed polygamy make it impossible to hear anything other than a confusion of voices. Orwell's conclusion is worth noting: 'I listened for twenty minutes, anxious to learn something about Mormonism, but the meeting never got beyond shouts. It is the general fate of street meetings' (Orwell 1997a: 137). On the one hand, it may be read as Orwell at his most short-sightedly unwilling to accept the mores of those whom he is observing. He seems to regret the fact that the East End crowd will not allow him to listen as he would like; that they have as much—or rather *more*—right to speak than two uninvited preachers is not taken into account. This is in sharp contrast with his judgement on the 'slumming-party' that 'invades' (the verb is clearly deliberately pejorative) one of the lodging houses where he stays, when he concludes that it 'is curious how people take it for granted that they have a right to preach at you and pray over you as soon as your income falls below a certain level' (ibid.: 183).

Given this contrast, the question arises whether Orwell may not be doing something rather more complex in the scene with the Mormon preachers than merely regretting poorer Londoners' lack of middle-class silence when listening to people speaking in public. I would suggest that Orwell is here, in fact, trying to strengthen his claim to being *truly* down and out rather than what he in fact is, an incognito social investigator. This works on two levels. First, paradoxically, the very fact of his not following the crowd insofar as he wishes to listen to the Mormons and is clearly irritated by his inability to do so can be read as making him belong *more* to the crowd, not less. This needs some explanation. By showing his readers his desire to hear the Mormons' talk, Orwell is individualizing himself, standing out from the crowd. The crowd in this case is not a single entity, but rather a clear collection of individuals—the lame, bearded atheist, the anti-polygamist, the man who continually shouts out to everyone not to 'get on the argue.' Had Orwell been more superficially sympathetic an observer and not mentioned his impatience with the lack of reactive silence, then he would, in fact, have been much more an external observer, wanting above all to fit in. Instead, by standing out, he is merely doing what everybody else whose voice in the crowd we hear is doing. In other words, Orwell is showing that his priority is not observation of the East End crowd here: he is there not through choice to observe but through necessity, and has, therefore, no need to *pretend*.

This stance of Orwell's is disingenuous pretense, but still a very subtle way of asserting his authority as one who has *truly* known poverty rather than another mere investigator in a long tradition. In this interpretation, the contrast between the scene with the Mormons and Orwell's reaction to it and that with the slumming party does not show inconsistency or hypocrisy. Rather, it shows that *Orwell has learnt something*. Again, this is a distancing of himself from those who have come before him and were openly incognito social investigators: the very fact that he does not notice the change suggests that it is 'real;' it is not something he has consciously learnt, with the implication that he has (subconsciously? deliberately?) set out to learn it, as is the case with the things he lists in the concluding chapter. Orwell learns things without noticing it because, he is suggesting, he is not an incognito social investigator but simply one whom poverty has forced into certain situations.

We have here to be careful. We can, of course, never truly know for certain whether in certain cases, such as that described above, Orwell was being subtle and using contradictions in his text to convince readers of his *bona fides* or simply not noticing his tyro's inconsistencies. I would argue, however, that the very proximity of contrasting attitudes at certain points in *Down and Out in Paris and London* does suggest an awareness on the author's part of what he is doing, which is always reminding us that he is an individual, with all an individual's contradictions. He is deliberately unprofessional, so to speak, in order to underline how much deeper he has gone into the down-and-out world than those more expert and more professional incognito social investigators who observed with a clearer eye and endeavored to stop their individuality from intruding between them and the object of their gaze. He is inconsistent because he is real. As an example of the proximity that I believe suggests Orwell's deliberate use of this technique, it is instructive to look at Chapter XXVI, in which Orwell goes to 'Romton' (almost certainly Romford), meets an old Irish tramp and goes with him to a chapel that hands out tea to tramps after prayer. The degree of inconsistency in this chapter, I would suggest, is too great to be casual or attributable to inability on the author's part: it is a deliberate ploy to have the reader accept Orwell's version of his account as a true story of an unlooked-for descent into poverty. This is not to say that Orwell's mask does not ever slip, as we shall see.

When he arrives in the market place in Romton, Orwell meets an old Irish tramp, whom he offers tobacco. The ensuing conversation is curious:

> 'By God,' he said, 'dere's sixpennorth o' good baccy here! Where de hell d'you get hold o' dat? *You* ain't been on de road long.'
> 'What, don't you have tobacco on the road?' I said.
> …
> 'D'you come out o' one o' de London spikes (casual wards), eh?' he asked me.
> I said yes, thinking this would make him accept me as a fellow tramp, and asked what the spike at Romton was like (ibid.: 140).[6]

Orwell distances himself from the tramp on one hand—the second-person pronoun in his bizarrely incredulous question is anything but inclusive. Notwithstanding this, the tramp's question would appear to mean that he remains of his first opinion, that the man in front of him is newly on the road rather than simply not being a tramp. In other words, Orwell is once again playing up his naïveté to underscore his genuineness. In the interpretation here of Orwell's technique of presenting himself as one genuinely poor rather than an investigator, the strangeness is, in fact, not in his question, nor in his later ones about different types of workhouse or what 'skilly' is, as all of these fit into his strategy. The mask of poverty does slip here, however, to show us a glimpse of the incognito social investigator beneath, but it is in his aside to the reader about his motivation in saying that he had come from a London casual ward: 'thinking this would make him accept me as a fellow tramp.' What is the point of his adding this? He has otherwise presented himself to the reader as he is presenting himself to the Irish tramp: as one honestly in need. If what Orwell has been recounting up to this point has been true, then he quite simply *is* a tramp at this point, albeit an inexperienced one lucky enough to know that his state is temporary. Orwell's ingenuous questions to the tramp have shown his lack of experience; this he has already seen does not make the Irishman doubt him. To include such an aside to the reader can only risk sowing a seed of doubt over the veracity of Orwell's account. It is because I consider the inclusion of this aside as a genuine error of judgement on Orwell's part that allows me to read his other inconsistencies as deliberate, as they can be fitted into a structure of strategy in a way that this cannot.

If we remain within this chapter, we shall find an excellent example of Orwell's deliberate 'carelessness,' as I read his inconsistencies in *Down and Out in Paris and London*. When describing the prayer meeting, Orwell says: 'We hated it. We sat around fingering our caps' (ibid.: 142); the inclusive pronouns are significant. He is now one of the tramps; but there follows another parenthetical statement addressed to the reader: '(a tramp feels indecently exposed with his cap off)' (ibid.) that might once again suggest a slipping of the mask as he suddenly and briefly switches voice and assumes that of an anthropologist noting an interesting detail of some savage tribe. I would, of course, argue that this, included as it is in the same sentence where the repetition of 'we' makes it seem a particularly glaring piece of authorial carelessness, is, in fact, another declaration of Orwell's individuality and thence his genuineness. He can allow himself this flash of pseudo-scientific interest, just as he allows himself the luxury of a non-narrative chapter of 'notes, as short as possible, on London slang and swearing' (ibid.: 176) because it is personal interest, personal curiosity, personal pleasure and even, if you will, astonishment, that causes him to blurt out, as it were, these observations. He can afford to be personal because he is (he wants us to believe) living not observing: he observes such things through passion and intellectual curiosity, not because he is seeking them out.

The same sleight-of-hand may be seen in two comparisons that Orwell makes a few sentences later in this chapter, which is something of a goldmine in terms of looking at his strategy for establishing his genuineness. He talks of a 'spry, red-nosed fellow looking like a corporal who had lost his stripe for drunkenness' (ibid.: 142) and extols the qualities of the chapel tea by saying that it is 'as different from coffee-shop tea as good Bordeaux is from the muck called colonial claret' (ibid.: 143). These phrases, stereotypically reminiscent of the sort of people who would never find themselves in a suburban chapel dressed as a tramp in order to drink free tea before a casual ward opened for the night, are another variation on the technique already identified. They allow Orwell to assert his strangeness to the situation in which he finds himself, and thus, paradoxically, his right to be there as an inhabitant, albeit temporary, of that world rather than as a visitor.

READERS' RESPONSES AND 'TRUTHFULNESS'

A related question regarding Orwell's truthfulness (or rather, his 'truthfulness') is a much wider epistemological one, and it is worth opening a parenthesis to look at it here, although treatment of it must necessarily be relatively superficial. To what extent can a reader (whether the most superficial and naïve of casual browsers or the most acute and profound of critics matters not) recognize a description of lived experience as 'truthful'? The common answer (and most useful) is, of course, insofar as that description tallies with the reader's own experience. Whilst this is reasonably unproblematic both for descriptions that one may fairly presume to be common to author and reader, at least when they both come from the same or similar cultures (certain emotional states, certain situations purportedly universal within that culture) and for descriptions of things so alien (cultural specificities that cannot legitimately be expected to be shared by the reader, experiences recorded only because they so *outré* as to make them putatively unique) that one must simply either accept the author's reliability or deny it, in the case of descriptions of the lives of the poor we find ourselves in a grey area *vis-à-vis* our acceptance or otherwise of authors' reliability.

Rare would be the reader who had never experienced poverty in some way, whether through personal experience or simple observation: the difficulty in gauging the veracity of reports from incognito social investigators such as Orwell lies in the high degree of specificity of the reader's personal history allowing recognition of a detail's being true to life or not. This is a problem that concerns not so much the reader as the critic. The degree to which an individual reader recognizes a description as accurate or false may be interesting, but when that individual reader is a critic basing parts of his or her argument upon that recognition of veracity, as in the example that you are reading, then the problem is clear. Modern academic practice rather frowns upon the intrusion of the critic's biography, but in this case it is useful, I think, to bear in mind that my reaction to Orwell's text and the problem of its veracity can only ever be a result of my own lived experience with regard to the questions of poverty treated therein: a text such as *Down and Out in Paris and London* has, I would argue, a wider range of possible reader responses *vis-à-vis* its 'truthfulness' than a 'normal' reportage text.

As an example of this issue, let us consider a detail from the Paris section. At his lowest ebb, Orwell notes a discovery about what happened to his saliva when he had not eaten for three days:

> Complete inertia is my chief memory of hunger; that, and being obliged to spit very frequently, and the spittle being curiously white and flocculent, like cuckoo-spit. I do not know the reason for this, but everyone who has gone hungry several days has noticed it (ibid.: 36).

I—the personal, autobiographical I and not the relatively anonymous critical voice—recognize this as 'true.' It is also possible, however, to make an appeal to authority here regarding the 'accuracy' of the observation: although there is a certain dearth in the scientific literature of studies on the effects of fasting on saliva, that which there is agrees that it causes a decrease in the production of saliva.[7] It is also the case that fasting, like a similar drop in liquid intake, would tend to make spittle thicker and gummier—more 'flocculent,' therefore.[8]

This, at first sight, would suggest that Orwell is partially 'right': one's spittle when one fasts does undergo the changes in texture that he notes, but its production decreases, which might suggest that he is wrong about being obliged to spit more frequently. However, fasting spittle, being thicker, is less easy to spit—therefore leading (again, in my own experience) to the impression of having to spit more often, even when one is in fact spitting less in terms of volume. The 'truth' of this in Orwell's case can only ever be conjecture: Orwell says that this was his case; whether the reader believes him hinges on the twin poles of previous experience of fasting that matches or does not match Orwell's and previous experience of Orwell and the degree to which one finds him and has found him reliable—where one's conviction or lack of it in his reliability comes from (personal experience, analysis of his writings, the secondary literature ...) matters not.

This epistemological problem is in itself far from new, and one can usually safely pass over it in silence. In this case, however, where we have to deal with questions of reliability as well as presumptions regarding experience and where, above all, the great selling point of incognito social investigation is to communicate secret experience, that is, experiences otherwise unknowable to the investigators' readerships, then the problem is crucial. Furthermore, it is not a factor that can be ignored when our interest lies in an analysis not of Orwell's 'truthfulness,' 'reliability' or 'honesty' *per se*, but instead of the methods that he uses to *convince* his readers thereof.

ORWELL'S REPORTAGE OR ORWELL'S FICTION?

Our examination of how Orwell increases his authority and concomitantly his readers' faith in the claim that what they are reading is reportage rather than fiction leads us to a question that has never been settled: to what extent is it true that Orwell's accounts of incognito social investigation *are* reportage, and what parts (if any) of are fiction(alized)?[9] Orwell exacerbates this situation with his vagueness (partially prompted by a fear of libel proceedings) regarding the practical details of his forays into the world of tramps; this, combined with the disappearance of documents such as the admissions books for the casual wards of Romford and Edmonton (almost certainly the spikes given as Romton and Edbury),[10] has meant that Orwell's most sustained body of work where there are issues of possible interplay between fact and fiction has remained stubbornly resistant to informed analysis in these terms.

However, the discovery of documentary evidence regarding one of his incognito social investigation exhibitions does now offer us some insight into this fraught question. This is Orwell's failed attempt in December 1931 to be sent to prison, given the title 'Clink' but not published, the writing of which Davison dates to August 1932 (Orwell 2000d: 254). His plan was to be arrested for being drunk and incapable, and, he says, after four or five pints and the best part of a bottle of whisky he was picked up and taken to Bethnal Green police station.[11] As he was arrested on a Saturday, he had to wait until Monday to be taken to Old Street Police Court to be seen by a magistrate. He describes those whom he saw there waiting to go in front of the judge, as well as his relative disappointment that even though he was unable to pay the six-shilling fine imposed upon him, his time in custody during the Monday was enough to spare him further incarceration.

The discovery of the Register of the Court of Summary Jurisdiction sitting at Old Street Police Court for December 1931 shows that in this, the only case as yet for which we can compare his account against documentary evidence, Orwell was consistently accurate; the one case in 'Clink' where this may not be the case is best thought of as an interpolation of matter collected during another expedition and put in to fill up space (Seaber 2014). We know that Orwell's account of why and how he found himself reduced to penury in London is fiction, but the evidence from 'Clink' suggests that the reportage itself may be relied upon as an accurate account of what he experienced and witnessed.

It is also worth our while to pause to look at Orwell's own statements about his book and his status as described therein—whether an incognito social investigator or one genuinely forced into poverty, however temporarily. In a November 1932 letter (that in which the name 'George Orwell' first appears) to his agent, Leonard Moore, written whilst the details of publication were being finalized, he wrote a PS suggesting *The Confessions of a Dishwasher* as a title, as 'I would *rather* answer to "dishwasher" than "down & out."' (Orwell 2000c; italics in original). The day before, he had also written to his friend Eleanor Jaques with the same message: 'I don't answer to the name of down & out' (Orwell 2000b: 273). This was certainly private honesty; but had Orwell had his way and seen his first book published under a different title, then it would have been a form of public honesty as well, as Orwell's dishwashing truly was through necessity in a way that his down-and-outery was not. The only point that I am aware of where Orwell in any way *publicly* made this point, however, was in the 'About the author' paragraph on the dust jacket of the Harper & Brothers American edition of *Down and Out in Paris and London*, published in June or July 1933, of which Davison rightly says that it was 'almost certainly based on material supplied by Orwell' ('Publication' 2000: 318). This brief biographical note mentions Orwell's career up to his resignation from the police in Burma, going on to conclude:

> Subsequently he has earned his living by schoolmastering and private tutoring, and he has also worked in a Paris hotel, picked hops, pushed a barrow in Billingsgate and done other varied jobs. Soon after he came home from Burma he became interested in the lives of destitute people and began to make expeditions among tramps. It was only after he had done this a number of times that it occurred to him that his experiences could be used for literary purposes. Later on when he was genuinely hard up he was glad to know the ropes in the world of the destitute ('Publication' 2000: 318–319).

Here, uniquely, Orwell recognizes that it was not mere misfortune that took him to the casual wards. However (and in this, I think, we can see Orwell's hand in the writing of the note), the details are disingenuously presented in such a way as to suggest a chain of events resembling that described in the book rather than what biographically occurred; this, though, is done in such a way that at no point can one accuse Orwell (or whoever was the note's putative author) of falsehood. The obvious reading is that the various jobs done by Orwell are unrelated to his 'expeditions among tramps;' we know, of course, that this was not the case, and he picked hops and ported fish in order to have the experiences of doing so, not through need. Nonetheless, this still stands as the only admission that Orwell was, indeed, at points an incognito social investigator, and as such is of great interest for the issues that we have been examining.

The 'London' section of *Down and Out in Paris and London* in the ultimate analysis shows a far greater degree of rhetorical subtlety than the book's reputation as a simple, perhaps even naïf, description might suggest. Orwell's description of the world of the London poor and suburban casual wards shows a level of rhetorical sophistication, in various forms, aimed not so much at convincing the reader of the truth of the tale being told as of the truthfulness of the teller.

NOTES

1. The research leading to this article has received funding from the People Programme (Marie Curie Actions) of the European Union's Seventh Framework Programme (FP7/2007–2013) under REA Grant Agreement No 298208.
2. There is currently no generally accepted term for this phenomenon. Other possibilities include 'slumming,' 'down-and-outery,' 'undercover investigation,' 'class passing,' 'complete participation' and 'incognito social exploration'.
3. Regarding 'A Night in a Workhouse' and the Greenwoodian tradition, see Freeman and Nelson (2008).
4. It will be noted that I normally use 'Orwell' regardless of whether I am talking about the period before or after his adoption of that pseudonym. Nothing should be read into this; it is merely for ease of reference.
5. See http://www.workhouses.org.uk/Rowton/, accessed on 17 October 2013.
6. The parenthesis translating 'spike' is Orwell's.
7. See Rahim and Yaacob (1991: 207): 'salivary flow rate decreased by almost 50% on fasting'.
8. Personal communication with Professor Stephen Porter, of the UCL Eastman Dental Institute, whom I thank for his time.
9. This is a problem not limited to Orwell's incognito social investigation, as Sonia Orwell's celebrated *cri de cœur* that 'of course he shot a fucking elephant' testifies. See Crick (1998: 164–167).
10. See http://www.workhouses.org.uk/Romford/ and http://www.workhouses.org.uk/Edmonton/, accessed on 16 October 2013.
11. Records for Bethnal Green are now lost. See Bridgeman and Emsley (1990: 104–121).

REFERENCES

Bridgeman, Ian and Emsley, Clive (1990) *A Guide to the Archives of Police Forces in England and Wales*, Leigh-on-Sea: Police History Society.

Crick, Bernard (1998) Orwell and the business of biography, Louis, Wm Roger (ed.) *More Adventures with Britannia: Personalities, Politics and Culture in Britain*, Austin: University of Texas Press and London: I.B. Tauris & Co pp. 151–167.

Freeman, Mark and Nelson, Gillian (eds) (2008) Editors' Introduction, Freeman, Mark and Nelson, Gillian (eds) *Vicarious Vagrants: Incognito Social Explorers and the Homeless in England, 1860–1910*, Lambertville: The True Bill Press pp. 7–47.

Orwell, George (1997a [1933]) *Down and Out in Paris and London, The Complete Works of George Orwell. Vol. 1*, Davison, Peter (ed.) London: Secker & Warburg.

Orwell, George (1997b [1937]) *The Road to Wigan Pier, The Complete Works of George Orwell, Vol. 5*, Davison, Peter (ed.) London: Secker & Warburg.

Orwell, George (2000a) Letter to Steven Runciman, August 1920, *A Kind of Compulsion: 1903–1936, The Complete Works of George Orwell, Vol. 10*, Davison, Peter (ed.) London: Secker & Warburg pp. 76–77.

Orwell, George (2000b) Letter to Eleanor Jaques, 18 November 1932. *A Kind of Compulsion: 1903–1936, The Complete Works of George Orwell, Vol. 10*, Davison, Peter (ed.) London: Secker & Warburg pp. 272–273.

Orwell, George (2000c) Letter to Leonard Moore, 19 November 1932, *A Kind of Compulsion: 1903–1936, The Complete Works of George Orwell, Vol. 10*, Davison, Peter (ed.) London: Secker & Warburg p. 274.

Orwell, George (2000d) Clink, *A Kind of Compulsion: 1903–1936, The Complete Works of George Orwell, Vol. 10*, Davison, Peter (ed.) London: Secker & Warburg pp. 254–260.

Publication of *Down and Out in Paris and London* in the United States (2000) *A Kind of Compulsion: 1903–1936, The Complete Works of George Orwell, Vol. 10*, Davison, Peter (ed.) London: Secker & Warburg pp. 318–319.

Rahim, Z. H. A. and Yaacob, H. B. (1991) Effects of fasting on saliva composition, *The Journal of Nihon University School of Dentistry*, Vol. 33, No. 4, pp. 205–210.

Seaber, Luke (2014) Edward Burton, fish porter, drunk and incapable: New evidence on Orwell's 'honesty' from the records of his 1931 conviction, *Notes and Queries*, Vol. 61, No. 4, pp. 597–602.

CHAPTER SEVEN

Orwell's Socialism

JOHN NEWSINGER

In *George Orwell: English Rebel* (2013: 1), Robert Coles refers to Orwell as being what 'they used to call a "socialist."' This, of course, begs many questions. What kind of socialist: reformist, revolutionary, rhetorical, gradualist, catastrophic, statist, fake? … We could go on. Coles himself demonstrates the problem when he ascribes a range of different meanings to Orwell's socialism from 'present society with the worst abuses left out' to 'a form of upper-middle-class charity for the poor' (ibid.: 67). Indeed, we are assured that the nearest Orwell ever came to describing 'the sort of socialism he wants lies in liberty and justice … and more help for the unemployed' (ibid.: 188). And, of course, on top of this, Orwell was also, according to Coles, 'nearly' or 'not quite' a Tory! His final resting place politically, however, was his embrace of British Labourism. Obviously dazed and confused by all this, Coles concludes 'that it is hard to find a consistent political voice in Orwell' (ibid.: 193).

What this chapter will attempt to show is that this confusion is actually in the eye of the beholder. In fact, Orwell developed an understanding of socialism out of his experiences during the civil war in Spain (1936–1937) that placed him firmly on the far Left, and, moreover, he remained remarkably consistent in adhering to this understanding until his early, indeed sadly premature, death. What perhaps has led to at least some of the confusion surrounding his beliefs is that although he continued to believe socialism as he understood it, to be desirable, indeed, necessary, he came to the conclusion during the Second World War that it was, on the most optimistic assessment, some way in the future. In the meantime, the best that could be hoped for in Britain was the Labour Party, although the contention here is that Orwell never took seriously the claim that even the Labour government of 1945–1951 was socialist. His support for that government should not be confused with the idea that he believed it was socialist. Whether, if he had lived, into the 1950s, the 1960s and beyond, he would have remained a socialist is another matter. His beliefs would have had to survive the remarkable post-war expansion of British capitalism and the intensification of the Cold War. How we assess his likely political trajectory had he lived really depends more on where we ourselves stand and is purely speculative.

'SOCIALISM MEANS A CLASSLESS SOCIETY OR IT MEANS NOTHING'

As far as George Orwell was concerned, by the end of the 1930s, socialism was not just a theory, an ethos or an attitude. He had actually seen socialism in practice in Spain, experienced it, fought for it, seen men and women die for it, watched it defeated and narrowly escaped with his life to tell the tale. In Barcelona, he saw for the first time, as he famously put it, 'a town where the working class was in the saddle'. His description is worth quoting at length because what he saw in Barcelona became the touchstone of his socialism:

> Practically every building of any size had been seized by the workers and was draped with red flags or with the red and black flags of the anarchists, every wall was scrawled with the hammer and sickle and with the initials of the revolutionary parties, almost every church had been gutted and its images burned … Every shop and café had an inscription that it had been collectivised; even the boot blacks had been collectivised and their boxes painted red and black. Waiters and shop-walkers looked you in the face and treated you as an equal … There were no private motor cars, they had all been commandeered, and all the trams and taxis and much of the other transport was painted red and black … In outward appearance it was a town in which the wealthy classes had practically ceased to exist … All this was queer and moving. There was much in it that I did not understand, in some ways I did not even like it, but I recognised it immediately as a state of affairs worth fighting for (Orwell 1985 [1937]: 8–9).

Barcelona really looked like 'a workers' state' where 'the entire bourgeoisie had either fled, been killed, or voluntarily come over to the workers' side.' As he later realized, many were, in fact, in hiding, waiting for the tide to turn (ibid.). He was already on the left when he arrived in Barcelona, but his experience of working class men and women in Britain was of people who had been defeated, whom he saw as victims. Barcelona was very different. Here the woman he saw poking a drain in Wigan about whom he wrote in *The Road to Wigan Pier* (2000 [1937]: 66) had been transformed into the woman on the barricades. He wrote enthusiastically to Cyril Connolly on 8 June 1937 (Orwell 1968 [1937]: 301): 'I have seen wonderful things and at last really believe in socialism, which I never did before.' His service in the Trotskyist Partido Obrero de Unificacion Marxista (POUM) militia had a similarly powerful impact on him. Here he experienced 'a foretaste of socialism, by which I mean that the prevailing atmosphere was that of socialism.' He wrote contemptuously of the 'huge tribe of party hacks and sleek little professors ... busy proving that socialism means no more than a planned state-capitalism.' Fortunately 'there also exists a vision of socialism quite different from this.' For most people, he insisted, 'socialism means a classless society, or it means nothing at all.' The militia he served in were 'a sort of microcosm of a classless society.' The experience 'was to make my desire to see socialism established much more actual than it had been before' (Orwell 1985 [1937]: 28–29).

There can be no serious doubt as to the importance of seeing the workers in the saddle in Barcelona for Orwell. He had actually seen a revolution in action, he knew from first-hand experience that the working class could take power into their hands and that this was what socialism looked like. It was not just a theoretical proposition or an account in someone else's book. He had seen it for himself. Equally important, of course, for his later political development was the manner of its destruction. This socialism was destroyed, not by Franco's army, but by the communists. Far from being in the vanguard of the struggle for socialism, Orwell saw the communists crush the revolutionary left and dismantle the institutions of workers' power in Spain—all in the interest of Soviet foreign policy. The Russians wanted an alliance with Britain and France against Nazi Germany and a revolutionary Spain would have scared them off. He escaped with his life, but others were not so lucky. The knowledge that if he had fallen into communist hands in Spain, he would almost certainly have been killed, was to give his anti-communism a very personal intensity. As he later complained, 'few people in England have yet caught up with the fact that Communism is now a counter-revolutionary force' (Davison 1998a: 42). But, of course, he had remarkably little success in convincing anyone on the Left of this at the time. The POUM and its supporters were relentlessly slandered by the communists as being in league with the fascists right up until Stalin allied with Hitler in August 1939. One last point worth making here is that Orwell, who is often remembered for his celebration of 'Englishness,' came back from Spain very much an internationalist.

Once back in Britain, he not only tried to expose communist conduct in Spain, but also to understand why they had behaved the way they did. He had gone to Spain believing that whatever their differences, he and the communists were on the same side, but returned regarding them as enemies. As part of his investigation into why they had crushed those to their left and lied so readily about it, he set about trying to understand the nature of the Soviet Union. He quickly concluded that what existed there bore no relation to the workers' state he had seen in Barcelona. The communists in Britain had willingly, indeed eagerly, subordinated themselves to a brutal, murderous dictatorship that had reduced the Russian working class 'to a status resembling serfdom.' They lied without any shame whatsoever in defence of this regime. The Russian dictator, Stalin, was, moreover, 'worshipped in terms that would have made Nero blush' (ibid.: 160). Whatever Russia was, it was not socialism as Orwell understood it. From this time on Orwell was to make every effort he could to combat the very idea that Soviet communism was to be supported, let alone emulated. As he later put it, Spain had 'turned the scale and thereafter I knew where I stood.' Since 1936, everything he had written had been 'directly or indirectly against totalitarianism and for democratic socialism' (Davison 1998f: 319).

'WHEN THE RED MILITIAS ARE BILLETED IN THE RITZ'

Orwell returned to Britain from Spain convinced that the world was charged with revolutionary possibilities. Initially, this saw him adopt an anti-war stance. War with Nazi Germany would be nothing more than a clash of empires with Britain moving in a fascist direction very likely under Popular Front auspices. Those opposed to war would get the same treatment that the communists had handed out to the POUM and the anarchists in Spain. The Hitler-Stalin Pact, the German-Russian partition of Poland and the Russian attack on Finland together smashed the Popular Front and provided absolute vindication for Orwell's rejection of Stalinism. With the German conquest of Western Europe, the character of the war changed or rather had another dimension added. It was now a war of liberation against a fascist tyranny that was allied with the Soviet Union, a war that could only be won if there was a socialist revolution in Britain with a revolutionary government putting itself at the head of a European-wide resistance movement. And Orwell believed that this revolution was already underway by the summer of 1940. In retrospect, of course, this all looks completely unrealistic, but at the time it was a much more credible scenario. In the summer of 1940, across Europe the conservative establishment was rushing to collaborate with the Nazis, powerful elements within the British establishment were in favor of surrender, the Russians were congratulating Hitler on his victories, and there was no likely prospect of US intervention. In these circumstances, the idea of a socialist Britain as being necessary to defeat of the Nazis and their communist allies was certainly not that farfetched to many on the left. But what did Orwell understand by a socialist Britain and how was it to be achieved?

In his essay, 'My Country, Right or Left,' published in the autumn of 1940, Orwell proclaimed that only revolution 'can save England,' that this revolution had, in fact, already began, and that while it would be a distinctively English revolution, nevertheless 'I dare say the London gutters will have to run with blood. All right, let them if necessary' (Orwell 2001 [1940]: 247). He went on to imagine 'the red militias ... billeted at the Ritz' (ibid.). It is important to remember here that Orwell had seen a revolution in Spain and that as far as he was concerned it was really inconceivable that a socialist revolution could be accomplished without bloodshed even in Britain. The reason was quite simple. Orwell believed, quite correctly, that the ruling class would resist any fundamental challenge to their position, any serious attempt to strip them of their wealth and power, by force. He was quite adamant about this. In February 1941, he wrote in *Left News*, the monthly magazine of the Left Book Club, that if a Labour government were elected with a clear majority and tried 'at once to establish socialism by act of parliament ... the monied classes would rebel.' There was, he argued more generally 'no strong reason for thinking that any really fundamental change can ever be achieved peacefully' (Davison 1998b: 269–272). At the time he wrote this, the last thing Orwell would ever have expected was that any Labour government would ever try to establish socialism. The 1924 and 1929–1931 Labour governments hardly inspired any confidence in Labour's radicalism, and in 1941 Labour was part of Churchill's coalition government and had agreed an electoral truce with the Conservatives. Instead, he looked for the emergence of a new socialist movement that 'which meant business' and was 'both revolutionary and democratic.' Such a movement would, he believed, have at its disposal a potential revolutionary militia in the shape of the Home Guard which would be able to put down any attempted coup à la Franco, and some of those militiamen would, of course, be billeted at the Ritz! (ibid.: 376–381).

Orwell did, of course, make a contribution to the formulation of the program that his hoped-for socialist movement would put into practice in his booklet, *The Lion and the Unicorn: Socialism and the English Genius* (1980 [1941]: 527–564). This was, it is important to remember, not an idiosyncratic work, the product of individual genius, but was rather one of a Searchlight series of booklets that he co-edited. These were propagandist interventions intended to help pull British politics to the left, to help create a new socialist movement and to provide it with arguments and with a program. There were volumes on Germany and Spain, on Africa, on the Blitz and on the Home Front and much else. Orwell's own contribution, *The Lion and the Unicorn*, was the longest statement of his stand regarding British politics that he ever wrote. Here he has much to say about Englishness which is of considerable interest, but more pertinent to the argument here is his rejection both of a Labourism which had never attempted any fundamental change and of 'the nineteenth century doctrine of class war,' that is of the politics of both the Stalinists and the Trotskyists. The new socialist movement that he envisaged would be led by the skilled educated section of the working class, into which he subsumed many jobs usually identified as middle class. It would implement a new model of revolutionary change. Whether this movement would have to use violence too would be 'an accident of time and place,' but if it proved necessary then the movement would use violence (ibid.: 560).

What *The Lion and the Unicorn* called for was the nationalization of the mines, railways, major industries, banks and financial institutions without compensation. All urban land was to be nationalized and rural landownership was to be limited to 15 acres (ibid.: 549). This would have effectively stripped the ruling class of all their wealth and power. They would have been abolished. It is really inconceivable that such a radical program would not have been forcibly resisted. Orwell also called for the compulsory limitation of income inequality with no one receiving more than ten times the lowest income. He called for the democratization of the educational system with the nationalization of the public schools and the closing down of most other private schools (ibid.: 556–557). And he called for the transformation of the Empire into a socialist federation of free and equal states (ibid.: 558). Any attempt at resisting this revolution would be put down by force and as far as Orwell was concerned the means was already available in the shape of the Home Guard. Certainly his program was far more radical than anything the Labour Party proposed, has ever proposed or will ever propose.

'THE COMMON MAN WILL WIN HIS FIGHT SOONER OR LATER'

In 1942, Orwell wrote an important essay, 'Looking Back on the Spanish War' (1968 [1943]: 286–306), that demonstrates the extent to which his Spanish experiences still influenced his thinking. The Spanish War was, he argued, 'in essence a class war. If it had been won, the cause of the common people everywhere would have been strengthened'. When it was lost, 'the dividend-drawers all over the world rubbed their hands.' From this, he argues as a general proposition that 'in the long run—the working class remains the most reliable enemy of Fascism, simply because the working class stands to gain most by a decent reconstruction of society' (ibid.: 298). He did make the point that this was 'only' in the long run. This was 'not to idealise the working class.' Indeed, in every struggle since the Russian Revolution, the working class had been defeated 'and it is impossible not to feel that it was their own fault.' Workers in Britain, for example, stood by while 'their comrades' were massacred 'in Vienna, Berlin, Madrid or wherever.' Indeed, they showed more interest in 'yesterday's football match' (ibid.: 299). Nevertheless, he insisted, this did not alter the fact 'that the working class will go on struggling against Fascism after the others have caved in.' But while working class consciousness 'ebbs and flows,' the working class remains, like a plant, 'blind and stupid,' but relentlessly growing 'towards the light, and it will do this in the face of endless discouragements' (ibid.).

Orwell remembered the Italian militiaman he had met in the Lenin barracks in Barcelona, 'probably a Trotskyist or an anarchist,' whom he had written about so dramatically at the start of *Homage to Catalonia* (of 1937)—by now very likely dead at the hands of either the Gestapo or the GPU, the Soviet secret service (ibid.: 303). This man, whom he only saw for a few minutes, nevertheless 'symbolises for me the flower of the European working class, harried by the police of all countries, the people who fill the mass graves of the Spanish battlefields and are now to the tune of several millions, rotting in forced-labour camps' (ibid.). He concludes by making a declaration of what the current war was about:

> ... the struggle of the gradually awakening common people against the lords of property and their hired liars and bumsuckers. The question is very simple. Shall the common man be pushed back into the mud, or shall he not? I myself believe, perhaps on insufficient grounds, that the common man will win his fight sooner or later, but I want it to be sooner and not later—some time within the next hundred years, say, and not some time within the next ten thousand. That is the real lesson of the Spanish War, and of the present war, and perhaps of other wars yet to come (Davison 1998c: 510).

'THE FORCES OF REACTION HAVE WON HANDS DOWN'

There never was a British revolution, of course. Orwell acknowledged that his belief in the inevitability of either revolution or military defeat had been proven wrong in his 'London Letter,' dated 3 January, that appeared in the March–April 1943 issue of the US dissident Marxist and literary Trotskyist journal, *Partisan Review* (Orwell 1968: 317–324). Here he contrasted the situation when he had written his first 'London Letter' for the journal in January 1941 with the current situation. At the end of 1940, while England was in 'desperate straits' militarily, at the same time the country 'appeared to be on the edge of rapid political advance.' Today, however,

> ... the military situation is enormously better but the political outlook is blacker than it has ever been ... the forces of reaction have won hands down. Churchill is firm in the saddle again ... it is hard to see how any revolutionary situation can recur till the Western end of the war is finished. We have had two opportunities, Dunkirk and Singapore, and we took neither ... the growing suspicion that we may all have underrated the strength of Capitalism and that the Right may, after all, be able to win the war off its own bat without resorting to any radical change is very depressing to anyone who thinks (ibid.: 317).

One of the indications of how politics was moving to the right that Orwell singles out for discussion is the *Beveridge Report on Social Security* (ibid.: 318). He described it as 'this very modest measure of reform' and regarded the support the report got from the left as indicating how much political hopes and ambitions had shrunk. If this was the best that people could hope for then the left really was in retreat! This attitude towards Beveridge is itself a good indication of how radical Orwell was at this time and how far politics had moved from that radicalism by the time Labour took office in 1945. The implementation of this 'very modest measure of reform' was to be trumpeted as one of the great achievements of the Attlee government (Davison 1998d: 292–293).

He returned to this theme in another 'London Letter' published in the Winter 1944 issue of *Partisan Review* (Davison 1998e). By now he had become the literary editor of the left-wing Labour newspaper, *Tribune*, a step that signalled his final abandonment of any hope for the emergence of a new socialist movement. In this 'Letter,' he once again acknowledged that he had misjudged the situation in Britain, putting it down to the 'political analysis which I had made in the desperate period of 1940 and continued to cling to long after it should have been clear that it was untenable.' His belief that without revolution in Britain the Nazis would win the war was clearly wrong long before he acknowledged it. He wrote that there were ...

> ... excuses for this belief, but still it was a very great error. For after all we have not lost the war, unless appearances are very deceiving, and we have not introduced socialism. Britain is moving towards a planned economy, and class distinctions tend to dwindle, but there has been no real shift of power and no increase in genuine democracy. The same people still own all the property and usurp all the best jobs (Davison 1998e: 112).

The British ruling class had been saved by the German attack on Russia and the Japanese attack on the United States. This had decisively changed the balance of forces in the war so that now the Nazis could be defeated without any radical change being necessary in Britain. Instead, the ruling class was able to ride the war out. In 1940–1941, Orwell had been very critical of the Labour Party for going to the assistance, as he saw it, of the Conservatives and refusing to give a lead to the socialist movement that was developing. He was not surprised by this, but nevertheless considered that it placed the Labour Party on the other side, as one of the obstacles to a socialist revolution. As part of his coming to terms with the failure of his revolutionary hopes, Orwell turned to this same Labour Party and the Labour Left as the best that was possible in Britain.

'AS I PLEASE'

A number of writers have welcomed Orwell's involvement with *Tribune* as him coming home, finally seeing sense and at last adopting a realistic attitude towards British politics and what was and was not possible. Bernard Crick, in what is still the best biography of the man, wholeheartedly endorsed his embrace of '*Tribune* socialism.' According to Crick, Orwell's *Tribune* years 'were happy days' (1980: 449). Paul Anderson is much more careful and nuanced in the 'Introduction' to his excellent collection of Orwell's *Tribune* contributions (2006: 1–39). But for Robert Coles, Attlee's government 'was Orwell's revolution made real' (Coles 2013: 178).

He argues that by 1943, Orwell was 'a pretty straightforward supporter of the Labour Party,' who recognized that Labour was 'a responsible party, attuned to real lives rather than ideological postures' (ibid.: 223). What Crick and Coles assume is that Orwell's involvement with *Tribune* somehow involved a repudiation of his revolutionary politics and that his Spanish enthusiasms were finally laid to rest. This is to fundamentally misunderstand his political development. Instead, the argument that will be put forward here is that Orwell's belief that socialism involved the working class taking power and establishing a classless society never changed, but that he recognized this was not practical politics and so gave his support to the Labour left as the best option available in the circumstances. He certainly did not consider that the 1945–1951 Labour government was introducing socialism, but nevertheless supported it because of its reforms and because of its opposition to Stalinism, both at home and abroad. And, of course, *Tribune* offered him an opportunity to put his ideas and idiosyncrasies in front of a large section of the British left.

One other point worth making about the champions of Orwell's conversion to Labourism is that they neglect Orwell's contributions to *Partisan Review* and, instead, privilege his *Tribune* contributions. This distorts his politics. Orwell wrote 80 of his 'As I Please' columns together with various other articles and reviews for *Tribune* between 1943 and 1947. Many of his contributions were not actually concerned with politics. Certainly none of this should be neglected in any assessment of his intellectual biography. What of his contributions to *Partisan Review*? From the March–April 1941 issue until the summer of 1946 issue, Orwell contributed fifteen 'London Letters' to *Partisan Review*, all of them specifically concerned with British political developments, and subsequently two important articles, 'Reflections on Gandhi' (Orwell 1980: 835–840) that appeared in the January 1949 issue and his crucial, as we shall see, 'Towards European Unity' that appeared in the July–August 1947 issue. The fact is that he wrote more political journalism and commentary for *Partisan Review* than he did for *Tribune,* and yet it is the *Tribune* contributions that are taken as defining his politics. This is not to attempt to deny his support for the Labour left but rather to insist that he was still engaged in a dialogue with dissident Marxism. And, indeed, one can go further and say that while he supported the Labour government, he certainly did not believe that it was introducing socialism and it was still socialism, the creation of a classless society where the rich had been altogether dispossessed, that was the political cause he still gave allegiance to.

One other point worth making about *Partisan Review* is the influence that it had on Orwell. His understanding of the Soviet Union and Stalinism was heavily influenced by the theory of 'bureaucratic collectivism,' a Trotskyist heresy, advanced by the journal. It was this particular understanding of the Soviet Union that informed *Nineteen Eighty-Four* (Newsinger 1999: 124–128).

'A LABOUR GOVERNMENT WITH A CRUSHING MAJORITY'

Orwell was very disappointed by the performance of the Labour government that took office in July 1945. In the last of his 'London Letters' that appeared in *Partisan Review* in the summer of 1946, he wrote:

> Even allowing for the fact that everything takes time, it is astonishing how little change seems to have happened as yet in the structure of society. In a purely economic sense, I suppose, the drift is towards socialism, or at least towards state ownership. Transport, for example, is being nationalised. The railway shareholders are being bought out at prices they would hardly get in the open market: still the control of the railways is being taken out of private hands. But in the social set-up there is no symptom by which one could infer that we are not living under a conservative government. No move has been made against the House of Lords ... if any effort has been made to democratise education, it has borne no fruit as yet ... the upper class are still living their accustomed life, and though they certainly dislike the Labour Government, they don't appear to be frightened of it ... I think almost any observer would have expected a greater change in the social atmosphere when a Labour Government with a crushing majority had been in power for eight months.

Even allowing for the fact that Britain was certainly not 'on the verge of violent revolution, or even that the masses have been definitely converted to socialism,' he would have expected more. Why had the generals and top civil servants not been replaced? Why were the public schools still tolerated? (Davison 1998f: 285–289). The mistake he was making, of course, was to take the Labour left's rhetoric too seriously, when, in fact, the Labour government's objectives were to restore the fortunes of British capitalism, introduce a limited program of social reforms, that in retrospect amounted to welfare capitalism, and maintain Britain's position as a great power. Far from Labour's nationalizations signalling some sort of attack on the capitalist class, they involved taking bankrupt industries off their hands with more than generous compensation and then modernizing them for the benefit of the capitalists generally. And the huge sums that the government spent on trying to maintain Britain's position as a world power were at the expense of the working class, and not in any way for their benefit. Certainly, Orwell regarded the government's social reforms as important, but he never made the mistake of regarding them as amounting to socialism. They improved the position of working class and middle class people but within a capitalist society still dominated by the rich and powerful.

While Orwell was himself still a socialist, in the day to day world of politics, he found himself being pulled to the right while Labour was in power. Two factors account for this. First, his support for the Labour government as the best that was possible at the time saw him becoming an apologist for it even when it came into conflict with sections of workers. Second, his hostility to Stalinism saw him, as we shall see, getting into some unsavoury company. Orwell took a 'lesser evil' stance as the Cold War began, deciding that in the event of another war, he would support the United States against the Soviet Union. Whether he would have followed through on this and become a fully-fledged Cold Warrior or drawn back once he was aware of the company he was keeping we do not know and there is evidence pointing in both directions. My own evaluation of the evidence is that he would have drawn back, but inevitably one's judgements on such hypothetical questions reflect where one stands personally as much as it does the available evidence.

There is no doubt that Orwell's disappointments of 1946 were put aside in 1947–1948. He became much less critical in his support for the Labour government. Why was this?

'THE STRUGGLE BETWEEN COLLECTIVISM AND *LAISSEZ-FAIRE* IS SECONDARY'

Context is all here. In August 1947, the government found itself having to deal with the worst financial crisis since 1931. The response to this was something we are familiar with today although not as grim as the late 1940s: austerity. This began with Hugh Dalton's November 1947 Budget but was greatly intensified under his successor as Chancellor of the Exchequer, Stafford Cripps, through to 1950, when Hugh Gaitskell took over. Austerity was combined with a massive rearmament programme. One other similarity with today is that all of these wealthy men imposing austerity on the working class were former public schoolboys, two Wykehamists (Cripps and Gaitskell) and an Old Etonian (Dalton). Orwell gave them his full support. There was also an important difference from the situation today: the Attlee government was introducing a modern welfare state alongside austerity whereas the Cameron government has been dismantling it alongside austerity.

In October 1948, Orwell published an article, 'Britain's Struggle for Survival: The Labour Government After Three Years' in *Commentary* (Davison 1998g). Here, he argued that the past three years had been lived 'in a state of almost continuous crisis' that had been postponed 'by American loans, by "austerity", and by the spending of reserves.' However, the fundamental problem 'of making Britain genuinely solvent without sinking the standard of living to an unbearably low level remains untouched.' Britain was engaged in a very real fight for 'national survival' and in these circumstances 'the struggle between collectivism and *laissez-faire* is secondary'. As Orwell pointed out, working people voted Labour 'for full employment, bigger old age pensions, the raising of the school leaving age, more social and economic equality and more democracy all round.' The government, he recognized, 'cannot afford to disappoint its supporters altogether,' but the fact was that at his time of writing 'the average British citizen is probably somewhat worse off than he was three years ago.' One of the problems, he discusses, is how to get the workers to actually work hard enough for the good of the country in these circumstances.

This is something completely new, indeed unique, in Orwell's political writing. Whereas before he had always sided with the working class, even when at his most critical, his identification with the government is so complete that we find him discussing the problems the working class are causing it. He writes: 'If wages are evened out, labour drifts away from the more disagreeable jobs: if especially high rates are paid for these jobs, absenteeism increases, because it is then possible to earn enough to live on by working only three or four shifts a week' (ibid.). He identifies a 'problem' that the socialist movement has always been reluctant to face up to: 'that certain jobs which are vitally necessary are never done except under some kind of compulsion. As soon as you have full employment ... you have to make use of forced labour.' He even makes the point that it could be called 'by some more soothing name.' This is really quite astonishing, not least coming from someone who elsewhere scathingly condemned political euphemisms. Clearly, Orwell's commitment to the Labour government had pulled him quite dramatically to the right at least as far as his attitude towards working class people was concerned. One can comfortably assume that he was not thinking in terms of public schoolboys being conscripted to do the jobs no one else wanted to do. Absenteeism was not the only problem. There were also 'the innumerable stoppages and unofficial strikes of the past few years,' many of them, he conceded, caused by 'sheer exhaustion quite as much as any economic grievance.' Whereas successful strikes had once 'brought concrete benefits to the working class,' now strikes were 'a blow against the community.' It would, he argues, be a disaster for the Conservatives to take power, but only because they could not persuade the working class to accept the necessary sacrifices peacefully! (ibid.: 436–443).

It is interesting to contrast Orwell's thinking here with the stance that he took in 1940–1941, another crisis period. Then the answer was for the working class to take power, for the rich to be dispossessed and for socialism to be established. Now with Labour in power all this is forgotten. The rich no longer figure in his thinking, instead the working class is the problem, and he condemns strikes and actually contemplates forced labour. This is not the whole story, of course, but nevertheless it is an aspect of Orwell's support for Labour that is too often neglected.

'THEY APPEAR TO HAVE CONSIDERABLE FUNDS AT THEIR DISPOSAL'

Orwell's support for the Labour government together with his anti-Stalinism led him into a relationship with the Information Research Department (IRD), a propaganda organisation set up by the government in 1947 to combat Soviet influence (see Lashmar and Oliver 1998). Orwell has been quite correctly criticized for this, but it is important to put his conduct into perspective (Lucas 2004). The notorious list that he handed over to the IRD was not a blacklist that was then passed on to MI5 but was, in fact, a list of people he recommended as unsuitable for the sort of work the IRD was engaged in because of their Stalinist sympathies. Nevertheless, the list is an unsavoury indication of where his anti-Stalinism might have led him. It is, however, nowhere near as reprehensible as the conduct of those communists and their sympathisers who were busy apologizing for Stalin's murderous regime at this time.

Even more problematic was his little-known flirtation with a US intelligence front, the International Relief and Rescue Committee (IRRC), although in his defence he was misled as to the nature of this organisation (see Chester 1995). On 16 March 1946, he wrote to Arthur Koestler about an approach he had received from Francis Henson about affiliating with the IRRC. Henson had assured him that the committee existed to help 'the victims of totalitarianism' and that it was strongly 'anti-Stalinist to the extent that the people they assist are largely Trotskyists etc.' As Orwell observed, these people 'appear to have considerable funds at their disposal,' which was something of a clue (Davison 1998f: 154–155). Nothing has so far come to light that indicates that his relationship with the IRRC went any further than tentative approaches on their part.

On the other side of the equation, however, Orwell publicly opposed any importation of McCarthyism into Britain and was actively involved in campaigning to protect the civil liberties of communists, anarchists, Trotskyists and others through the Freedom Defence Committee. In the late 1940s, he condemned the execution of communist prisoners both in Franco's Spain and in Stalin's East European empire, whereas British communists, of course, only condemned the executions in Spain (see his support for Spanish prisoners: Davison 1998h: 164–165). Whatever the dubious nature of his involvement with the IRD and the IRRC, his position is still infinitely superior to that of Stalin's apologists.

CONCLUSION: 'THE ONLY WORTHWHILE POLITICAL OBJECTIVE TODAY'

Even while Orwell's support for the Labour government pulled him to the right, he still maintained his engagement with the far left and his belief that hope for the future lay with the working class. This is demonstrated in a very powerful way in *Nineteen Eighty-Four* (1989 [1949]). When Winston Smith says: 'If there was hope, it lay with the proles,' this is not just empty rhetoric. Watching the working class woman hanging out her washing, he eulogizers such women all over the world as 'the same solid unconquerable figure, made monstrous by work and childbearing, toiling from birth to death and still singing. Out of those loins a mighty race of conscious beings must one day come' (ibid.: 216). Smith famously ponders the problem of working class consciousness in the novel: 'Until they become conscious they will never rebel and until after they have rebelled they cannot become conscious' (ibid.: 229–230). This problem is never resolved, but its very formulation places the novel firmly on the left. Both *Nineteen Eighty-Four* and the earlier *Animal Farm* (of 1945) were to be attacked by the left, but this was because most of the left, even the Labour left, remained sympathetic to the Soviet Union, especially in the aftermath of the Second World War.

This engagement was not confined to fiction. *Partisan Review* ran a series on 'The Future of the Left' to which Orwell was asked to contribute. His 'Towards European Unity' appeared in the July–August 1947 issue (Davison 1998g). The essay owes considerably more to his continuing engagement with the ideas of the far left than it does with *Tribune* socialism. Here he wrote of how hopeless the situation looked as far as the socialist cause was concerned. Indeed, he was pessimistic regarding the survival of civilization at all. Clearly, however, the success of Stalinism, for Orwell, only strengthened the enemies of socialism, but what is also interesting is that there is no championing of the Labour government. Whatever his support for the government, he did not consider it to be building socialism. Indeed, he identifies as one of the obstacles to socialism the fact that under Labour, Britain had become 'almost a dependency on the USA.' Still, he insisted that 'our activities as socialists only have meaning if we assume that socialism *can* be established.' What then was the way forward? Now while 'Socialism cannot properly be said to be established until it is world-wide … the process must begin somewhere.' He went on: 'A Socialist United States of Europe seems to me to be the only worth-while political objective today.' He thought the prospect of success 'unlikely … but I also can't at present see any other hopeful objective' (ibid.: 163–166).

REFERENCES

Anderson, Paul (2006) *Orwell in Tribune: 'As I Please' and Other Writings 1943–7*, London: Politico's.

Chester, Eric Thomas (1995) *Covert Network: Progressives, the International Rescue Committee and the CIA*, New York: M. E. Sharpe.

Coles, Robert (2013) *George Orwell: English Rebel*, Oxford: Oxford University Press.

Crick, Bernard (1980) *George Orwell: A Life*, London: Penguin.

Davison, Peter (ed.) (1998a) *George Orwell: Facing Unpleasant Facts 1937–1939*, London: Secker and Warburg.

Davison, Peter (ed.) (1998b) *George Orwell: A Patriot After All 1940–1941*, London: Secker and Warburg.

Davison, Peter (ed.) (1998c) *George Orwell: All Propaganda Is Lies 1941–1942*, London: Secker and Warburg.

Davison, Peter (ed.) (1998d) *George Orwell: Keeping Our Little Corner Clean 1942–1943*, London: Secker and Warburg.

Davison, Peter (ed.) (1998e) *George Orwell: I Have Tried to Tell the Truth 1943–1944*, London: Secker and Warburg.

Davison, Peter (ed.) (1998f) *George Orwell: Smothered Under Journalism 1946*, London: Secker and Warburg.

Davison, Peter (ed.) (1998g) *George Orwell: It Is What I Think 1947–1948*, London: Secker and Warburg.

Davison, Peter (ed) (1998h) *George Orwell: Our Job Is to Make Life Worth Living 1949–1950*, London: Secker and Warburg.

Lashmar, Paul and Oliver, James (1998) *Britain's Secret Propaganda War 1948–1977*, Stroud: Sutton.

Lucas, Scott (2004) *The Betrayal of Dissent: Beyond Orwell, Hitchins and the New American Century*, London: Pluto Press.

Newsinger, John (1999) *Orwell's Politics*, Basingstoke: Macmillan.

Orwell, George (1968 [1937]) Letter to Cyril Connolly, Orwell, Sonia and Angus, Ian (eds) *The Collected Essays, Journalism and Letters, Vol. 1: An Age Like This*, Harmondsworth, Middlesex: Penguin pp. 300–301.

Orwell, George (1980) *George Orwell*, London: Martin Secker and Warburg.

Orwell, George (1985 [1937]) *Homage to Catalonia*, London, Penguin.

Orwell, George (1989 [1949]) *Nineteen Eighty-Four*, London, Penguin.

Orwell, George (2001) My country right or left, Davison, Peter (ed.) *Orwell's England*, London: Penguin pp. 242–248.

CHAPTER EIGHT

Sectarians ON Wigan Pier

George Orwell and the Anti-Austerity Left in Britain

PHILIP BOUNDS

Whenever there is a whiff of austerity in the air, many of us on the British left set our sights on Wigan Pier. Written in the middle of the deepest depression that Western capitalism has ever known, George Orwell's *The Road to Wigan Pier* (1937) still powerfully conditions our sense of how austerity should be portrayed.[1] Its searing and mordant images of overworked miners, whey-faced proletarian housewives and quietly desperate dole claimants have long since acquired archetypal status. Each new generation of British socialists has sought to update them in an effort to evoke the economic and social problems of its own times. Indeed, there is now a lengthy tradition of books, articles and pamphlets in which the conditions described in Orwell's masterpiece are explicitly compared with those of the present. The most substantial recent addition to this body of work is Stephen Armstrong's *The Road to Wigan Pier Revisited* (Armstrong 2012), a deft travelogue which comes close to concluding that conditions in the North of England are almost as bad now as they were in Orwell's day.[2]

Most latterday attempts to revisit Wigan Pier focus on the first half of Orwell's book, which deals with such matters as housing, working conditions and unemployment. The focus of the present chapter is slightly different. In the second half of *The Road to Wigan Pier*—especially in Chapters XI and XII—Orwell tries to explain the distressing failure of the inter-war left to win much support for a socialist solution to the crisis. His emphasis is not so much on structural or objective factors as on the *cultural* deficiencies of the various left organizations. The contemporary relevance of this part of his book scarcely needs underscoring. Although there were many people on the radical left in Britain who thought that their time had come when international capitalism lurched into crisis in 2008, there has been no revival of socialist politics over the last five years. The innumerable small Marxist parties and the radical wing of the Labour Party are still weak, fragmented and marginalized. To what extent does *The Road to Wigan Pier* help us to understand the modern left's lack of effectiveness? Does its diagnosis of the left's cultural malaise still speak to our contemporary political practices or should we be seeking new explanations? These are among the questions I shall try to answer.[3]

ORWELL'S ATTACK ON THE LEFT

George Orwell was not a political theorist and never claimed to be one. When he tried to account for the failure of the socialist left to capitalize on the crisis of the inter-war period, he made no attempt to deploy any heavy philosophical artillery. His approach was that of a highly intelligent, unusually independent-minded journalist who based most of his conclusions on his personal observations of the left. He was not interested in analyzing the deep structures of capitalist society or the forms of consciousness to which they give rise. Instead, he focused on those comparatively superficial aspects of socialist politics which too often induce a neuralgic response on the part of ordinary working people. His superficiality was at once his biggest strength and his greatest weakness. Aware of the importance of first impressions, he had an unrivalled ability to understand the ways in which the surface characteristics of the left tend to 'drive away the very people who ought to be flocking to its support' (Orwell 2001 [1937]: 159). By the same token, his big drawback as a socialist thinker was that his obsession with political surfaces prevented him engaging in sufficient depth with issues of structure, organisation and ideology. If we look to him for help in trying to understand the weaknesses of today's left, we have to realize that his ideas can only provide a starting point for the debate. Other and weightier writers will also need to be consulted.

The circumstances in which Orwell launched his attack on the left are well known.[4] After being commissioned by the publisher Victor Gollancz to write a book about the contemporary working class, Orwell spent nearly eight weeks in early 1936 travelling through the so-called 'distressed areas' in the North of England. His exposure to such harrowing levels of poverty, unemployment and industrial dereliction went a long way towards crystallizing his exasperation with the left. Given that the deepest crisis in capitalism's history had inflicted such misery on ordinary people, why was it that 'Instead of going forward, the cause of socialism is visibly going back'? (ibid.: 159). Orwell's most famous answer to that question was that the left had alienated potential recruits with its sheer crankiness.

His searing attack on the fruit-juice drinkers, nudists and sandal wearers of the organized socialist movement is still widely quoted. Less famous but probably more important were his discussions of three other things which served to limit the left's appeal—its officiousness, its ambivalent commitment to achieving real change and its uncritical embrace of modernity.

Orwell's attack on the left's officiousness was rooted in a contrast between the socialist movement's working-class sympathizers and its more articulate middle-class spokesmen. Although he always believed that working-class socialists had sound political instincts, not least because they realized that socialism was ultimately about 'justice and common decency' and 'nobody bossing you about,' he also believed that their commitment to the left was neither 'complete' nor 'logically consistent' because of their lack of interest in political doctrine (ibid.: 164). His real targets were the intellectually sophisticated middle-class socialists who represented the public face of the left. His main concern about the 'mingy little beasts' who populated the Communist Party, the Independent Labour Party and the Labour left was that their radicalism seemed wholly devoid of libertarian impulses. What attracted them to socialism was not a love of freedom but an overdeveloped desire for order. Offended by the unpredictable and chaotic nature of free markets, they embraced the idea of economic planning because they thought it enabled governments to subject every last aspect of people's lives to precise administrative control. Their vision of socialism had nothing to do with workers' self-management and everything to do with the subordination of the masses to enlightened but essentially bloodless officials. Orwell even suggested that their 'hypertrophied sense of order' (ibid.: 166) had its roots in a sort of visceral dislike of working people. Their desire to abolish poverty arose not so much from a sense of compassion as from the feeling that the poor were 'contemptible and disgusting' (ibid.). The politics of the middle-class left were ultimately an expression of the desire for social hygiene.[5]

After pouring scorn on the vision of socialist society to which his contemporaries subscribed, Orwell went on to question whether the middle-class left really wanted socialism at all. He strongly suspected that its desire to change society was at best somewhat ambivalent. Although many middle-class radicals nursed an almost pathological hatred for the bourgeoisie, they could not be relied upon to support a challenge to capitalism when the chips were down. This was partly because so many of them were slaves to political fashion. According to one of Orwell's less accurate predictions, many of the young men and women who called themselves socialists in 1936 would cheerfully go over to fascism when the pendulum of political opinion swung to the right. Their tendency to equivocate also arose from a highly recognizable species of old-fashioned snobbery. Usually reasonably affluent and addicted to the status which their professional positions conferred upon them, middle-class radicals secretly regarded the socialist idea as a grave threat to their wealth and prestige. Hence Orwell's devastating judgement that the 'typical socialist' was:

> ... a prim little man with a white-collar job, usually a secret teetotaller and often with vegetarian leanings, with a history of Nonconformity behind him, and, above all, with a social position which he has no intention of forfeiting (ibid.: 161).

Perhaps the most interesting symptom of the middle-class left's insincerity was its attitude towards political doctrine. Implicit in Orwell's description of left-wing culture was the belief that bourgeois radicals used socialist theory as a means of symbolically asserting their superiority to their working-class comrades. Whereas working-class socialists engaged only superficially with the rarified world of theory, the 'intellectual, book-trained socialist' mugged up on Marx, Engels and Lenin in order to shore up his sense of entitlement and establish his right to lead. Orwell was especially suspicious of what he regarded as the socialist intellectual's deeply inhumane quest for absolute consistency. On the assumption that Marxism and other radical ideologies provided an integrated explanation for every last aspect of human existence, intellectuals often supposed that there was a distinctively socialist way of seeing everything and doing everything. Their horror of inconsistency tended to transform them into aridly cerebral creatures, secure in a sense of their own intellectual eminence but utterly divorced from the humanizing passions of everyday life. Like his great Tory contemporary Michael Oakeshott, Orwell clearly believed that nothing erodes common decency quite as badly as too much thought.[6]

When Orwell was writing *The Road to Wigan Pier*, British socialism was closely associated with a deep faith in the liberating power of science and technology. J. D. Bernal, J. B. S. Haldane and other members of the so-called Social Relations of Science movement had popularized the idea that socialism's main function was to free scientific research from the constraints imposed upon it by capitalism. As long as the market system prevailed, or so it was argued, the potential of science would be held in check by a debilitating divorce between pure and applied forms of research. Only socialism could revive the intellectual vitality of the sciences and renew humanity's dream of imposing its will on nature through the use of advanced technology.[7] This was the context in which Orwell accused the intellectual left of associating itself too uncritically with the forces of modernity. Unlike Bernal and his co-thinkers, Orwell believed that there was something *intrinsically* dehumanizing about advanced technology. The ultimate effect of the cutting-edge machinery to which socialists attached such significance was to rob work of its creativity, erode the human capacity for heroism and generally make life insipid, complacent and soft. While accepting that nothing could prevent the onward march of science and technology, Orwell insisted that the left had made a tragic error of judgement in embracing the vision of a 'completely mechanised, immensely organised world' (ibid.: 175). The main duty of a socialist intellectual was not to worship technology but to warn against its dangers. The culture of a socialist society would somehow have to brush against the grain of its technological base, seeking to preserve the most vital human qualities by continually drawing attention to the dire cultural consequences of machinery. It was not simply officiousness and insincerity which had prevented the left from winning much support. The effete technophilia of men such as Bernal had gone a long way towards alienating a working class whose culture was altogether less anaemic and deracinated.[8] It is here, perhaps more than anywhere else, that Orwell's attack on the left speaks most powerfully to the contemporary world. Its pertinence to a culture positively saturated in ecological dogma scarcely needs underlining. This provides us with the cue we need to turn our attention to *The Road to Wigan Pier*'s relevance to the modern left.

SECTARIANISM AND THE CONTEMPORARY LEFT

The politics of the radical left in Britain have been dominated over the last few years by the theme of austerity. After the international financial system came close to collapse in the autumn of 2008, Gordon Brown's Labour administration spent trillions of pounds in an effort to underwrite the solvency of Britain's banks.[9] By the time Brown was ousted from office in 2010, there was something approaching a consensus among politicians that Britain's most urgent task was to reduce the size of the national deficit by cutting public expenditure. The responsibility for introducing a rolling program of cuts fell to David Cameron's Conservative-Liberal Democrat government, which argued that public spending had to be driven down if Britain was to retain its creditworthiness and embark on a new cycle of economic growth. (Cameron's Conservatives have governed on their own since winning the 2015 general election.) Opposition to the cuts has been spearheaded primarily by the trade unions, several of which have taken industrial action in defence of their members' living standards. Opposition of a less visible but more explicitly political kind has come from Britain's dense network of Marxist organizations and parties. Although British Marxists are as fragmented now as they ever were, they all tend to agree that the cuts pose a massive threat to Britain's public sector and need to be resisted *in toto*. The most energizing contributions to the campaign against the cuts have been made by the Socialist Workers Party (SWP), the Socialist Party (SP), the Communist Party of Britain (CPB), the Scottish Socialist Party (SSP) and Counterfire (a breakaway from the SWP). Some of these groups have tried to reach out to ordinary members of the public by working through front organizations such as the Right to Work Movement, the National Shop Stewards Network and Coalition of Resistance. Members of the various groups have often displayed a heartening willingness to work with each other. Activists from all parties and none have come together to form broad anti-cuts movements in many towns and cities. The most important symptom of this cautious desire for unity has been the establishment of the so-called People's Assembly Against Austerity in 2013.[10]

Marxist campaigners against the cuts have acquitted themselves honorably and have notched up a number of minor victories. The Right to Work Campaign's success in forcing several large companies to withdraw from a government workfare scheme is particularly impressive (see Sawer and Mendick 2012). Nevertheless, only the most purblind activist would deny that the left has had a very small impact on public opinion in the years since the crisis began. Recent opinion polls indicate that a clear majority of the British people accept the need for cuts.[11] The left is no nearer to sinking deep roots in British society now than it was in Orwell's day. So let us return to the questions with which we began. To what extent can Orwell's attack on the hard-left of the 1930s help us to come to terms with our own predicament? Have we learned any lessons from the failures of the interwar period, or must we conclude that our latterday campaign against austerity is tainted by all the old errors of officiousness, ambivalence and technophilia?

OFFICIOUSNESS

At first sight, the contemporary left seems to have little enough in common with the left depicted by Orwell. The typical activist is no longer a 'prim little man' whose Nonconformist background conspires to make him officious and insincere in equal measure. Modern hard-leftists bear all the hallmarks of the cultural revolution which has swept traditional morality aside over the course of the last 50 years. Shaped by the hedonism of the consumer age as well as by its countercultural alternatives, their structure of feeling is characterized by a very distinctive combination of studied informality, post-hippie authenticity and down-at-heel defiance. Ours is an age in which the seller of *Socialist Worker* or the *Morning Star* (a daily newspaper associated with the Communist Party) seeks to endear himself to his comrades by going unshaved and conveying an air of having slept in his clothes. On the other hand, the waning influence of Nonconformity does not mean that officiousness has disappeared from the left. The authoritarian reflexes to which Orwell drew attention are still disturbingly prevalent. Sometimes they take the form of gross intolerance towards dedicated activists who refuse to accept every dot and comma of the party line. At others they manifest themselves in contempt for parliamentary democracy, a bovine determination to have the spokesmen of the far-right excluded from the media or sycophancy towards authoritarian Latin American leaders such as Hugo Chávez or Fidel Castro. One of the most interesting things about the current crisis is that the hard left's officiousness is increasingly taking a novel form. These days, in a way that was rarely true in the past, activists have reinforced their illiberal reputation by identifying themselves with the patterns of authority associated with the welfare state.

It is not difficult to understand how this situation has arisen. Convinced that the cuts represent the first stage in the dismantling of the welfare state, activists have felt obliged to launch a fairly simplistic defence of collective provision of essential goods and services. For the last five years their propaganda has pivoted around the claim that the state is infinitely better than the private, voluntary or charitable sectors at allocating such things as healthcare, education and unemployment relief. In itself this claim is perfectly justified. At a time when the right is seeking to exploit the crisis to advance the neoliberal agenda, there has certainly been a need for an energetic public defence of collective provision. But what is remarkable about the hard left's recent interventions is that their attitude towards the welfare state has seemed so uncritical. The necessary defence of state provision has long since been drowned out by trite, sentimental and disingenuous tributes to the workers and officials who run the welfare system. Teachers, nurses, social workers and even policemen and welfare bureaucrats have increasingly been portrayed as selfless public servants, heroically serving the indigent and the needy in appallingly difficult circumstances. The following passages are entirely typical:

> 'Stand up for education—Gove must go!' is what hundreds of teachers were chanting as they marched through Nottingham on the day of their strike. The well-supported march and rally was applauded by passers-by as it made it's [sic] way through the streets into the city centre. This made a big difference to the teachers who were saying 'it's good that parents realise we're striking for their children' (Socialist Party Nottingham 2013).

> Cuts are hitting women at their most vulnerable and when support is most required ... Humberside police force planned to replace five constables specialising in rape and child sex abuse cases with civilians as part of its scheme to save £2 million by 2013. The volunteers have five weeks training instead of the two years the police undergo (Sachs-Eldridge 2011).

The problem with sentiments such as these is that they overlook the highly contradictory nature of the welfare state. It is one thing to acknowledge that teachers, social workers or claims advisers provide an essential service and work hard on behalf of the people they serve. It is quite another to elide the fact that they exercise their authority in such a way as to reinforce support for the *status quo*. As countless radical analysts have pointed out, the welfare state in Britain has 'always been regulative, coercive and oriented towards the imperatives of the labour market' (Pierson 1999: 180). The relationship between the providers and the users of services is often an extremely hierarchical and intrusive one, intended to reconcile people who rely on the welfare state to their subordinate status in society. The existing patterns of authority also go a long way towards reinforcing patriarchal ideology and undergirding the oppression of women by men.[12] A long tradition of working-class suspicion of the welfare state suggests that 'ordinary' people are better attuned to this aspect of capitalist hegemony than the middle-class ideologues who claim to represent them. If the left becomes too closely associated with the welfare bureaucracy, it risks creating the impression that it is less interested in the self-liberation of the working class than in the shoring up of existing structures of power. It also makes it very difficult for the left to make a meaningful contribution to the current debate about the proper balance between collective provision and what is sometimes called 'self-help.'

Since the crisis began in 2008, many conservatives have justified the cuts by claiming that the welfare state has sapped society's moral fibre. By coercing people into helping the needy—or so the argument goes—the state has coarsened their moral outlook by depriving them of the opportunity to provide voluntary assistance to their fellow men and women. Although this argument strikes many people as a peculiarly blatant piece of special pleading, it has prompted some activists on the left to argue for the revival of the old traditions of working-class self-reliance. Their argument is that the welfare state has penetrated too far into the lives of working people and robbed their culture of at least some of its initiative, leaving no room for the sort of mutual aid that was once provided by trade unions, credit unions and friendly societies.[13] Whether or not this perspective is correct, it is clear that the left can do little to revive the tradition of working-class self-reliance while it identifies too closely with the interests of the welfare bureaucracy. The instincts of activists are simply too out of step with those of the constituency they aim to convert.

AMBIVALENCE

A certain officiousness is by no means the only characteristic that modern leftists share with their counterparts in the 1930s. The two lefts are also linked across the decades by their ambivalent attitude towards achieving real change, though here again it is necessary to update Orwell's analysis. As we have seen, Orwell believed that leftist equivocation was primarily a function of the elevated social position enjoyed by socialist intellectuals. If this argument no longer seems very persuasive, it is perhaps because the class composition of anti-capitalist parties has changed radically over the last forty years. The radical left of Orwell's day was largely composed of a mass of working-class adherents and a smaller but highly influential fraction of middle-class professionals. These days there are fewer workers and professionals but more members of the educated lower-middle class. Indeed, one way of understanding the culture of the modern left is to see it as a by-product of the post-war expansion of higher education. As has often been pointed out, not least by historians trying to explain the periodic outbursts of rebellion among students, the labor market no longer works to the advantage of university graduates in the advanced capitalist world. People with degrees often struggle to find the sort of well-paid, prestigious and stimulating positions for which their education equips them. This is the sort of constituency to which the modern radical left overwhelmingly appeals. Excluded from the professional world to which they aspire, disaffected graduates join Marxist parties in order to find an outlet for the skills acquired over twenty or so years of formal education. It is hardly surprising if some of them come to regard political self-advancement as intrinsically more important than the advancement of the socialist cause. The acquisition and retention of a prominent position in the party take precedence over the creation of a non-hierarchical society. To a degree that would have seemed unthinkable even forty years ago, the political effectiveness of Britain's Marxist parties is stymied by the fact that so many of their members regard activism as a sort of alternative career.

There is also a sense in which the radical left's ambivalence towards changing society is reflected in its approach to ideas. It sometimes seems as if organizations such as the SP or the SWP use ideology primarily for purposes of internal party management. Beleaguered by a deep sense of alienation from their fellow men and women, many people join radical organizations in the hope of finding a close-knit community in which their human sympathies can flourish. In embracing a particular set of ideas, activists bind themselves into a distinctive community by marking themselves off from the horde of unenlightened folk who fail to share their wisdom. The political dangers of all this are clear enough. If the most important function of an ideology is to unite an organization by sustaining a sense of 'us' versus 'them,' there will always be a powerful if unconscious temptation to make the ideology as controversial as possible. To the person in search of a community to which he or she can belong, political ideas matter less for their persuasiveness than for their capacity to unite a self-appointed vanguard around the defence of the party line. Telling the truth takes second place to the goal of keeping a small but fervent band of true believers in business.

The present crisis has thrown up its own examples of Marxist parties using ideology as a form of organizational cement. One in particular illustrates the sectarian temper of many sections of the left with considerable clarity. When anti-cuts movements were being formed across Britain in the wake of David Cameron's election victory, there was a lively and sometimes fractious debate about who should be eligible to participate in them. According to a vociferous group of activists—many of them associated with the Socialist Party—the movement should only embrace people who opposed *every last cut* in public expenditure. People who opposed certain cuts but accepted others were condemned for their divisiveness and their woeful lack of militancy.[14] Judged on purely political lines, this position was clearly absurd. If activists only choose to associate with people who reject the government's cuts program as a whole, they lose the opportunity to influence the hundreds of thousands of people whose opposition to the cuts is sincere but more limited in scope. They also create the misleading impression that activists have a duty to defend every last piece of public expenditure, whereas the left's historic position has always been that savings made in certain areas—defence is the obvious example—should be used to boost spending on health, education and other socially beneficial aspects of the welfare state. But to say all this is ultimately to miss the point. The real function of the oppose-all-cuts shibboleth is not to build a mass movement but to create a sense of political belonging. By drawing a rigid and highly tendentious distinction between principled militants who reject all cuts and wishy-washy dilettantes who reject only certain cuts, activists in organizations like the SP are engaging in a shamelessly sectarian exercise in political bonding. The fact that they are not fully conscious of what they are doing should not absolve them from criticism.

TECHNOPHILIA

Although officiousness and ambivalence are still prevalent on the British left, it is equally clear that technophilia has long since been jettisoned from radical culture. It would be quite impossible for a latterday Orwell to claim that modern socialism is suffused by a naive faith in the possibilities of science and technology. These days, even in those parties and organizations which ostensibly retain a belief in the principle of economic growth, there is a widespread assumption that technology is imposing an intolerable strain on the environment. Suspicion of science and technology has been central to the left's response to the current crisis, not least because cuts in public expenditure are seen as a grave threat to environmentally responsible forms of government. A particularly striking example of this occurred in January 2014 when various coastal areas of Britain were affected by severe floods. Looking on with a certain apocalyptic relish as ordinary people were evacuated from their water-logged homes, many anti-capitalists argued that the floods would never have happened in the first place if the government had not cut spending on flood protection:

> The Department for the Environment, Food and Rural Affairs (Defra) has already had its budget slashed by £500m, with a further £300m to be cut by 2016. Such cuts can only mean that, faced with extreme weather or natural disasters, Britain will be less prepared and less able to deal with the tasks at hand, with working people inevitably hit hardest (Anon 2014).

Arguments such as these reflect British Marxism's gradual rapprochement with Green politics over the last twenty-five years. Nearly every Marxist party now seeks to justify its hostility to capitalism by claiming that the environment can only be saved by the transition to socialism. One of the more surprising aspects of this engagement with Green politics is that it has not always been adequately thought through. Although eco-Marxists such as John Bellamy Foster, Fred Magdoff and James O'Connor have made a highly sophisticated attempt to synthesize Marxism and ecologism, activists in Britain have often seemed to absorb ecological arguments in a curiously unreflective manner. The tendency has been to accept the tenets of Green ideology without first assessing their compatibility with more traditional socialist assumptions. Nowhere is this more obvious than in the debate about economic growth. Many left-wing activists now take it for granted that continued industrial expansion will inevitably lead to irreparable despoliation of the environment. As such, their socialism is rooted in the belief that one of the main justifications for economic planning is that it will bring humanity's feverish quest for growth to an end. Whereas capitalism necessarily stimulates large-scale economic growth through the process of market competition, socialism—or so the argument goes—enables us to impose strict limits on industrial expansion by co-ordinating production and consumption.

Surprisingly few activists seem ready to acknowledge that this modish suspicion of science and industry conflicts with the perspectives of classical Marxism.[15] Insofar as the founders of Marxism addressed themselves to ecological themes, they generally drew a distinction between the creative potential of industry and the destructive powers of the market. In their view, adumbrated with particular force in Engels's great essay on 'The Part Played by Labour in the Transition from Ape to Man' (Engels 1968 [1876]),[16] there is no necessary tension between large-scale industrial expansion and environmental responsibility. Ecological problems are largely a consequence of the market's gravely distorting influence on production, not the result of the intrinsic limitations of advanced technology (ibid.). Speculating about life after capitalism, Marx and Engels argued that a planned economy would liberate technology from market distortions and thereby stimulate massive economic growth. The purpose of socialism was not to hold production in check but to create the circumstances in which the 'springs of co-operative wealth flow more abundantly' (Marx 1976 [1890–1891]: 18).

Many people believe that British Marxism has benefited from its embrace of Green ideology, but it is equally possible to argue that our political culture has been impoverished by it. Although Orwell was right to warn against the dangers of technophilia, there is surely a case for saying that contemporary socialists have gone too far in the opposite direction. British politics is currently in the grip of a sullen, life-denying and intolerant anti-scientific consensus. Even when they purport to favor economic growth, the major parties perpetuate the idea that technology has brought humanity to the verge of outright catastrophe. Given that Marxists have historically evinced a deep faith in the liberating power of science and technology, it is surprising that they have adapted themselves so unquestioningly to the new mood of environmental pessimism. Armed with the idea that environmental problems are precipitated more by markets than machines, British Marxists could have responded to the crisis of neoliberalism by arguing that a break with capitalism would greatly augment human wealth. They could also have served as cheerleaders for the various techniques which science has already devised to counter the environmental crisis, ranging from carbon sequestration schemes on the one hand to enhanced sunlight reflection schemes on the other.[17] Instead they have chosen to reinforce the mood of national gloom by parroting the idea that ours is an age in which human beings have no choice but to reduce their expectations. The environmental obsessions of the day have thrown up a series of questions which urgently need answering. Does the Green agenda necessarily result in a collapse of faith in humanity's creative powers? Is there a danger that the attempt to restrain industrial production could effectively put our economic evolution into reverse? Can we even be sure that a phenomenon such as global warming is caused by economic activity? So far—and in spite of the sterling efforts of a number of maverick left-libertarians—the most sustained and stimulating critique of Green orthodoxy has come from the right.[18] This means that the defence of economic growth is now largely associated in the public mind with support for free markets, deregulation and globalization. The left will only be able to make the progressive case for growth if it recovers some of the technological enthusiasms for which Orwell once attacked it.

CONCLUSION: THE CATASTROPHE OF CATASTROPHISM

It is a testament to Orwell's skills as a journalist that his attack on the British left still holds water, *mutatis mutandis*, more than seventy years after it was written. Everything he said about the left's officiousness, ambivalence and technophilia serves to focus our minds on the problems of contemporary radicalism. Having said all that, it would be unforgivably bland to end an essay of this sort with an unqualified tribute to Orwell's insight and perspicacity. A more authentically Orwellian strategy would be to turn the critical focus on to Orwell himself. Although his vision of socialism compares very favorably with that of most of his contemporaries—and although his personal integrity cannot reasonably be doubted—he shared some of the left's faults even as he tried to distance himself from them. To what extent do *The Road to Wigan Pier*'s unacknowledged flaws increase our understanding of the contemporary left's failures?

The principal weakness that occasionally appears in Orwell's book is a species of catastrophism. Writing in the middle of the worst recession in history and tormented by the growth of fascism, Orwell took it for granted that capitalism had entered a period of radical decline from which it could never recover:

It hardly needs pointing out that at this moment we are in a very serious mess, so serious that even the dullest-witted people find it difficult to remain unaware of it ... For enormous blocks of the working class the conditions of life are such as I have described in the opening chapters of this book, and there is no chance of those conditions showing any fundamental improvement ... Presently there may be coming God knows what horrors—horrors of which, in this sheltered island, we have not even a traditional knowledge (Orwell 2001 [1937]: 158).

Orwell's absolute conviction that capitalist civilization was beyond redemption echoed that of his socialist contemporaries. Virtually everyone in the Communist Party and the other left sects believed that humanity was faced with a choice between socialism or barbarism. The idea that capitalism could ever again embark on a period of sustained growth was dismissed as impossibly naïve. And yet, in spite of the horrors which the world had to endure in the decade or so after *Wigan Pier* was published, history did not unfold according to Orwell's predictions. After the defeat of fascism and the widespread acceptance of Keynesian techniques of demand management, world capitalism entered what Eric Hobsbawm has justifiably called its 'Golden Age' (Hobsbawm 1994). Rates of growth increased exponentially, full employment was easily maintained and consumerism flourished. The system's capacity to recover from trauma was greater than anyone on the left had imagined.

The left's taste for catastrophist rhetoric has done a great deal to undermine the appeal of radical ideas. Quite apart from burdening socialists with a reputation for not understanding how capitalism actually works, it has also created the impression that activists positively relish the idea that society is on the verge of outright disaster. The well-known charge that left-wingers are prone to 'scaremongering' resonates so deeply with the public because it so often turns out to be true. This makes it all the more regrettable that catastrophism has played such a central role in the left's response to the current crisis. Right from the start of the crisis, the left has staked its credibility on the claim that government cuts would plunge the British economy into a maelstrom of disinvestment, unemployment and stagnation. The idea that cuts would stimulate economic growth by boosting private investment was dismissed as a neoliberal fantasy, unworthy of being discussed by any serious commentator. Yet the weakness of the left's position is already becoming clear. Although the British economy is still in a fairly parlous state—and although the possibility of a second recession can by no means be dismissed—the embarrassing truth is that Britain currently boasts the highest rates of growth in the developed world. Predictions of stagnation and widespread social unrest have so far proved wide of the mark.[19] Wedded to an apocalyptic theory of capitalist crisis which has been proved wanting on so many occasions over the last 150 years, Marxists have been caught out by the fundamental Keynesian axiom that 'Things [always] happen, in the country or in the world, to revive business's "animal spirits"' (Skidelsky 2013).

It could even be argued that the left has massively overstated the extent to which ours is genuinely an age of austerity. As a number of Hayekian provocateurs have pointed out, public spending in Britain is currently running at more than 40 per cent of GDP. Spending on the National Health Service has been 'ring-fenced', and substantial amounts of money continue to be poured into the education system. It is one thing to claim that the government has introduced a number of cruel and unnecessary cuts, each of which needs to be resisted. It is quite another to claim that the New Right is intent on plunging us into an anarcho-capitalist dystopia. Perhaps one of the reasons why the public remains indifferent to the left is that the times are rather less austere than activists would have us believe. The lesson of all this is clear. Sometimes the knee-jerk Orwellian tendency to assume the worst is politically misguided. Sometimes things are a lot less catastrophic than they seem.

NOTES

1. See Orwell 2001 [1937]. See also Orwell 2010.
2. See also Taaffe 2010; Sharrock 2011. Mention should also be made of Beatrix Campbell's remarkable *Wigan Pier Revisited: Poverty and Politics in the 80s* (Campbell 1984), the most stimulating of the various attempts to update Orwell's book during the deep recession of the early 1980s.
3. I am focusing in this chapter only on the political culture of Britain's anti-capitalist parties and organizations. I am not focusing—except in passing—on the response of radical academics and intellectuals to the international crisis of the last five years. This is because my particular interest is in the failure of the organized left to win support for its perspectives. Like Orwell, I am primarily concerned with those sections of the left which purport to offer a socialist alternative to the capitalist mode of production. This means that my main focus is on the cluster of Marxist and semi-Marxist parties to the left of the Labour Party. I am aware that these parties are a highly varied bunch and that many of them are associated with distinct ideological positions, but I would also insist that their responses to the crisis have been remarkably homogeneous. I would be the first to acknowledge that my chapter is a highly polemical and impressionistic one, rooted as it is in my own involvement in the British left. I shall be satisfied if it starts some sort of debate.
4. Orwell's trip to the North has been described in detail by his many biographers. See, *inter alia,* Crick 1992 [1980]: Chapter 9; Shelden 1991: Chapter 12; Meyers 2000: Chapter 7; Taylor 2003: Chapter 9.
5. For Orwell's belief that the politics of the middle-class left were rooted in a craving for order, see Orwell 2001 [1937]: 166.
6. For Orwell's account of the obsessive intellectualism of the middle-class left, see Orwell 2001 [1937]: 162. For Oakeshott's account of the relationship between rationalism and morality, see Oakeshott 1981.
7. The single most important text produced by the Social Relations of Science movement was probably Bernal 1939. Bernal brilliantly summarized the main arguments of his book in Bernal

7. 1937. For a useful overview of the ideas of the Social Relations of Science movement, see Roberts 1997: Chapter 5.

8. For a longer discussion of Orwell's ideas about science and technology, see Bounds 2009: 50.

9. See http://www.theguardian.com/politics/reality-check-with-polly-curtis/2011/sep/12/reality-check-banking-bailout, accessed on 16 February 2015.

10. See http://www.thepeoplesassembly.org.uk/, accessed on 16 February 2015.

11. See https://yougov.co.uk/news/2013/05/22/brits-not-feeling-austeritys-bite/, accessed on 16 February 2015.

12. To say this in no way seeks to impugn the honor of the dedicated men and women who keep the welfare state going. It is simply to recognize that they have little choice but to obey the imperatives of the institutions for which they work.

13. Among the only British Marxists who have addressed this issue during the current crisis are the libertarian polemicists associated with the journal *Spiked*. See, in particular, O'Neill 2013.

14. The Socialist Party's position is outlined in Sell 2011.

15. For the sake of clarity, I have slightly oversimplified my account of the role of Green ideology in modern Marxist parties. It would perhaps be more accurate to say that the perspectives of classical Marxism coexist uneasily with Green ideology in the minds of many activists. Although Marxist parties are often suffused with skepticism towards modern technology, their members can still be heard making the case for economic growth on occasion. Moreover, it is not uncommon for the ideas promulgated by party leaders to conflict with those of the rank and file. Whereas official spokesmen on environmental issues often make the case for 'green growth,' ordinary party members tend to emphasize the dangers of economic expansion. For a stimulating defence of green growth by a leading member of a British Marxist party, see Dickenson 2007. Dickenson is a member of the Socialist Party.

16. See https://www.marxists.org/archive/marx/works/1876/part-played-labour/, accessed on 16 February 2015.

17. For a characteristically cynical eco-Marxist survey of scientific responses to the environmental crisis, see Magdoff and Bellamy Foster 2010: 20.

18. The most effective right-wing intervention in the British debate about the environment has been made by the Conservative politician Nigel Lawson. See, for instance, http://www.telegraph.co.uk/news/earth/environment/climatechange/10340408/Climate-change-this-is-not-science-its-mumbo-jumbo.html, accessed on 16 February 2015.

19. This is not to say that Britain has been entirely unaffected by social unrest over the last few years. The inner-city riots which broke out in 2011 have been widely interpreted on the left as a response to the problems of austerity. For a highly sophisticated account of the political significance of the riots, see Badiou 2012.

REFERENCES

Anon (2014) Cuts, floods and climate change, *Proletarian* [monthly paper of the Communist Party of Great Britain (Marxist Leninist)], February.

Armstrong, Stephen (2012) *The Road to Wigan Pier Revisited*, London: Constable.

Badiou, Alain (2012) *The Rebirth of History: Times of Riots and Uprisings*, London: Verso.

Bernal, J. D. (1937) Science and civilisation, Day Lewis, C.(ed.) *The Mind in Chains: Socialism and the Cultural Revolution*, London: Frederick Muller pp. 185–204.

Bernal, J. D. (1939) *The Social Function of Science*, London: Routledge.

Bounds, Philip (2009) *Orwell and Marxism: The Political and Cultural Thinking of George Orwell*, London: I. B. Tauris.

Campbell, Beatrix (1984) *Wigan Pier Revisited: Poverty and Politics in the 80s*, London: Virago.

Crick, Bernard (1992 [1980]) *George Orwell: A Life*, Harmondsworth: Penguin Books.

Dickenson, Pete (2007) *Planning Green Growth: A Socialist Contribution to the Debate on Environmental Sustainability*, London: CWI Publications and Socialist Books.

Engels, Friedrich (1968 [1876]) *The Part Played by Labour in the Transition from Ape to Man*, Moscow: Progress Publishers.

Hobsbawm, Eric (1994) *Age of Extremes: The Short Twentieth Century 1914–1991*, London: Michael Joseph.

Magdoff, Fred and Bellamy Foster, John (2010) What every environmentalist needs to know about capitalism, *Monthly Review*, Vol. 61, No. 10, pp. 1–30.

Marx, Karl (1976 [1890–1891]) *Critique of the Gotha Programme*, Moscow: Progress Publishers. Available online at https://www.marxists.org/archive/marx/works/download/Marx_Critque_ of_the_Gotha_Programme.pdf, accessed on 16 February 2015.

Meyers, Jeffrey (2000) *Orwell: Wintry Conscience of a Generation*, New York: W. W. Norton.

Oakeshott, Michael (1981) The Tower of Babel, *Rationalism in Politics and Other Essays*, London: Methuen pp. 59–79.

O'Neill, Brendan (2013) The great welfare myth, *Daily Mail*, 5 April.

Orwell, George (2001 [1937]) *The Road to Wigan Pier*, London: Penguin Books.

Orwell, George (2010) *The Road to Wigan Pier* Diary, Davison, Peter (ed.) *The Orwell Diaries*, London: Penguin Books pp. 23–71.

Pierson, Chris (1999) Marxism and the welfare state, Gamble, Andrew, Marsh, David and Tant, Tony (eds) *Marxism and Social Science*, London: Macmillan pp. 175–194.

Roberts, Edwin A. (1997) *The Anglo-Marxists: A Study in Ideology and Culture*, Oxford: Rowman and Littlefield.

Sachs-Eldridge, Sarah (2011) Women under siege in the age of austerity, *Socialism Today*, No. 152, October.

Sawer, Patrick and Mendick, Robert (2012) Tiny band of left-wing radicals bring jobs policy to its knees, *Daily Telegraph*, 25 February.

Sell, Hannah (2011) The cutbacks and the fightback, *Socialism Today*, No. 146, March.

Sharrock, David (2011) *The Road to Wigan Pier*, 75 years on, *Observer*, 20 February.

Shelden, Michael (1991) *Orwell: The Authorised Biography*, London: Heinemann.

Skidelsky, Robert (2013) Osborne may gloat about recovery, but his 'hard slog' will leave Britain worse off, *New Statesman*, 30 September.

Socialist Party Nottingham (2013) Stand up for education! Hundreds march in Nottingham on teachers strike, Nottinghamsocialists.org.uk., 1 October.

Taaffe, Peter (2010) Revisiting *The Road to Wigan Pier*, *Socialism Today*, No. 137, April.

Taylor, D. J. (2003) *Orwell: The Life*, London: Chatto and Windus.

Orwell: International Perspectives

First Encounters AND THE Writing OF Otherness IN *Burmese Days* AND *Keep* THE *Aspidistra Flying*

MARINA REMY

INTRODUCTION

As Raymond Williams (1984: 41) put it: 'Orwell's writing in the 1930s can be conventionally divided into the "documentary" and the "factual" work on the one hand, and "fictional" and "imaginative" work on the other ... Yet nothing is clearer as we look into the work as a whole, than that this conventional division is secondary.' That is why it may be interesting to focus on the link between the writing of alterity offered in his reportage and that offered in his early novels. In Orwell's reportage and documentaries what is fundamentally at stake in the constitutive encounter between self and other appears perhaps more clearly than anywhere else, due to the immediacy of the observational process.

This is shown through a series of revelatory face-to-face encounters depicted, for instance, at the start of *Homage to Catalonia* (1937) between the narrator and the Italian militiaman or between the exceptional character of Bozo and the 'I' of the narrator in *Down and Out in Paris and London* (1933). Yet Orwell's early novels also prove to be fruitful sources for the study of Orwell's writing of otherness and the understanding of what is fundamentally at stake in the constitutive encounter between self and other. This will lead us to examine the style Orwell develops in his novels which questions the fixity of ontology by challenging to a certain extent the ontological status of texts and the fixity of genres. His works, indeed, constantly question clear-cut dichotomies between both self and other, fact and fiction by staging, creating and re-creating encounters with others and considering the time of the other in the temporality of the novel. This requires a rhetoric which merits our attention, pointing both to the anthropologist as author—to borrow Clifford Geertz's (1989) title—and the author as anthropologist.

I have chosen to focus on *Burmese Days* (1934) and *Keep the Aspidistra Flying* (1936) because the third-person realist narratives in the two novels, 'both with neat protagonist/antagonist dialogues … make them so useful and revealing as a pair,' contrasting 'with the more experimental *A Clergyman's Daughter* [1935] and again with George Bowling's charming first-person nostalgia in *Coming Up for Air*' [1939] (Stewart 2003: 69). In the two novels, Orwell switches the perspective from face-to-face encounters between contemporaries as offered in his reportage to a confrontation between Burmese and English, between social classes and economic statuses and also between masculinity and femininity. Particularly in the latter, Orwell departs from the writing of alterity provided in *Down and Out in Paris and London*, *The Road to Wigan Pier* (1937) and *Homage to Catalonia* in the sense that the miners', the soldiers' worlds and that of the streets almost automatically excluded both the observer and the observed from the realms of femininity and sexuality. Moreover, the two main antithetical portrayals of feminine figures, in the form of Rosemary Waterlow and Elizabeth Lackersteen, in *Keep the Aspidistra Flying* and *Burmese Days*, along with the other figures of alterity studied here, will aim at questioning Orwell's writing on intersubjective relations, his ethics and his aesthetics of otherness.

This is why the fundamental questions for the present study now arise: is Orwell's humanist aesthetics, always hinting at its connectedness with an ethics which the other awakens in us, still present in the novels, namely in *Burmese Days* and *Keep the Aspidistra Flying*? What kind of writing of otherness is provided in these novels where the two main characters try to escape their stifling environment and are thus concerned with both a fear of and a desire for change? Does this desire for alteration coexist with a desire for alterity? Does the move towards the other appear as the only alternative, third way to escape the reassuring yet potentially claustrophobic confines of the self and the sterility of isolation so vividly and minutely described in the two novels? Or does the economic, mental, political, and physical isolation which affects both anti-heroes, the duality they experience in different yet comparable terms, lead to a negation of the other? Is the acceptance of the other's equality *and* otherness made impossible beforehand by the capitalist and colonial frameworks questioned in the novels?

I will endeavor to confront the status ascribed to figures of alterity in the two novels to determine whether a co-presence, a *coevalness* with the other is accepted, granted, dismissed, negated or present only in the form of a potentiality. The inherent duality at work in the texts, namely between the two anti-heroes and the capitalist and colonial structures they refute and accept at the same time also prolongs the reflection on otherness within. Indeed, Flory (in *Burmese Days*) both rejects and abides by colonial rules while Gordon Comstock's hatred of money, his monomania (in *Keep the Aspidistra Flying*), in turn becomes what could be called a *moneymania*.

This study is highly indebted to Johannes Fabian's ground-breaking work. The conclusions he reaches in *Anthropology with an Attitude* (2001) and *Time and the Other* (2002) proved essential in the analysis of a corpus where the frontiers between literature and anthropological perspectives, essay and reportage, reality and fiction are constantly at play. Fabian's theory is based on the notion of 'coevalness.' For him, the recognition and reciprocal comprehension are conditions of the exchange and the confrontation between observer and observed in the encounter which are made possible by the acceptance of the 'contemporaneity' (Fabian 2002: xi) and the 'coevalness' between its participants (Fabian 2002: 31). Yet time has often been employed in anthropological discourse as a means to keep the other at a distance, a wider temporal distance than that necessarily involved in the anthropological practice as a production based on remembrance.

Relying on a number of methodological tools which include the varied perspectives of anthropologists such as Fabian and philosophers such as Emmanuel Levinas (1961) may seem surprising when studying Orwell's writing but may open up fruitful avenues of research for, each in a different way, these works transcend their specific genres to embrace a wider vision of the reflection on alterity. Fabian highlights this in his own field of research when stating that anthropology's findings 'pose the same problems that philosophers, historians, and literary critics address when they think about representations of time' (Fabian 2001: 140).

For Levinas (1961: 9), one has to exit one's being through another way out,[1] by accepting the responsibility of the self as it is confronted with the other, whose face speaks to me and calls me (ibid.: 172). A fundamental aspect of Levinas's thinking and possibly of Orwell's writing, too, is this perception of the face-to-face encounter with the other as the beginning of an ethical relationship based on one's responsibility towards the other which does not in any way preclude but, indeed, requires an acceptance of the value—and the time—of the other (ibid.: 13). This, in my opinion, is shown with literary mastery in Orwell's endeavor to highlight the extraordinary in the encounters with seemingly ordinary people. Interestingly, in Orwell such encounters between self and other do not posit either self or other as fixed entities but rather display a set of complex and fragile relations, prone to uncertainty, instability and even failure.

THE BURMESE OTHER

One such encounter is that between Flory and Dr. Veraswami in *Burmese Days* which takes the form of 'a topsy-turvy affair' (Orwell 1934: 39). Flory, the misfit participant in the colonial undertaking, seeks an escape from the stifling world of the club in his periodical encounters with Dr. Veraswami, which enable him 'to be out of the stink of it for a little while' (Orwell 1934: 37). Unlike the others who avoid any real closeness with the other, a double predisposition towards the other seems to be at work. The first scene between the two characters is also valuable to the extent that it exposes the fallacy of the empire and the connection between colonialism and capitalism (see Young 1995: 167–170), as Flory wants to denounce the empire in private while Veraswami wants to defend its values and thus each man seeks to present himself as other.

This mirrors a series of confrontational encounters between opposed figures such as Dorothy Hare and Mr. Warburton in *A Clergyman's Daughter* (1935) who mix feelings of repulsion for the other's ideas and 'a certain shuddering pleasure' (Orwell 1934: 40) in hearing them uttered out loud. Indeed, 'the pious and the immoral drift naturally together' (Orwell 1935: 41). Dr. Veraswami's ambivalence is superimposed onto Flory's own in relation to the empire as both are presented as fundamentally split personalities. The doctor argues at length how the English have 'civilized' the Burmese out of 'self-sacrifice' (Orwell 1934: 40): it is he who denies any form of coevalness and co-presence between the Burmese and the English, as it was denied to him in the first place. He places the two peoples in distinct times, as the Burmese would be naturally behind the British, psychologically, mentally, economically and temporally. He even uses Old Mattu's presence, the Hindu *durwan*, to reinforce his point after Old Mattu told him, when asked his age, that he believed he was ten years old (ibid.: 44). These distinct temporalities turn Burma into an anachronism (in comparison with British time) or even into a complex allochronism (Fabian 2002: xi), which would mean that the denying of the shared present with the other is not initiated by the observer but that, here, it has been internalized by the other and reasserted through discourse. Indeed, the doctor tells Flory that 'your civilization at its very worst is for us an advance' (Orwell 1934: 42) whereas Flory insists that it is the British who deliberately prevented any form of progress.

Once more, the encounter with the other is made impossible, and this scene, like most other encounters with others, instances an unbridgeable gap and a certain familiarity which is not sufficient to redefine, reconfigure or profoundly disrupt the self. The other's presence initiates no epiphany in the self for it is not really an encounter with an alterity recognized as such: Dr. Veraswami plays the part of the English in place of the Englishman and pines for Flory's Englishness whereas Flory seeks Dr. Veraswami's *Burmeseness* as a means to lay his secret out in the open with the assurance that it will remain forever private.

Still, Dr. Veraswami's is the most audible Burmese voice in the novel. Even if he can be seen as wanting to 'realize himself as superior-inferior' (Carter 1985: 60) in comparison to his fellow Burmese thanks to his status as educated doctor and friend of the Englishman, he is characterized by a decency and a clear-sightedness when he warns Flory of the dangers of U Po Kyin's scheming which the Englishman lacks when believing that, as an Englishman, he is 'quite above suspicion' (Orwell 1934: 49). Even though the doctor's prestige increases every time Flory is seen 'to enter [his] house' (ibid.: 48), he does not exploit his friendship with Flory as a means to secure his honor which U Po Kyin is trying to destroy. Interestingly, the omniscient narrator tells us that 'the doctor was a little disappointed that Flory had not promised to propose him for the club, but he would have perished rather than to say so' (ibid.: 49). Thus he cannot be perfectly honest either, which sharply contrasts with the acknowledgment of intimacy made by the narrator in the preceding sentence.

Of course, Flory's inability to challenge one of the *pukka sahib* precepts, namely keeping out of '"native" quarrels' (Orwell 1934: 416) and his inability to face the 'row' (ibid.: 48) which he would need to endure to elect the doctor at the club also contradicts Dr. Veraswami's firm belief that the English are in Burma out of 'self-sacrifice'.

These encounters could have been privileged ones, momentarily removed from the rigidity of colonial encounters, but the doctor has internalized his inferiority so deeply that he is not really other, and his voice mimics, indeed parrots, that of the most fanatic agent of the Empire. This form of mimicry of the anglicized 'men who are not English' (McClintock 1995: 62) can be related to Homi Bhabha's initial definition of the term as McClintock (1995: 63) reminds us: 'The mimic men are obliged to inhabit an uninhabitable zone of ambivalence that grants them neither identity nor difference; they must mimic an image they cannot fully assume.' They are placed in an impossible situation and are condemned to 'mirror back an image of the colonials but in an imperfect form: "almost the same but not white"' (Bhabha 1984: 130 cited in McClintock 1995: 62).

ENCOUNTERING A SENSE OF SAMENESS

This text seems to show the possibility of friendship despite the differences between the two men, but even if there is some understanding (namely in the way they both share absolute, albeit opposite views), what prevails in this encounter between self and other is actually a sense of sameness. The conversation between the two men goes round in circles and, indeed, becomes a form of psittacism (speech or writing which appears mechanical and repetitive), as they parrot themselves and others, not unlike what goes on in the club. Variety and the possibility of change are replaced by a never-ending sameness which, as the rest of the scene reminds us, affects systems, places, people and the self. In a way 'the same tune' (Orwell 1934: 42) which defines the empire is also what the dialogue between the two men is, like the *havildar* 'saying the same thing' (ibid.: 38).

At the end of the novel, Flory's untenable situation summed up in the proleptic 'you've got to be a pukka sahib or die, in this country' (ibid.: 43) will lead to his suicide. The encounter with Veraswami becomes nothing but a momentary and fallacious parenthesis 'out of the stink,' one he cannot really escape. This scene displays the fallacies the British empire is based on and the depth of the psychological, mental damage it induces both in Flory and Dr. Veraswami. Even though the doctor is the only person with whom Flory can share his true feelings on the empire, he is not really heard either, thus reinforcing their two diametrically opposed views and the extent of their isolation.

The most important denomination in the novel, that of the *pukka sahib*, the tacitly agreed code of conduct of the British abroad, in itself encapsulates what is at stake in Flory's predicament and the fear and the pressure of sameness. It is also interesting that the first reference to the *pukka sahib* is made by Flory along with a French expression: 'The pukka sahib *sans peur et sans reproche*' (ibid.: 37) as the foreign nature of both parts of the expression hints at the hermeneutic effort required on the part of the reader to understand the intricacies of the term. Thus, in keeping with the work of literature, some sense of otherness is distilled in the text with the numerous references, puns playing with sounds, polysemy, similarity and opposition as well as the inclusion of other languages. Yet, despite this linguistic variety, the situation of both characters, like the atmosphere they live in, is untenable and oppressive, and thus it is only through verbal play that they can momentarily (pretend to) be other.

THE FEMININE OTHER

One can argue that a radical alterity is embodied in the figures of the feminine: indeed, as Levinas writes, 'l'absolument autre, c'est le *féminin*' (Levinas 1991 [1947]: 77). The presence of feminine figures serves to disrupt the predominantly male worlds depicted in Orwell's early fiction, and that of the club in *Burmese Days*, in particular. However, in Orwell's first novel, women such as Mrs. Lackersteen or Elizabeth tend to reinforce the *status quo* and the patriarchal hegemony of the empire over the Burmese. This negative force ascribed to many a feminine character has led feminist scholars such as Daphne Patai (1984) to study in depth the instances of what they see as Orwell's misogyny. As noted by John Newsinger (1999: 6), Orwell never went as far as relating racial/social and gender divisions fully: 'While Blair came to detest imperialism and any dominion of man over man, this radicalisation did not extend to gender relations,' for 'he never developed an understanding of the relation between empire and sexuality.'

Moreover, even if feminine figures could offer the masculine characters a privileged opportunity to access the realm of the other, *The Aspidistra*, in particular, abounds with instances of the contrary. The main purpose of Hermione's presence in the novel, an otherwise relatively insignificant character, seems to be to hamper Ravelston's attempts to escape his class and help out penniless writers and strangers. Significantly, it is the materiality of her body which works more effectively than discourse in taming Ravelston's moves towards the other: 'He thought of the unemployed in Middlesbrough, seven in a room on twenty-five bob a week. But the girl's body was heavy against him, and Middlesbrough was very far away' (Orwell 1936: 105). It is even her smell which prevents a move towards an other: 'The woman-scent breathed out of her a powerful wordless propaganda against all altruism and all justice' (ibid.: 106).

Not all women fit into that equation: Julia, Gordon's sister, even though she does not question the precepts of the money-god, is willing to sacrifice herself in order to help Gordon. Yet this sacrifice had been bestowed upon her from childhood as Gordon's studies meant that Julia would never be able to study: 'Gordon was "the boy" and Julia was "the girl," and it seemed natural to everyone that "the girl" should be sacrificed to "the boy"' (ibid.: 46). Patai (1984: 109) has denounced 'Orwell's consistently gender-typed approach to male and female existence.' If, in accordance with Judith Butler (1999: xxviii), one takes gender, sex and sexuality to be 'a cultural performance,' enacted through 'discursively constrained performative acts' (ibid.: xxix) which give the effect of 'naturalness' (ibid.: xxviii), it is important to note that these categories do not seem to be taken for granted or regarded as natural, quintessential ones, here at least, countering the illusion of naturalness of these categories represented by Gordon's family's mindset. Indeed, the use of inverted commas highlights the problematic status of these roles and, possibly, their artificiality.

However, it is clear that several other feminine figures in the novels hamper any move towards an alterity, as shown, for instance, by Mrs. Lackersteen's performance of the role of the *memsahib*. The latter is presented as a *moneymaniac* figure as suggested by her delight in reading the 'Civil List (which tells you the exact income of every official in Burma)' (Orwell 1934: 195). But Gordon, in *Keep the Aspidistra Flying*, also evaluates people according to their annual income, when he tells Ravelston, for instance, that his 'enemies' are 'anyone with over five hundred a year' (Orwell 1936: 96), incidentally turning Ravelston into a potential enemy according to that equation. Gordon believes that, without any money, he has no hold over Rosemary. 'In the last resort, what holds a woman to a man, except money?' (ibid.: 111). Human value becomes equated with financial value (see Eagleton 1970: 94). Rosemary is not considered for what she brings Gordon but merely for what she deprives him of: the 'inalienable right … to a sexuality (Orwell 1936: 110). Women become a commodity, as indirectly shown by the choice of location for the encounters with Rosemary and Elizabeth in the two novels: the market and the bazaar.

WOMEN AND THE THREAT OF EMASCULATION

The threat of emasculation appears when women are no longer bought or paid for in exchange for sexual intercourse as is the case with Ma Hla May, in *Burmese Days*, or the prostitutes, in *Keep the Aspidistra Flying*, but when it is women such as Rosemary who offer to buy or pay for things. This is noted by Rosemary who asks Gordon if he thinks they are still living 'in the reign of Queen Victoria' (ibid.: 126). Gordon tells Rosemary she has been brought up as a woman: '… and you can't help behaving like a woman, however much you don't want to' (ibid.). The expression '*behaving like a woman*' (ibid.: 127) is significantly italicized in Rosemary's cue to illustrate the fallacy of Gordon's point of view. Gordon's belief that 'every woman's the same' when it comes to whom they think should pay the bill is immediately countered by Rosemary and her actions throughout the novel (ibid.). Gordon and Rosemary initiate 'a violent argument upon the eternal and idiotic question of Man versus Woman' (ibid.: 124) which is derided by the narrative voice and shown to be 'always very much the same' (ibid.: 123), not unlike Ravelston and Gordon's quarrels on socialism or Flory and Dr. Veraswami's on the empire. Furthermore, through the reference to Queen Victoria's reign, it is actually Gordon who becomes an anachronism (see Stewart 2003: 85) as Rosemary herself stresses that they seem to stand in distinct, nearly incompatible times.

The difficulty in genuinely seeing the other is illustrated by one of the few truly first encounters in *Burmese Days*: that between Flory and Elizabeth (Orwell 1934: 79–88), which both counters and echoes the first scene between Gordon and Rosemary (Orwell 1936: 135–157). Both scenes enact a desire for and a distance with the other. They also make clear the sheer opposition between two figures of femininity and foreshadow the failure of the relationship between Flory and Elizabeth, whereas in *The Aspidistra* an alternative figure of femininity, Rosemary, or the embodiment of decency, emerges (Stewart 2003: 70).

In *Burmese Days*, Flory wishes for a companion, but her contours are vague and blurred: a 'friend. Or a wife? That quite impossible she' (Orwell 1934: 72). As Annie Verut-Plichon (1989: 71) argues: 'This dream, which is actually of an essentially negative nature, is only distantly related to femininity.' This is perfectly shown when Flory hears of Elizabeth's arrival and hopes that she spelled her name with a Z (Orwell 1934: 88). Even though her name is, indeed, spelled with a Z, this nonetheless points to the displacement of 'différance' (Derrida 1968) and to the predetermined image he has created of Elizabeth.

Elizabeth first appears as an 'English voice' (Orwell 1934: 79). The face-to-face encounter cannot really take place because Flory cannot 'see her face' at first and she cannot see his since, as usual, he turns himself 'sidelong' to avoid showing the reality of his marked face (ibid.: 80). Moreover, her face is not really seen as such but rather for its differences with other Englishwomen in Burma. When Flory protects Elizabeth from the harmless water-buffalo, she seems, by getting closer to him, to bring Flory back to his past for it had been 'several years since he had seen such a hand' (ibid.). Elizabeth thrusts Flory back to another place—England, and another time—his past. Yet an exceptional moment illustrates a closeness between the two, however ephemeral. Indeed, the moment when they stop to admire nature embodies the single instant when they really function in unison and feel a 'pang of unreasonable happiness' (ibid.: 82), echoing the few moments when Gordon is not reasoning about money in the countryside scene in *The Aspidistra* (Orwell 1936: 136–137). The narrator also stresses Flory's feeling of 'intimacy' (Orwell 1934: 80), only ever possible, paradoxically, between strangers, when he refers to Elizabeth's short hair and hatless head under the sun. Interestingly, it seems that to speak of it 'was like touching it with his hand' (ibid.), as a form of verbal intimacy acts as a replacement for physical intimacy. They then begin to 'chatter … with extraordinary eagerness' (ibid.: 83).

The initial moment of communion is short-lived for there always seems to be something coming in between them: the buffalo, the flowers, the leopard—a necessary intermediary for them to ever feel close. As this scene draws to a close, the insistence is on Flory's obsession with his age in comparison to her youth (ibid.: 84) and on the unbalance and superficiality of their dialogue. Each resorts to hackneyed hyperboles and creates in his or her mind a false 'picture' of the other (ibid.), Flory of Elizabeth as an artistic, curious, well-traveled girl bringing forth images of Parisian cafés and Marcel Proust (ibid.: 85) and Elizabeth of Flory as a perfect *pukka sahib*. Moreover, this heralds a series of interrupted scenes—during the *pwe*, in the bazaar, in Li Yeik's shop—as 'their pleasure evaporates' (ibid.: 86) when Ma Hla May enters the scene and they are forced to return to reality.

The reader's encounter with Rosemary in Chapter 5 does not appear to be as shattering for Gordon has invented 'an imaginary character for Rosemary' (Orwell 1936: 101) and has already presented her in ambivalent terms, with mingling grudge and affection—feelings which will be re-enacted on both sides in the first scene where they meet by chance in the market. This perfectly timed coincidence marks the appearance of a character defined by an energy and a life which nearly all the others lack. She is simultaneously characterized by her strength (ibid.) and her fragility (ibid.: 114, 115) in a portrait highlighting her face 'full of character' (ibid.: 115) and the fact that, unlike Gordon, she does not look her age (ibid.). Her appearance almost has a magical feel to it: it 'was as though his desire had called her into being' (ibid.: 114).

Even when Gordon realizes Rosemary's uniqueness, her otherness is reduced to a means to avoid the burden of his sameness: 'she alone of all women in the world was willing to save him from the humiliation of his loneliness' (ibid.). This mirrors Flory's belief in how important it is that Elizabeth 'should grasp the nature of the loneliness that he wanted her to nullify' (Orwell 1934: 179). Rosemary's affection for Gordon is marked in her speech—'I adore you' (ibid.: 117)—in which the unitalicized 'adore' marks, unlike Elizabeth's constant use of the term, a genuineness of feeling which is confirmed by the narrator. Despite that, the narrator thereafter emphasizes the distance between the two characters who stand on different temporal and sexual stages. While Gordon longs for sexual closeness and mainly focuses on her body—her hat conjures up images of her 'behind' (Orwell 1936: 116)—Rosemary is still in an indeterminate pre-sexual age. She focuses on his face – and makes 'him face her' (ibid.: 127), yet genuine face-to-face encounters require a willingness, a reciprocity. One learns that when they are 'body to body, it was as though there were a shield between them' (ibid.: 118). This echoes Gordon's poem quoted *in extenso* at the end of Chapter 7 as the money-god:

> ... lays the sleek, estranging shield
> Between the lover and his bride (ibid.: 162).

Like Flory and Elizabeth, there always seems to be something enhancing the distance between beings, as the physical proximity conjured up by sexuality actually becomes a motif of estrangement. However, after they have once more argued over the questions of money and women, they are able to unite their ambivalent feelings into a shared happiness which sharply contrasts with the beginning of the scene: even as they 'disputed, arm in arm, they pressed their bodies delightedly together. They were very happy. Indeed, they adored one another. Each was to the other a standing joke and an object infinitely precious' (ibid.: 124). For once a reciprocity of feeling is at work, as they become partners in this merry-war, 'two enemies breast to breast' (ibid.) but it is soon once more obliterated by another quarrel over money, used by Gordon as a shield, a means to protect himself from the anxiety of disruption. This nearly unbridgeable gap, materialized by their antinomic views on money, can be paralleled with Flory and Elizabeth's conflicting perspectives on the Burmese world.

The first encounter between Rosemary and Gordon wavers between closeness and distance, a distance which is at times physical, symbolic, mental *and* temporal. The physical and temporal distance is also stressed in the countryside scene by an oscillation between a detailed foray into both characters' feelings and states of mind, and an impersonality mingled with the narrator's subjectivity. This is visible, for instance, in the bird's eye view cast on the characters who become mere bodies: 'after all, the scene was grotesque—the naked woman lying on the grass, the dressed man standing moodily by with his hands in his pockets' (ibid.: 152). As for the temporal distance, it is enhanced by the fact that it is Rosemary who is constantly compared to a child (ibid.: 118, 119, 128) whereas Gordon is a prematurely aged man. Interestingly, in this scene, 'the marks of time ... upon her face' (ibid.: 136) become apparent as her dread of abandoning 'the youthful, sexless world in which she chose to live' (ibid.: 118) makes itself more tangible than ever.

She is caught up in an idealized pure past while Gordon is standing prematurely in a decaying future so that no real present seems shared. This is especially visible in the following comment: 'He wanted to have had her, but he wished it were over and done with' (ibid.: 147). Despite a brief moment of communion and ecstasy over the beauty of nature (similar to Elizabeth and Flory's) during which the couple gently quarrels 'about similes and metaphors' (ibid.: 137), as if wishing to be the authors of their own existences, the balance is soon broken when Gordon wants to re-assert his power over Rosemary. What matters is the knowledge that he has possessed Rosemary, not the actual moment of their encounter. This is shown by his constant pressure to extort from Rosemary the promise of sex, namely, at the end of Chapter 6 (ibid.: 129). Thus, the countryside scene is once more a scene of sexual—and textual—interruption.

Only at the end, through the mediating presence of their future baby, do Gordon and Rosemary share a 'moment of sympathy such as they had never had before' (ibid.: 241). When she announces the news to him, for once, his eyes meet hers (ibid.) as this constitutes a truly decisive and disrupting moment which maintains its strangeness and aura of mystery while hinting at the possibility of a common ground and future.

Indeed, the presence of the future in the present appears in the encounter with the other (Levinas 1991 [1947]: 69). Paternity is experienced as an 'epiphany' (Levinas 1987 [1972]: 50) as Gordon grasps, when seeing pictures of a foetus, the fundamental humanity beyond its somewhat 'monstrous' (Orwell 1936: 249) appearance. At the same time, he sees Rosemary because 'a bit of himself' is 'growing in her' and feels that they are like 'one flesh' (ibid.: 241), which runs the risk of once more denying her radical alterity. But for once Gordon relates to the other and thus one can posit that with this, time is in motion and he is once more in the realm of human beings (ibid.: 254). His previous outlook is completely reversed so that the fickleness of his rebellion and the predictability of this transformation are revealed. The significance of the aspidistra is completely reversed and becomes the 'tree of life' (ibid.: 255). Even though this ending has often been deemed inconsistent, what I am interested in here is the genesis of a feeling of 'responsibility' (ibid.: 249), an ethical relationship initiated with Rosemary and the baby which makes him see the threat of war and the future in a wholly different light (ibid.: 246). Thereby, he experiences 'an extreme vulnerability' (Levinas 1987 [1972]: 109), and possibly, at last, a challenging of the self: 'man is woven by responsibilities. They lacerate his essence' (ibid.).

As for Rosemary, she appears as a positive force throughout the novel, as she never manifests a desire to subjugate Gordon's pseudo-rebellion against the money-god and accepts his otherness without forcing onto him any form of alteration. She validates an alternative positioning of genuine decency and manifests the ability to place oneself in the shoes of others, while at the same time, not dismissing their radical alterity, an alterity which cannot be subsumed in the self. This is why, despite the ambivalent perspective on femininity and certain shortcomings, the postures of Rosemary, like Julia's in *Nineteen Eighty-Four* and that of secondary characters such as Ma Kin and her 'gentle heart' (Orwell 1934: 144) in *Burmese Days*, may help us qualify univocal interpretations of Orwell's view of women and femininity in his works.

CONCLUSIONS

'If the fiction is an attempt to represent a larger-than-personal world, it neverthe-less assumes an almost entirely personal standpoint' (Levenson 2007: 67). Gordon and Flory are, indeed, the two fundamental focuses in the novels through which the other characters appear; their voices sometimes seem to become mingled with the narrator's thanks namely to the use of 'free indirect thought' (in the first half of *Aspidistra*, in particular, see Fowler 1995: 144) and the risk is that they drown and mute the voices of the other, even more so than the persona does in Orwell's docu-mentaries. Nevertheless, the alternative readings provided by the narrator and then, possibly, the reader also offer a (limited) 'heteroglossia' (styles of voices, range of discourses) (see Fowler 1995). This plurality of voices—which, of course, may both apply to and show its limits in any novelistic (and documentary) form—reminds us of 'the narrative of how an author (as a dialogic, non-psychological self) constructs a relation with his heroes (as others)' (Holquist 1991: 30).

This can point to another form of dialogism in the interstices of certain peremptory and authoritative statements, thus furthering the novels' reflection on coercive, oppressive and authoritarian systems which blur the face of the other while attempting to supply some of the otherness and the communication which these systems constantly seek to deny. This can lead the reader to '… re-evaluat[e] his whole sense of reality' (Knapp 1975: 29) in accordance with Orwell's wish for alteration through writing and reading, visible in the use of the verb 'alter' in his essay 'Why I Write': writing 'to *alter* other peoples' idea of the kind of society that they should strive after' (2000 [1946]: 1082–1083).

NOTE

1. All translations from the original French by the author.

REFERENCES

Bhabha, Homi K. (1984) Of mimicry and man: The ambivalence of colonial discourse, *Discipleship: A Special Issue on Psychoanalysis*, Vol. 28, pp. 125–133.

Butler, Judith (1999) *Gender Trouble: Feminism and the Subversion of Identity*, New York: Routledge.

Carter, Michael (1985) *George Orwell and the Problem of Authentic Existence*, London: Croom Helm.

Derrida, Jacques (1968) La Différance, *Bulletin de la société française de philosophie*, Vol. 62, No. 3, pp. 73–101.

Eagleton, Terry (1970) *Exiles and Emigres: Studies in Modern Literature*, London: Chatto & Windus.

Fabian, Johannes (2001) *Anthropology with an Attitude*, Stanford: Stanford University Press.

Fabian, Johannes (2002) *Time and the Other: How Anthropology Makes its Object*, New York: Columbia University Press.

Fowler, Roger (1995) *The Language of George Orwell*, London: Macmillan.

Geertz, Clifford (1989) *Works and Lives: The Anthropologist as Author*, Cambridge: Polity Press.

Holquist, Michael (1991) *Dialogism: Bakhtin and His World*, London: Routledge.

Knapp, John (1975) Dance to a creepy minuet: Orwell's *Burmese Days*, precursor of *Animal Farm*, *Modern Fiction Studies*, Vol. 21, No. 1, pp. 11–30.

Levenson, Michael (2007) The fictional realist: Novels of the 1930s, Rodden, John (eds) *The Cambridge Companion to George Orwell*, Cambridge: Cambridge University Press pp. 59–75.

Levinas, Emmanuel (1987 [1972]) *Humanisme de l'autre homme*, Paris: Librairie générale française.

Levinas, Emmanuel (1991 [1947]) *Le Temps et l'Autre*, Quadrige, Paris: Presses Universitaires de France, fourth edition.

Levinas, Emmanuel (1961) *Totalité et Infini: Essai sur l'Exteriorité*, La Haye: Nijhoff.

McClintock, Anne (1995) *Imperial Leather: Race, Gender, and Sexuality in the Colonial Contest*, New York: Routledge.

Newsinger, John (1999) *Orwell's Politics*, Houndmills, Basingstoke: Macmillan.

Orwell, George (1934) *Burmese Days*, San Diego: A Harvest Book, Harcourt.

Orwell, George (1975 [1935]) *A Clergyman's Daughter*, Harmondsworth, Middlesex: Penguin.

Orwell, George (1962 [1936]) *Keep the Aspidistra Flying*, Harmondsworth, Middlesex: Penguin, in association with Martin Secker and Warburg.

Orwell, George (2000 [1946]) Why I write, Carey, John (ed.) *George Orwell, Essays*, London: Everyman's Library pp. 1079–1085.

Patai, Daphne (1984) *The Orwell Mystique: A Study in Male Ideology*, Amherst: University of Massachusetts Press.

Regard, Frédéric (2002) *L'Ecriture féminine en Angleterre*, Paris: Presses Universitaires de France.

Stewart, Anthony (2003) *George Orwell, Doubleness and the Value of Decency*, New York: Routledge.

Verut-Plichon, Annie (1989) Images de la femme dans l'oeuvre romanesque de G. Orwell, No. 10, pp. 69–79.

Williams, Raymond (1984) *Orwell*, London: Flamingo, second edition.

Young, Robert (1995) *Colonial Desire: Hybridity in Theory, Culture and Race*, London: Routledge.

CHAPTER TEN

'Pukka Sahibs' AND 'Yellow Faces'

Reassessing Ambivalence in Orwell's Burma

SREYA MALLIKA DATTA AND UTSA MUKHERJEE

'You've got to be a pukka sahib or die, in this country.'

—ORWELL (2009 [1934]: 42)

In a private conversation with the Indian Dr. Veraswami, John Flory, timber merchant and main protagonist of George Orwell's *Burmese Days*, succinctly puts forth a statement that may serve as the point of entry through which we can re-evaluate the politics of the colonial project in early twentieth century Burma. This chapter seeks to engage with the dynamics of race, gender and 'modernity' through the lens of Postcolonial Studies, focusing on Orwell's writings on Burma including his novel *Burmese Days* and some of his essays such as 'Shooting an Elephant' (1968 [1936]). Orwell is a British writer whose chronicling of the Burmese way of life has its own set of ambivalences. The chapter examines Orwell's works on colonial Burma in order to analyze the interactions between the 'colonizer' and the 'colonized' and to scrutinize the gaps and incongruences within this curiously ambivalent sphere. As a postcolonial critique of Orwell's works on colonial Burma, the chapter looks into the problem of the distorted tropes of identification and the slippages in stereotyping which reveal the inconsistencies in the colonial authoritative discourse, thus preventing an 'essentialization' of the colonial exchange. Orwell's writings provide a telescopic view of the multiple possibilities of a colonial encounter, going beyond the pigeon-holes of binaries into a reexamination of the colonial dialogue. This chapter, therefore, analyzes the kaleidoscopic nature of colonial exchange in the context of Orwell's writings on colonial Burma, and through that, attempts to reassess Orwell's position in the polemics of postcolonialism.

THE *'DANSE DU PUKKA SAHIB'*: THE COLONIAL INTERFACE IN ORWELL'S BURMA

The colonial interface can be seen in terms of an interaction between the colonizer and the colonized, where each looks upon the other in an attempt at identification. However, the reflexive nature of the 'Self-Other' is mirror-like, in that one is not the complete visual representation of the other but is only a half-view, where the unseen aspects remain as an uneasy void, fraught with incongruences.

According to Homi Bhabha (1986): 'The question of identification is never the affirmation of a pre-given identity … it is always the production of an "image" of identity and the transformation of the subject in assuming that image.' The process of identification entails a 'splitting'—where the image, on the one hand, becomes a construction of the colonizer and, therefore, something that *must* be present, and on the other, stands as a metonym for an absence or loss; not a representation of 'reality' but an illusory fulfillment of the colonial desire for a definite 'Other.'

The production of the 'Colonized Other' is, however, not simply a reflection of the 'Colonialist Self.' It is a *poor* reflection, the colonialist desire to firmly establish the 'Orient' as all that the 'West' is *not*. In order to maintain this, the colonizer brings certain stereotypical catalogues to *fix* the native in his position of inferiority. In *Burmese Days*, some of the sensory registers commonly attributed to the natives are garlic, coconut oil and sandalwood; Burma is hot, unhygienic and stifling whereas England is fresh, cool and free. We find such instances in 'Shooting an Elephant' as well. The natives are repeatedly referred to as 'yellow faces;' the entire population seems to have been relegated to the homogenous denotation of a 'sea of yellow faces.' In order to formulate stereotypes, the colonizer tries to bring the colonized *within* his discourse, labelling him as belonging to a backward, almost bestial race, a race to be ruled over and civilized. In producing such stereotypes, however, the colonizer concurrently tries to *expel* him from his discourse, as the 'other' *needs* to be exotic, mysterious and defamiliarized. Therefore, there is an attempt both to reduce as well as maintain the distance between the colonizer and the colonized, to produce the colonized as a 'social reality' which is simultaneously an 'other' as well as 'entirely knowable.' Therefore, as Bhabha (1994) says: 'The "fullness" of the stereotype—its image as identity—is always threatened by a "lack."'

Albert Memmi (1965) attempts a categorization of the colonizer where 'a colonizer who refuses' is one who recognizes how unjust the colonial system is. On the other hand, the 'colonialist' is the colonizer who enjoys a higher status and an 'illegitimate' privilege in the colony and hence is not interested in going back 'to being a mediocre man' in his homeland. Does Mr. Flory, the protagonist of *Burmese Days*, act upon such a generalization? Ambiguously situated in his liking for Burma, Mr. Flory, on the one hand, typifies the Burmese as a unique but generally inferior race, but on the other hand, he sows his roots in a foreign country, and makes it his own, thereby falling into the ambivalent position of both distancing as well as associating himself with Burma. Similarly, the protagonist in 'Shooting an Elephant' recognizes the injustice of the system on one hand but on the other asserts his heroic virtues to impress the colonized.

Even conscious colonial interactions are characterized by ambivalence. The colonizer creates a 'caste' of educated men in administrative positions, like U Po Kyin of *Burmese Days*, in order to propagate further the colonial mission. These men become almost like their colonizers, becoming a part of the colonial machinery and performing similar functions. However, the presence of the 'mimic man' who is *almost* like his master but *not quite* reveals the gaps in the authoritative discourse. As Bhabha (1994) says: 'The look of surveillance returns as the displacing gaze of the disciplined, where the observer becomes the observed and "partial" representation rearticulates the whole notion of *identity* and alienates it from essence.' U Po Kyin, in *Burmese Days*, acts as such a 'mimic man,' a native who has risen from poverty to become an official in the colonial service. Throughout the novel, he tries to gain access to the only European club in his district, as proof that he has successfully emulated his master. However, his position is not obsequious but subversive as he is willing to go to any length against anyone, even an Englishman, who tries to stand as an obstacle to his path of ultimate success, i.e., entry into the club. In the repetition of the colonizer's rules, the colonized becomes menacing, in the sense that while his resemblance to the colonizer is authorized, as it were, he becomes a threat to the colonial structure at the same time. Mimicry, in its 'double vision' reveals the slippages in such a structure, since the 'native' occupies the ambivalent position of being like his 'master' while at the same time, retaining his nativity. The very notion of mimicry not only gives rise to ambivalence, but itself revolves around an uneasy contradiction where the emergence of the colonial discourse is rooted in a lack *within* itself, the limitation of partial representation. A significant instance in *Burmese Days* is the club scene, where the butler is harshly rebuked by Ellis for replying in the language of the white man:

'Don't talk like that, damn you—"I find it very difficult!" Have you swallowed a dictionary? "Please, master, can't keeping ice cool"—that's how you ought to talk. We shall have to sack this fellow if he gets to talk English too well. I can't stick servants who talk English. D'you hear, butler?' (Orwell 2009 [1934]: 23).

What is more interesting is the fact that he is not reprimanded for using English, but essentially for using *correct* English, and not the broken, ungrammatical English he is supposed to use. The language of the colonizer, therefore, returns to him as a veiled threat, and reasserts Bhabha's point that to be Anglicized is emphatically not to be English.

We also find another possibility in Orwell's writings on Burma, i.e., the *reversal of the gaze*, where the colonizer becomes the object of the colonized. The colonial interaction ceases to be a one-way process but encapsulates a dialogue, where both parties simultaneously give and take. Mr. Flory, of *Burmese Days*, calls the Englishmen governing British India 'pukka sahibs'; he argues that the behavior and attitude of the colonialist is determined by the code of 'pukka sahibdom' or that they 'dance the *danse du pukka sahib*' as he puts it. Orwell, in his essay 'Shooting an Elephant' sharply brings alive the state of the white man who is trapped in his whiteness, courtesy of the social role that he is supposed to fulfil as a colonizer. In a moment of epiphany, he recognizes that he will have to shoot an elephant which has gone loose only because the natives expect it of him as a valorous colonizer. He says: 'I perceived in this moment that when the white man turns tyrant it is his own freedom that he destroys' (1968 [1936]): 194).

Orwell does not directly involve himself in a spatial construction of Burma through his writings. But by examining the weather, architecture and other features in vivid detail through his protagonists, he engages in a comparison of these colonial sites with Britain. In *Burmese Days*, Flory's habit of growing English flowers in his garden and keeping 'honey scented orchids' in the verandah are attempts at constructing an imagined British homeland around himself. Allaine Cerwonka (2004) notes how geography is a key component in constructing a nation. In Orwell too, race, culture and the ethnographic identity of the Burmese are imagined by means of geography. In 'Shooting an Elephant,' the space which the narrator enters becomes a geographical determinant of identity. According to James A. Tyner (2005), Orwell's narrator undergoes a temporary displacement, where he comprehends the inextricability of his sense of self from the alterity of the colonized. Therefore, 'Geographic allegorization becomes a central constituent of identity' and the landscape becomes a 'situational marker of subjectivity' (Tyner 2005: 264).

THOSE 'HORRIBLE BROWN HANDS'—THE POLITICS OF RACE IN *BURMESE DAYS*

Burmese Days tries to address the question of modernity by simultaneously unpacking and reasserting the epistemic archetypes of Western knowledge. The struggle of Mr. Flory represents the struggle of British imperialism in its colonialist ambition. Starting from the claim to dominion, as illustrated by Flory's early involvement with Burma after his schooling in Eton, proceeding to a more encompassing and penetrative entry into the Burmese way of life, with Flory sending his roots deep into a foreign country and ultimately ending in suicide, *Burmese Days* anticipates the gradual exit of Britain from its empire. Flory acts, at times, as the mouthpiece of the colonial empire, in a way stereotyping and essentializing the native population. At other times, he is vituperative in his attacks against the empire, intent on exposing its decadence. This dualistic tendency to both conform to as well as revolt against the empire lends itself to an understanding of Flory's ambivalent nature. The worth of the 'civilizing' mission is not entirely discarded, yet its discrepancies are revealed. For instance, in his conversation with the Dravidian doctor, Veraswami, Flory comments: 'But we're not civilising them, we're only rubbing our dirt onto them' (Orwell 2009 [1934]: 40).

The emphasis lies in the struggle for achieving a benevolent modernity on the part of the colonizers. There is hardly any illustration, on the other hand, except an ambivalent intimation towards the end of the novel (during the riot), of any kind of nationalistic feeling or thought among the native population. During the revolt, the natives are not explicitly shown to be protesting against their imperial masters. Rather, it seems to be the result of a personal feud between the colonizer and the colonized that does not have much to do with ideas of the nation. The natives' reaction to the narrator is two-fold: on the one hand, they push and jeer at him and on the other they look upon him with awe. As Bhabha (1986) mentions: 'The fantasy of the native is precisely to occupy the master's place while keeping his place in the slave's avenging anger.' This is best illustrated when, in a moment of crisis, the rioting Burmese do not know what to do with an Englishman in their midst; Flory, having plunged himself into the middle of the chaos is met with ambivalence:

> Flory pushed his way into the crowd … A sea of bodies closed in upon him and flung him from side to side, bumping his ribs and choking him with their animal heat … The whole riot had been ludicrous from the start, and what was most ludicrous of all was that the Burmans, who might have killed him, did not know what to do with him now he was among them. Some yelled insults in his face, some jostled him and stamped on his feet, some even tried to make way for him, as a white man (ibid.: 262).

The text does not offer any avenues of knowing whether there is any national consciousness among the Burmese let alone any possible discourses of nation-building or institutionalized nationalism. *Burmese Days*, therefore, addresses the question of modernity by assessing the pitfalls of the same from a Western standpoint. Even though it critiques colonialism and its ramifications (through Flory's lens), it still circulates within the colonialist ambit.

Burmese Days presents the character of Ellis, who is the local manager of a company, and that of Mr. Macgregor, the deputy commissioner, as well as the secretary of the European club at Kyauktada, and other members of the club. As has been pointed out before, the debate on racial superiority, on sustaining the divide with non-Europeans and efforts at an imaginative recreation of the 'homeland' through engagements in British sports or drinking habits, imparts a distinctive character to the space of the European club at Kyauktada. In one of the conversations at the club, Macgregor and Ellis debate the entry of a non-European into the club, wherein the anxiety of racially profiling the Burmese and Indians at Kyauktada as 'Aryan brothers' or even into a pejorative category like 'niggers' is brought to the fore. What characterizes the scene is an interesting set of arguments and observations about the racial categorization of the Burmese and, by extension, the Indians, and a number of associated anxieties. As Orwell writes:

> Mr. Macgregor stiffened at the word 'nigger' which is discountenanced in India. He had no prejudice against Orientals; indeed, he was deeply fond of them. Provided they were given no freedom he thought them the most charming people alive. It always pained him to see them wantonly insulted (ibid.: 28).

The protagonist Flory doubts whether it is appropriate 'to call these people niggers—a term they very naturally resent—when they are obviously nothing of the kind. The Burmese are Mongolians, the Indians are Aryans or Dravidians, and all of them are quite distinct' (ibid.). Ellis then sums up his stance: 'Call them niggers or Aryans or what you like. What I'm saying is that we don't want to see any black hides in this club' (ibid.). These exchanges bring to light the anxieties that underlie the inability of the 'white man' to fix the racial profiles of the Burmese, the Indians, the Eurasians and other non-Europeans who inhabit Kyauktada into rigid racial categories, thereby producing an apparent *racial ambiguity*.

The discrepancies in the supposedly water-tight categories are also vividly brought forward in the passage where Flory and Elizabeth come across the Eurasians, i.e., men of mixed parentage. Nicknamed 'yellow-bellies,' they literally represent the notion of 'hybridity' or, in this case, a 'third space,' indicative of the cultural dynamics of any colonial interaction. Being partly white and yet living in poverty, Elizabeth calls them 'degenerate.' They are excluded from society at large and do not enjoy the privileges on either side, their difference in appearance posing as a threat to the imperial, Manichean order. In a sense, the Eurasians become outsiders in their own home, occupying the 'in-between' space of two cultures, an embodiment of the ambiguity generated by the problematics of the colonial interface.[1]

Flory and Elizabeth, during a sojourn in the local bazaar, visit the shop of an old Chinese grocer, Li Yeik, where Flory gets her a cup of tea. What unfolds thereafter, encapsulates another poignant instance of the 'race' debate. It starts with the physical appearance of Li Yeik's shop as the narrator describes it: '[T]he European look of Li Yeik's shop-front—it was piled with Lancashire-made cotton shirts and almost incredibly cheap German clocks—comforted her somewhat after the barbarity of the bazaar' (Orwell 2009 [1934]: 131).

Inside the shop, Elizabeth notices a naked child, who is said to crawl 'about the floor like a large yellow frog' and the artificially deformed 'small feet' of the two Chinese women. She exclaims that these people 'must be absolute savages!' to which Flory replies: 'Oh no! They're highly civilized; more civilized than we are, in my opinion. Beauty's all a matter of taste' (ibid.: 133). Later on in the scene, Elizabeth asks Flory whether it is not a 'sort of *infra dig*' to sit down in 'these people's house.' Flory re-assures her: 'It's all right with a Chinaman. They're a favored race in this country. And they're very democratic in their ideas. It's best to treat them more or less as equals' (ibid.: 134).

How to understand these statements regarding the relative racial standing of the Chinese? Certainly, the cultural politics of racially profiling the 'Other' is enmeshed within the colonialist/imperialist ideological framework. It has to be understood that colonial Burma was an integral part of British India until 1 April 1937 when it became a separate British colony. Though a Burmese was readily distinguished from an Indian or more specifically from an 'Aryan' or a 'Dravidian' as is exemplified by the text; such a distinction was more a product of the phenotypic difference etched on the physical appearance of the inhabitants of Burma, or as Flory calls them 'Mongolians.'

Thant Myint-U (2011) argues with a historical perspective on trade and diplomatic relations between China and India, that Burma forms the 'missing link' between the two countries. He documents historical anecdotes dating from 122BC to trace the ways in which Chinese envoys travelled to the kingdom of Dian in an effort to open up direct relations with India, via the Burmese territory. Thus, there lies a long and complex history of China's interactions with Burma over the years and of how India had been a point of interest in such efforts. The various racial and ethnic identities within Burma, however, are never acknowledged nor understood in the text, as is evident from the use of the term 'Burmans' as a synonym for 'Burmese.' Smith and Allsebrook (1994) argue that any institutional effort to yield a 'Burmese' identity, has to be predicated upon a supposedly shared history and religious experiences of the people. They further point that the interchangeable usage of the terms 'Burman' and 'Burmese' is problematic and contentious. 'Burman' stands for the largest ethnic group which forms the majority in the ethnic landscape of Burma, whereas 'Burmese' refers to the linguistic community or generally to the citizens of Burma.

THE SET OF 'DAMN BLACK SWINE': WHERE DO THE NON-EUROPEANS GO?

As Swapna Bhattacharya (2007) notes, Indians in various capacities—laborers, professionals and bureaucrats—had made significant contributions to the British administration in particular, and to colonial Burmese society in general. Dr. Veraswami, in *Burmese Days*, represents one end of the spectrum while the other end is peopled by the butler in the novel or the coolie in 'Shooting an Elephant', with many other characters occupying the space in between these extremes. Though the power dynamics within this community are not well developed in these writings, the Indians are still clearly positioned ambivalently in between the space of the colonizer and colonized. Thus, Orwell presents an important dimension to the historiography of colonial Burma, hitherto largely unnoticed by writers and historians alike.

Interestingly, the only non-European characters who enjoy generous mention in the text are, in many ways, more intricately expressive of the colonial machinery than the Europeans of the club. They are introduced in such a manner as to demonstrate their connection to the center of power that is the European club. U Po Kyin, the Burmese sub-divisional magistrate of Kyauktada and the quintessential mimic-man, is shown to encourage a riot simply in order to defame Veraswami and attain entry into the club. The desire for elevation to a status almost but never the same as the white man forms the crux of his machinations: 'Something noble, glorious! Something that is the very highest honour an Oriental can attain to' (Orwell 2009 [1936]: 146).

In his attempt to gain entry into the colonizer's space, U Po Kyin reveals the slippages that are inherent in the working of colonialism. These slippages are brought forcibly to light by the issuing of the circular that mandates the election of a native to the club. Veraswami, the doctor considered to be the most viable option, considers membership to the club an instance of extraordinary prestige that vividly illustrates the dignity issued to an inherently inferior 'Oriental' by the superior race. Unlike U Po Kyin, he shows complete devotion towards Flory and entirely ingratiates himself within the colonizer's discourse. Veraswami does not wish to use the facilities of the club, but feels that the protection which whiteness lends to the native protects him against the onslaught of U Po Kyin: 'In affairs like this, where a native official's reputation is at stake, there is no question of proof, of evidence. All depends upon one's standing with the Europeans' (ibid.: 154).

The prospect of Veraswami's election to the club prompts the dissonance between its present members to come to the surface. Ellis's deep-seated hatred towards the natives, for instance, clashes with Macgregor's feudal benevolence and Mr. Lackersteen's opportunism. It also prompts Flory, a silent and reticent protestor throughout the novel, to emerge as a *parrhesiastes* (one who speaks the truth) towards the end, when he finally musters the courage to face the agents of power and suggests Veraswami's name in the hostile presence of the other club members. Michel Foucault reworks the ancient Greek notion of *parrhesia*, as it appears in Euripides's writing, to imply a kind of 'free speech' in order to 'tell the truth' even at the cost of personal danger. According to Foucault (1999): 'If there is a kind of "proof" of the sincerity of the *parrhesiastes*, it is his courage. The fact that a speaker says something dangerous—different from what the majority believes— is a strong indication that he is a *parrhesiastes*.' In a sense, the election exposes the skewed power equations that exist within the all-white club and implodes the apparent stability of the power center.

Importantly, even when non-Europeans appear in the book, they do so to cement the idea of a flawed modernity, a modernity which is nevertheless Western. In its emphasis on the inter-personal dispute between certain individuals in power, and others who get embroiled in the dispute, Burmese Days is significantly silent about the subaltern voice. There is hardly any intimation of the discourse of the Burmese who are outside the power nexus, and this disproportionate representation further problematizes the postcolonial aspect of the text. For instance, it is briefly mentioned that Ko S'la, Flory's devoted servant, is the father of five children and is 'one of the obscure martyrs of bigamy' (Orwell 2009 [1936]: 50). There are only cursory allusions to the domestic quarrels within Flory's household between the wives; significantly, their voices are not registered in the main narrative and they remain only as squabbling wives of little interest to the 'main' story. Similarly, the *mali*, or gardener, is described as a 'lymphatic, half-witted Hindu youth' who not only occupies a marginal position, but who literally cannot speak because 'he [speaks] some Manipur dialect which nobody else [understands]' and because his 'tongue [is] also a size too large for his mouth' (ibid.: 76–77). U Po Kyin's wife, Ma Kin, holds a significant position in her household, and is shown to be the only person who can appeal to U Po Kyin's conscience. Her agency, too, is confined within the four walls of her house and does not, in any way, impact the larger narrative. The epistemic violence inflicted upon these characters becomes clear once we assess their marginal positions within the household but in the narrative as well, thereby indicating, in their silence, the politics of the text.

'DUTCH DOLLS' AND '*BURRAMEMSAHIBS*': DISCOURSES ON GENDER AND SEXUALITY

Frantz Fanon (1986: 127) interestingly analyzes racial domination in sexual terms: 'The civilized white man retains an irrational longing for unusual eras of sexual license, of orgiastic scenes, of unpunished rapes … Projecting his own desires on to the Negro, the white man behaves as if the Negro really had them.' The colonial impulse of penetration, impregnation and rape is clearly evident in *Burmese Days*. An insidious threat running throughout the novel is a phobic fear of Burmese sexuality which is represented as an impending atrocity. The Burmese are viewed as beasts, who have mysteriously terrifying love lives. U Po Kyin identifies Mrs. Lackersteen's 'weak spot' in his anonymous letter to her, fabricating Veraswami's involvement in instigating natives to rape and abduct European women. As the narrator says:

> To her mind the words 'sedition,' 'Nationalism,' 'rebellion,' 'Home Rule,' conveyed one thing and one only, and that was a picture of herself being raped by a procession of jet-black coolies with rolling eyeballs (Orwell 2009 [1936]: 142).

Even Flory's mistress Ma Hla May, who is Burmese herself, exclaims at the possibility of those 'horrible brown hands' touching her. Ma Hla May enjoys a pivotal role in the novel. Starting from the visceral, almost pungent images associated with her from the beginning, such as the smell of garlic, coconut oil and sandalwood as well as her painted, doll-like face, she gradually turns into a vicious, almost spectral presence as the novel proceeds, finally becoming violent and hysterical towards the end. Her motive, according to the omniscient third person narrator, is fuelled by her need to incorporate 'whiteness' into/onto her body, be it in the form of the clothes or jewelry that she buys with Flory's money or, at the very least, be acknowledged by Flory as his mistress. Flory's inability to quell her anger signifies his failure as the male colonial subject. Even though Ma Hla May ends up working in a brothel, her position as the paradoxical and almost oxymoronic legal mistress, continuously unnerves Flory from his position of colonial masculinity.

By virtue of her subject position, Ma Hla May seems to invite the exploitation of her body by the colonizer in order to survive, thereby outwardly upturning the colonial premise of the frail, stagnant female body waiting to be penetrated against her will. Flory's colonial masculinist sentiment is shaken by her boldness, while he still recognizes the larger symbolic violence of which Ma Hla May is part, where the demand for sexual favors in exchange of social standing does not necessarily mean assent—once again, pointing towards an ambiguity in his characterization. For Ma Hla May's gender marginalizes her in Burmese society. Yet, her access to the private chamber of the white man, her 'thakin,' and her attempts to convince the villagers that she is a white man's 'wife,' or 'bo-kadaw,' generates her sense of privilege. This becomes clear in the light of the statements made by the narrator about the opinions held by KoS'la, who is himself Burmese, on Ma Hla May. The narrator says: 'KoS'la always called her [Ma Hla May] *the woman*, to show his disapproval—not that he disapproved of Flory for keeping a mistress, but he was jealous of Ma Hla May's influence in the house' (ibid.: 50).

Moreover, the narrator comments that the ideal of a Burmese woman is that they are not supposed have 'breasts.' This observation is made in the very same paragraph in where Flory puts his hand on her breasts:

> He put his hand on her breast. Privately, Ma Hla May did not like this, for it reminded her that her breasts existed—the ideal of a Burmese woman being to have no breasts. She lay and let him do as he wished with her, quite passive yet pleased and faintly smiling, like a cat which allows one to stroke it (ibid.: 53).

In another instance she is said to kiss Flory and the narrator comments that kissing is 'a European habit which he had taught her' (ibid.: 52). Moreover, it is also mentioned that there is no Burmese equivalent for the word 'kiss.' These instances point out the ways in which discursive notions culturally construct the materiality of the 'body.'

Ma Hla May's position is further nuanced with references to her racial identity such as when the narrator observes that the whiteness of Flory's skin had a fascination for her; because of its 'strangeness and the sense of power it gave her' (ibid.: 54). Afterwards Flory finds a 'white' female companion in Kyauktada and Ma Hla May ceases to be important in any way in his life. Instead, an attempt can be perceived, on the part of the narrator, at a sympathetic portrayal of Flory, by focusing on how Ma Hla May tries to blackmail him and extort from him money and other valuables. Flory wants her to go away to her village and tries to make sure that Elizabeth never comes to know about her. The reply that Ma Hla May offers to Flory needs to be quoted at length to bring out the nuances of not only Flory's treatment of his Burmese mistress but also the predicament of such women in Burmese society when she is no more given access to the white man's life:

> How can I go back, to be jeered at and pointed at by those low, stupid peasants whom I despise? I who have been a bo-kadaw, a white man's wife, to go home to my father's house, and shake the paddy basket with old hags and women who are too ugly to find husbands! Ah, what shame, what shame! Two years I was your wife, you loved me and cared for me, and then without warning, without reason, you drove me from your door like a dog. And I must go back to my village, with no money, with all my jewels and silk longyis gone, and the people will point and say, 'There is Ma Hla May who thought herself cleverer than the rest of us. And behold! Her white man has treated her as they always do.' I am ruined, ruined! What man will marry me after I have lived two years in your house? You have taken my youth from me. Ah, what shame, what shame! (ibid.: 158).

At the close of the novel, Ma Hla May ends up in a brothel. The trajectory of her life and the interventions brought therein because of her association with Flory, reflect the complicated terrain where colonialism, gender and 'modernity' interact in complex configurations.

Flory's only other relationship with a woman in the novel is also fraught with ambivalence. Elizabeth, the Lackersteens' niece, forms the center of his romantic interest for a major part of the novel, and later, Flory is shown to be even obsessively in love with her, ending his own life after she rejects his advances. He seeks Elizabeth as an anchor for his conflicted view of Burma; he attempts to address the crisis of his identity by gaining a worthy companion in her:

> Elizabeth, by coming into his life ... had brought back to him the air of England—dear England, where thought is free and one is not condemned forever to dance the *danse du pukka sahib* for the edification of the lower races (ibid.: 156).

On the one hand, she reminds him of 'dear England,' i.e., possibly of the 'modernity' that Flory searches for. He, however, forms a predetermined idea of Elizabeth, as the almost angelic figure who can deliver him from his painful solipsism. Flory's search for 'modernity,' therefore, becomes gendered and problematic. On the other hand, he wants her to engage actively in the way of Burmese life, a life that he both despises as well as attaches himself to. Flory expects Elizabeth to involve herself in his world as an exponent of European progressive 'modernity', while at the same time appreciating the multi-variant quality of Burmese life. Elizabeth, however, becomes yet another emblem of failed modernity. Her interest in India is piqued by the mental picture she has of the idle life of the colonial masters:

> She was going to love India, she knew. She had formed quite a picture of India, from the other passengers' conversation; she had even learned some of the more necessary Hindu-stani phrases, such as 'idherao,' 'jaldi,' 'sahiblog,' etc. In anticipation she tasted the agreeable atmosphere of Clubs, with punkahs flapping and barefooted white-turbaned boys rever-ently salaaming; and maidans where bronzed Englishmen with little clipped moustaches galloped to and fro, whacking polo balls. It was almost as nice as being really rich, the way people lived in India (ibid.: 98).

Her way of thinking is described by the narrator as being defined by a peculiar binary 'code' comprising the 'good' and the 'bad':

> Thereafter her whole code of living was summed up in one belief, and that a simple one. It was that the Good ('lovely' was her name for it) is synonymous with the expensive, the elegant, the aristocratic; and the Bad ('beastly') is the cheap, the low, the shabby, the labo-rious (ibid.: 92).

Subsequently, Elizabeth reduces everything she experiences in Burma to either of the two categories. Her insistence with the sphere of the 'body' is striking. The Burmese are physically revolting to her and are 'beastly:' 'Aren't they too simply dreadful? So *coarse*-looking, like some kind of animal' (ibid.: 122).

In Chapter 8, when Flory and Elizabeth watch the performance of the 'pwe' dancer, it is pointed out that her face 'was powdered so thickly that it gleamed in the lamplight like a chalk mask with live eyes behind it. With that dead-white oval face and those wooden gestures she was monstrous, like a demon' (ibid.: 108). This is followed by a blow-to-blow description of her dance moves and how with her 'strange bent posture the girl turned round and danced with her buttocks pro-truded towards the audience' (ibid.: 108). Soon afterwards, Flory explains to an apparently angry Elizabeth that '[t]hese people's sense of decency isn't the same as ours' (ibid.: 110) and it is further noted that:

> It was not the pwe girl's behaviour, in itself, that had offended her; it had only brought things to a head. But the whole expedition—the very notion of *wanting* to rub shoulders with all those smelly natives—had impressed her badly. She was perfectly certain that that was not how white men ought to behave (ibid.).

Elizabeth is sickened not only by the fact that Flory seems to be going against the code of 'whiteness' but also that Flory does not act as a white *man* should. She con-stantly questions his masculinity, and after every encounter with the Burmese that she has to experience because of Flory, she thinks him 'ungentlemanly' or unmanly.

She, however, responds favorably whenever Flory undertakes any 'traditional' masculine activity; for instance, she is drawn closer to him after they go out to a hunt and Flory displays his skill. As Angelia Poon (2014) argues: 'In the novel, again and again, we are shown the equation between a particular version of the modern—a more open, self-conscious, even proto-cosmopolitan disposition toward the world with a premium placed on the aesthetic—and a lack of "true" masculinity.'

Interestingly, Flory and Veraswami share a joke where they compare the British empire to a dying female patient; here, Flory himself becomes a weak masculine subject of the ailing and *female* empire, showing an uneasy juxtaposition of gender roles, where a ruthless and marauding empire is feminized as is its masculine agent. Flory's masculinity is further destabilized by the entry of the young military officer Verrall as a contender for Elizabeth's affections. Verrall, 'lank but very straight,' with his 'buckskin topi and his polo-boots,' cuts the prototypical figure of colonial masculinity and enters the text as the archetype of everything Flory fails to be and therefore makes Flory feel 'uncomfortable in his presence from the start' (ibid.: 190). Moreover, Elizabeth reminds Flory of his greatest insecurity, the birthmark on his face, the disfigurement becoming emblematic of Flory's final failure in white colonial masculinity. Suitably, at the end of the novel, Elizabeth marries Macgregor who is a much older man and fulfils her role as the '*burramemsahib*.' According to Poon (2014): 'Flory's tragedy in *Burmese Days* is the result of a longing for modernity that can find no suitable form or release within the oppressive and repressive machinery of empire where (gendered) subject positions have become fossilized.'

CONCLUSION

Alyssa Phillips (2003) points out that not everything that is known about Burma is a product of the colonial history making-project, but a significant portion of what has been understood about Burma or the Burmese people comes filtered through the various literary works and political institutions, all of which are a product of the British colonial enterprise.

Interestingly, Orwell's chronicling of the Burmese way of life etches out an alternative discourse—with deliberations on race, gender, colonialism and 'modernity' highlighting significant ambiguities and contradictions.

NOTE

1. Significantly, the essay 'A Hanging' (of 1931)—dealing with the execution of a prisoner—also employs racial profiling to etch out the characters. The Dravidian head jailer, the 'Hindu' convict

who is to be hanged, the Indian warders and the Eurasian jailer are all identified and character-ized by their racial profile. Though the essay is a critique of the death penalty, in the course of developing its plot, the idea of 'race' is constantly re-created and reinforced.

REFERENCES

Ashcroft, Bill; Tiffin, Helen; Griffiths, Gareth (1998) *Key Concepts in Postcolonial Studies*, London and New York: Routledge.

Bhabha, Homi K. (1994) *The Location of Culture*, London and New York: Routledge.

Bhabha, Homi K. (1986) Foreword, Fanon, Frantz *Black Skin, White Masks*, London: Pluto Press p. xxix.

Bhattacharya, Swapna (2007) *India–Myanmar Relations 1886–1948*, Kolkata: K. P. Bagchi & Co.

Cerwonka, Allaine (2004) *Native to the Nation: Disciplining Landscapes and Bodies in Australia*, Minneapolis: University of Minnesota Press.

Fanon, Frantz (1986) *Black Skin, White Masks*, London: Pluto Press.

Foucault, Michel (1999) The meaning and evolution of the word *parrhesia*, Pearson, Joseph (ed.) *Discourse and Truth: The Problematization of Parrhesia*. Available online at http://foucault.info/documents/parrhesia/foucault.dt1.wordparrhesia.en.html, accessed on 3 January 2014.

Gandhi, Leela (1998) *Postcolonial Theory*, London: Allen and Unwin.

Memmi, Albert (1965) *The Colonizer and the Colonized*, London: The Orion Press.

Myint-U, Thant (2011) *Where China Meets India: Burma and the New Crossroads of Asia*, London: Faber and Faber Limited.

Orwell, George (1931) A hanging, *Adelphi*. Available online at http://george-orwell.org/a_hanging/0.html, accessed on 2 January 2015.

Orwell, George (2009 [1934]) *Burmese Days*, London: Penguin Books.

Orwell, George (1968 [1936]) Shooting an elephant, Thorpe, Michael (ed.) *Modern. Prose*, Oxford: Delhi/Oxford University Press pp. 190–197.

Phillips, Alyssa (2003) *'The Mirror Cracked': The Colonial History-Making Project and its Legacy in Burma, 1900 to the present*. Phd dissertation, Monash University, Melbourne, Australia. Available online at http://www.soas.ac.uk/sbbr/editions/file64293.pdf, accessed on 2 January 2015.

Poon, Angela (2014) Against the 'uprush of modern progress:' Exploring the dilemma and dynamics of modernity in George Orwell's *Burmese Days*, *Concentric: Literary and Cultural Studies*, Vol. 40, No. 1, pp. 79–95.

Smith, Martin and Allsebrook, Annie (1994) *Ethnic Groups in Burma-Development, Democracy and Human Rights*, London: Anti-Slavery International.

Tyner, James A. (2005) Landscape and the mask of self in George Orwell's 'Shooting an elephant,' *Area*, Vol. 37, No. 3, pp. 260–267.

CHAPTER ELEVEN

Critiquing Communist Dictatorship East AND West

George Orwell's *Animal Farm* and Chen Jo-hsi's *Mayor Yin*

SHU-CHU WEI

INTRODUCTION

George Orwell famously subtitled his *Animal Farm* (1945)[1] 'a fairy story.' However, as John Rodden points out, it is in fact 'a political allegory of the history of the USSR … written in the form of a beast fable,' and he also notes that, in doing so, Orwell offered 'a stinging moral warning against the abuse of power' and 'a brilliant work of political satire' (Rodden 2011: 7–10). At least four literary terms—fairy story, beast fable, political allegory and satire—have been used to describe *Animal Farm*, and much of its success and brilliance results from the skillful interplay of these various generic models. While it is true that children have enjoyed reading this 'fairy story,' Orwell himself was concerned to stress its serious intent. In a letter to his agent Leonard Moore from 1946, for instance, he described the main purpose of the book as follows: '*Animal Farm* is intended as a satire on dictatorship in general but *of course* the Russian Revolution is the chief target. It is humbug to pretend anything else' (Quinn 2009: 53). These statements underscore the essence of the story as a satire on the Russian Revolution.

In keeping with Orwell's comment that *Animal Farm* aims at satirizing 'dictatorship in general,' John Rodden points out that *Animal Farm* 'reads today like a startlingly accurate indictment of Chinese Communism too, not just Stalinism' (Rodden 2011: 10). This understanding of Orwell's masterful satire opens up meaningful cross-cultural perspectives and makes room for comparative studies of *Animal Farm* and Chinese fiction regarding the Communist Revolution in China, in particular the Cultural Revolution. This is generally defined as lasting from

1966 to 1976, the so called 'Ten Lost Years,' and is arguably the most disastrous period in the history of Communist China. One author who immediately comes to mind in this respect is the Taiwanese author Chen Jo-hsi (also spelled Chen Ruoxi) and her anthology of stories entitled *The Execution of Mayor Yin and Other Stories from the Great Proletarian Cultural Revolution* (尹縣長) (1976). In these stories, some of which are semi-autobiographical and others eye-witness reports presented as stories, Chen Jo-hsi presents many similar practices of communist dictatorship explored by Orwell such as propaganda and indoctrination, systematic spying and surveillance, show trials and the complete subordination of citizens to the needs of the Party.

In addition to contents, Orwell and Chen also share some similarities in their presentational methods. As noted above, Orwell gave his tale the 'fairy story' treatment and, as John Rossi comments, this enabled him 'to show the absurdities of a failed revolution with irony and even humor' (Rossi 2003: 151). Stephen J. Greenblatt explains this point further by saying: '*Animal Farm* does, indeed, contain much gaiety and humor, but even in the most comic moments there is a disturbing element of cruelty or fear that taints the reader's hearty laughter' (Greenblatt 1974: 106). This is also true of Chen's stories, which, though generally regarded as presentations of realism, similarly make use of irony, humor and satire and in doing so, achieve a memorable anatomy of the absurdities of the Cultural Revolution. Irony and satire, to be sure, are related to categories such as the comic and the absurd. Northrop Frye explores their interrelationship and notes that 'satire is irony which is structurally close to the comic: the comic struggle of two societies, one normal and the other absurd, is reflected in its double focus of morality and fantasy.' Frye also asserts that the satirist 'has to select his absurdities, and the act of selection is a moral act' (Frye 1970: 224). Absurdities, then, are at the core of both Orwell's *Animal Farm* and Chen's stories.

This chapter explores how the practices of communist dictatorship are exposed and satirized and offers a comparative study of Orwell's *Animal Farm* and Chen's *The Execution of Mayor Yin* by discussing two pairs of representative characters: Mollie in *Animal Farm* and P'eng Yu-lien in 'Residency Check' from *The Execution of Mayor Yin*, as well as Boxer in *Animal Farm* and Mayor Yin in 'The Execution of Mayor Yin.' I also discuss recurring themes of cover-ups and propaganda in both books. In close reading the texts, more plot synopses will be provided of the stories in *Mayor Yin* as they are not as well known to readers as *Animal Farm*.

AUTHORIAL BACKGROUND

George Orwell, as he stated himself, 'never visited Russia' and his knowledge of the country consisted 'only of what can be learned by reading books and newspapers' (Orwell 1987a: 111). Nevertheless, he had direct experience fighting in Spain (1936–1937) with the Partido Obrero de Unifición (POUM), a Marxist militia and was blacklisted for this by mainstream communists for the rest of his life. In the 'Preface to the Ukrainian Edition of *Animal Farm*,' he presents this experience as follows:

> These man-hunts in Spain went on at the same time as the great purges in the USSR and were a sort of supplement to them. In Spain as well as in Russia the nature of the accusations (namely, conspiracy with the Fascists) was the same and as far as Spain was concerned I had every reason to believe that the accusations were false. To experience all this was a valuable object lesson: it taught me how easily totalitarian propaganda can control the opinion of enlightened people in democratic countries (Orwell 1987a: 111).

It is evident that Orwell came back from Spain with a firm grasp of Russian communist methods and a ready determination to expose them. Chen Jo-hsi, for her part, spent seven years in China during the high time of the Cultural Revolution and witnessed how the Chinese people were ruthlessly exploited by the authorities. Chen's personal exposure to life in a communist society was, therefore, even more intense and prolonged than that of Orwell. In fact, nothing in Chen's background initially suggested that she would ever have to live in a communist country. She was born in 1938 in Taiwan, obtained a BA degree in English from Taiwan University, then went to the United States to pursue a degree in Creative Writing. Her life took a dramatic turn, however, when—gripped by idealistic enthusiasm—she moved to China with her husband in 1966 just after the Cultural Revolution had been launched by Mao Zedong. In 1973, she and her family, totally disillusioned, were lucky enough to get permission to leave China. They settled temporarily in the then-British Hong Kong where she started to publish stories about her experience in China. She became the first writer to tell the world outside China what had happened under the much-glorified Chairman Mao's rule (Leys 1978: xii–xiii). She did not read *Animal Farm* until the 1980s, long after her experience of the communist dictatorship in China and 'felt deeply touched' reading it.[2]

The crucial point about her stories is that she was a direct observer of and participant in the Chinese Cultural Revolution and yet had also seen the world outside China, thus giving her a unique and sharp perspective with which she could compare and contrast the two worlds and see how vicious and absurd the Chinese Cultural Revolution was. C. T. Hsia emphasizes this aspect in his preface to Chen's *Selected Stories*: 'After she went to mainland China, what she saw were not only individual tragedies and misfortunes, but the absurdity of the whole society' (Hsia 1976: 30, my translation). Exposing and satirizing the tragic absurdity of the events during the Cultural Revolution is, in my view, the most important contribution Chen has made to the history of modern Chinese literature.

MOLLIE IN *ANIMAL FARM* AND P'ENG YU-LIEN IN 'RESIDENCY CHECK'

Turning now to specific examples of what may be called Orwellian themes in the respective fiction of both authors, I first focus on Mollie, the white mare in *Animal Farm*, and Yu-lien, one of the narrator's close neighbors in 'Residency Check' in *The Execution of Mayor Yin*. Despite some shortcomings, both of them are captivating females highly conscious of their attractiveness. Mollie, though 'foolish,' is 'pretty' with her 'white mane,' while Yu-lien, though 'very short,' has 'large and curvaceous' breasts as well as 'big and bright' and 'expressive' eyes. In addition to these qualities, they pay special attention to making themselves look even more attractive. As a result of all their attractive qualities and beautifying efforts, Mollie is stroked on her nose by men and men are 'captivated' by Yu-lien's 'all manner of allurements' (Orwell 1987a: 2–3; Chen 1978: 91–92).

Mollie has other problems besides being foolish. She is 'not good at getting up in the mornings' and has a way of 'leaving work early' with an excuse (Orwell 1987a: 18). She also goes into hiding when the fight against the humans breaks out (ibid.: 28). One would suppose that being lazy and being cowardly are serious vices for a worker among the revolutionary animals. Strangely, Mollie is not punished nor even admonished for these vices. Instead, she is 'reproached ... sharply' by the other animals only when she is found holding 'a piece of blue ribbon ... against her shoulder and admiring herself in the glass in a very foolish manner' (ibid.: 14). After she is seen allowing a man to 'stroke [her] nose' and 'a little pile of lump sugar' and 'several bunches of ribbon of different colours' are found under the straw of her stall, she runs away from the farm, obviously of her own volition. Some weeks later, the pigeons report that they have spotted her with human beings, appearing 'to be enjoying herself,' and she is wearing 'a scarlet ribbon round her forelock' (ibid.: 30–31), possibly referring to Hawthorne's *Scarlet Letter* (of 1850). Afterwards, the animals never mention Mollie again; that is, she is punished as a complete outcast 'in the best Victorian tradition' in dealing with 'the fallen woman' (Reilly 1999: 67).

Mollie, with her follies and vices, clearly is not a worthy comrade in the revolution. On Animal Farm, Mollie's colorful ribbons are considered as 'the badge of slavery' (ibid.: 10) and as 'clothes, which are the mark of a human being' (ibid.: 13). Human beings, as Old Major points out at the beginning of the story, represent the evil capitalists who are slave drivers and enemies of the animal—and of the proletariat, figuratively speaking. In the communist revolution against the oppressive capitalists, anything related to or showing a slight sign of capitalism is viewed as vice and is not tolerated. Consequently, Mollie's ribbons have to be cast away as 'the mark of a human being.' If she does not cast away her ribbons, then Mollie herself has to be cast out.

Being fond of good food such as sugar and of beautiful things such as ribbons, flowers, and clothes, or even being interested in being beautiful, is simply human nature; and 'Residency Check' also focuses on such inborn aspects of human nature. The narrator comments on how Yu-lien's 'lovely and enticing' clothes in 'bright colors' and her attractive appearance have captivated men, so that '*naturally* many of the women [look] upon her with envy and malice' (Chen 1978: 92, emphasis added). The fact that the women are 'naturally' envious of Yu-lien's attractiveness indicates that they themselves want to be attractive, too, and their desire to be attractive, especially to men, is only 'natural.' Since the earliest times in human history, men have always pursued beautiful women, and women have never stopped worshiping heroic men. Compared with the abuse of power, vanity is a minor vice. When we see the power abusers persecute the vain women, the irony is all too obvious.

In Yu-lien's case, the power abusers are the women of the Neighborhood Committee. This is a political, moral and watch-dog committee and, in fact, an all-encompassing committee made up of mostly elderly women in the neighborhood. These women, who used to be powerless but are newly bestowed with unrestrained power to supervise and spy upon the neighborhood after the revolution, work extra hard to carry out their assignments from the authority, so much so that they tend to abuse their power. Since many of these women are envious of Yu-lien's attractiveness to begin with, they resort to 'malice' when they suspect that she is having an extramarital affair while her university professor husband is sent away on a farm for re-educational labor. One wonders how a socially and politically insignificant little woman's suspected adultery, regardless of its supposed immorality, has anything to do with the success of a revolution. Nevertheless, the committee women keep her 'under surveillance' and set up a scheme, or rather a mouse-trap farce, to catch her on the spot of her crime. Once she is caught, they will 'hold a big group session and soundly criticize her' (ibid.: 97–100). To be criticized in such a session was a matter of 'devastating' 'humiliation' (Fairbank 1986: 336) during the Cultural Revolution as court trials were non-existent and the unlucky or physically weak could be, and often were, tortured to death.[3]

Yu-lien escapes the 'big group session' because, to the great disappointment of the committee women and to our great amusement, her husband does not care whether she has an extramarital affair or not, nor does he want the divorce suggested by his political leaders. However, she has no other alternatives but to continue being closely watched by the Neighborhood Committee. Regarding this kind of torture, Northrop Frye observes that 'the lust for sadistic power on the part of the ruling class is strong enough to last indefinitely.' Consequently, poor Yu-lien has to endure 'the humiliation of being constantly watched by a hostile or derisive eye' (Frye 1970: 238).

In sum, the zealotry of the committee's irrational work in trapping Yu-lien is much ado about something that is none of their business. Unlike Yu-lien, lucky

Mollie can choose to either run away or self-exile. Mollie may be 'foolish,' but, sticking to her instinct, she knows what she wants and has an option and the courage to go for it. As the story of the animals' revolution turns out, Mollie's life of being men's slave, ironically, is much better than her animal comrades' lives as Napoleon's slaves, though her animal comrades may not be aware that they are slaves, too, and very bitter ones.

BOXER AND MAYOR YIN

An even more striking example of the analogous moral visions of Orwell and Chen can be found in the fates suffered by the horse Boxer in *Animal Farm* and Mayor Yin in Chen's 'The Execution of Mayor Yin.' Boxer, the symbol of 'the hard work, endurance and patriotic loyalty of the working class' (Dickstein 2007: 141), and his Chinese equivalent Mayor Yin both end their lives miserably and unjustly when they are eliminated by the political authorities they have served faithfully.

Boxer, an 'enormous' horse 'nearly eighteen hands high, and as strong as any two ordinary horses put together,' has a white stripe down his nose, which gives him 'a somewhat stupid appearance,' and, in fact, he is 'not of first-rate intelligence.' However, he is 'universally respected for his steadiness of character and tremendous powers of work' (Orwell 1987a: 2). This portrayal of Boxer puts him into the category of a strong, hard-working simpleton. With his great strength and devotion, he qualifies as a first-rate worker; with his level of intelligence, he is doomed to be exploited by vicious, smart rogues no matter how much respect he garners. Boxer's fate reveals Orwell's criticism of Lenin's belief 'that the proletariat must be led by an intellectually elite corps of party members who would direct and secure the revolution' (quoted in Quinn 2009: 49).

Mayor Yin is similar to Boxer in many ways. When the narrator first encounters him in 1966 in a backward area, he is observed as 'very tall ... dark and thin, about fifty years old.' His back is 'straight and strong' and his facial expression 'diffident and gentle.' The narrator also finds out that Mayor Yin 'was commended for his meritorious service during the [1949] Revolution and became the acting mayor,' and everyone in the county continues to address him as Mayor Yin. He is considered a selfless hero who contributed tremendously to the successful establishment of Mao's China as he was originally an officer under Chiang Kai-shek during the civil war between the Nationalist and Communist parties, but led his troops over to the Communist side (Chen 1978: 5–8). However, this hero is attacked during the Cultural Revolution as a 'class enemy,' 'underworld criminal' and 'warlord' of the Chiang Kai-shek era (ibid.: 15) by a group of 'arrogant Red Guards' led by his distant nephew Hsiao Wu, a high school sophomore (ibid.: 3). Though it may be ridiculous at first sight that a senior, well-respected party cadre should be attacked by a green, seventeen-year-old lad over events that took place before the 1949 revolution, such attacks did indeed take place during the Cultural Revolution as the young were consistently encouraged by the authority to turn against their elders. The latter is also something that would be seen in Orwell's *Nineteen Eighty-Four* as children are encouraged to spy on their own parents.

Disturbed by the new campaign and this personal attack, Mayor Yin goes to the narrator to voice his puzzlement and feeble protest:

> I still don't see what this Cultural Revolution has to do with me … I've never been involved with organization, propaganda work, or any policy making. Whatever the Party told me to do, I did. I only have one head, which the Party can reform any way it wishes to. As for my family history, I've already reported it five or six times since Liberation. What's there to cover up, to lie about? (ibid.: 18).

The truth is that, although he has nothing to cover up or to lie about, the Party does. The highest Party leadership created an ambiguous Cultural Revolution so as to bend the revolutionary movement anyway it wished. Just as Napoleon summons his dogs to help him establish his absolute control over Animal Farm, Mao bestowed unrestrained power on the youthful and reckless Red Guards, a more savage group of political pawns than the Neighborhood Committee, in order to pull down the established party leaders so that he would be the supreme leader.[4] Yet, the poor mayor who always does 'whatever the Party [tells him] to do' does not suspect the Party to which he is totally devoted. In fact, when problems occur, he blames himself, saying: 'I come from a lowly background and didn't have much book learning as a child … I never could understand the doctrines of Marxism' (ibid.: 20).

Such is also the problem with Boxer. After Napoleon's bloody show trials and execution of animal comrades, Boxer blames himself and provides an unbelievable solution. He says: 'I do not understand it. I would not have believed that such things could happen on our farm. It must be due to some fault in ourselves. The solution, as I see it, is to work harder' (Orwell 1987a: 57). Boxer's self-sacrificing spirit for the general good of the farm is noble and admirable, but he is unable to see the true faces of Napoleon and Squealer. His 'fidelity is inseparable from stupidity' (Reilly 1999: 79) after all. He is so loyal to Animal Farm and trusting of its leader that he chooses to believe 'Napoleon is always right.' Only once does he voice his disbelief when Squealer accuses Snowball of treason. Boxer feels uneasy about the accusation and insists: 'I do not believe that Snowball was a traitor at the beginning' (Orwell 1987a: 55). It is unusual for Boxer to be so disagreeable; it gives us a glimpse of hope that he is capable of telling right from wrong and that a strong enough figure on the farm is going to stand up against the exploiters. To our great disappointment, when Squealer announces firmly that Napoleon has said it, Boxer gives in completely, saying: 'If Comrade Napoleon says it, it must be right' (ibid.: 55). In doing so, he offers 'proof of how suicidally credulous he is (Reilly 1999: 78). This surrender of Boxer also foreshadows his ultimate downfall. Having worked himself to exhaustion, the unsuspecting fool, believing that he is being sent to the hospital for treatment, steps into the van of the Horse Slaughterer and, despite all the other animals' efforts to get him out of the van, he is unable to escape:

> [T]here was the sound of a tremendous drumming of hoofs inside the van. He was trying to kick his way out. The time had been when a few kicks from Boxer's hoofs would have smashed the van to matchwood. But alas! his strength had left him; and in a few moments the sound of drumming hoofs grew fainter and died away (Orwell 1987a: 82).

Thus, the huge horse, which was once powerful enough to pin down Napoleon's blood-thirsty dogs with his hoofs (ibid.: 56), is now too weak to kick his way out of this death trap. Since Boxer's hoofs symbolize the great working power of the proletariat, this moment when 'the sound of drumming hoofs grew fainter and died away' marks the death toll for the proletariat under totalitarian tyranny.

Mayor Yin is similarly unable to escape his death sentence. Although he may not be as foolishly faithful to the party leader as Boxer, he is not as lucky as Mollie who can run away because personal registry was tightly controlled during the Cultural Revolution. What is more, his execution is desperately desired by the young Red Guards who are eager to grasp power. Hsiao Wu's cousin, one of the Red Guards at the execution scene, explains: 'At the time everyone felt it was a necessary step for the sake of the revolution. If they didn't execute a few people they couldn't establish their authority and extend their influence ... Yin Fei-lung wasn't the only case; there were many more like him' (Chen 1978: 33). The Red Guards, therefore, execute Mayor Yin and 'many more like him' for the sake of a naked power grab and self-interest. It may be useful at this point to note that Chen's story accurately reflects the methods of the Red Guards and the manner in which they persecuted party members. Fairbank states: 'Allowing for many variations, the purge rate among the party officials was somewhere around 60 per cent. It has been estimated that 400,000 people died as a result of maltreatment ... Many more were physically and mentally crippled ...' (Fairbank 1986: 320). Orwell's counterparts to the Red Guards are Napoleon's dogs. These dogs are taken from their mothers shortly after birth and bred to serve as secret police under Napoleon's command. In the movement 'from revolution to totalitarian state,' these secret police become the necessary 'imposition of state terror to ensure the continued acquisition of power' (Quinn 2009: 56).

Mayor Yin is not only executed on far-fetched charges by the Red Guards; he is, in fact, slaughtered, much like Boxer. While Boxer is slaughtered secretly, Mayor Yin is executed in broad daylight and in public:

They tied Mayor Yin to a wooden stake that had been stuck in among the rocks. As they pointed their rifles at him, he raised his head and shouted again, 'Long live the Communist Party! Long live Chairman Mao!' His eyes were bulging as though they would burst from their sockets, and his lips were bleeding from biting them ... (Chen 1978: 35).

This scene again presents a striking comparison with a similar detail in *Animal Farm* when Squealer, the 'spokespig' of Animal Farm, reports to the animals that the last words from the ever-loyal Boxer were: 'Long live Animal Farm! Long live Comrade Napoleon! Napoleon is always right' (Orwell 1987a: 83). Boxer's so-called 'last words' are of course Squealer's lies, whereas Mayor Yin's are uttered by himself, but the remarkable parallelism of the slogans casts a bitterly ironic light on these death scenes. Squealer's propagandist rendition of the death of Boxer is cunningly executed and successfully comforts the foolish animals, and this, in turn, strikes the reader as both heart-breaking and maddening at the same time.

The execution scene of Mayor Yin, meanwhile, also offers troubling complexities as it is hard to decipher what Mayor Yin really means by his last shouting. His bulging eyes and bleeding lips indicate that he is intensely agitated and even infuriated by the injustice inflicted upon him. Why, then, does he shout the familiar slogans that glorify the Communist Party and Chairman Mao? Could he be hoping against hope that his life will be spared as the Red Guards may not dare to shoot a person chanting these sacred slogans? Is he still asserting his innocence by reminding people how loyal and devoted he has been to the Party and Chairman Mao? Or is he perhaps cynically venting his anger at his beloved Party and Chairman? Maybe he is being sarcastic because he now finally realizes that he has been fooled? The truth is that we do not know the answer, nor perhaps does Mayor Yin himself, and this makes the howling all the more disturbing and unforgettable. The slogans, the same ones which were chanted numerous times every day by everyone in Mao's China, have lost their literal meaning. The combination of the loud howling and of the meaninglessness of the slogans reminds one of King Lear's maddening 'Howl, howl, howl' at Cordelia's death. As Wylie Sypher reflects, when men are pushed into 'the direst calamities,' that is, the 'inherently absurd,' they reach 'the stage of the inarticulate' (Sypher 1965: 18–19). They can only howl, or in Boxer's case, kick.

COVER-UPS AND PROPAGANDA

In *Animal Farm* and some of Chen's stories, the political authorities force their subjects to hide internal deficiencies from outside visitors so as to give these visitors positive but false impressions of their true condition. In both cases humor is used to expose the folly of such schemes. On Animal Farm, there is a food shortage one bitter winter. The animals are cold and hungry and Napoleon is concerned about 'the bad results that might follow if the real facts of the food situation were known.' Therefore, it is '*vitally necessary* to conceal this fact from the outside world' (Orwell 1987a: 50, emphasis added). Napoleon then takes swift action in order to mislead Mr. Whymper, the businessman who trades with Animal Farm on a weekly basis.[5] The cover-up involves the following procedures. First, a few 'selected' animals, mostly sheep, are 'instructed to remark casually in [Mr. Whymper's] hearing that rations [have] been increased.' Then, Napoleon orders the 'almost empty bins' in the store-shed 'to be filled nearly to the brim with sand' and then they are 'covered up' with what remains of the grain and meal. Finally, on some 'suitable pretext,' Whymper is to be 'led through the store-shed and allowed to catch a glimpse of the bins' (ibid.: 50). The plan is executed to perfection, and Mr. Whymper is deceived and reports to the outside world that Animal Farm is flourishing. As noted earlier, Orwell learned from his experiences in Spain 'how easily totalitarian propaganda can control the opinion of enlightened people in democratic countries' (Orwell 1987a: 111). Something of this nature is at work here as there seems to be some guilty complicity between the tricksters and their gulls who are too 'easily' misled.

Such large-scale programs to falsify one's situation are also in evidence in Chen's stories. It should be noted in this respect that the most important visitor from 'the outside world' to Communist China during the time of the Cultural Revolution, specifically in 1972, was President Nixon, of the United States of America, the most important and powerful capitalist country. China had actually wanted to establish better relations with the US for years, but finding the right opportunity proved difficult as it had openly criticized the US for decades as an imperialist enemy. Now that President Nixon was coming, however, it became 'vitally necessary' for China to look more than perfect to this visitor and his entourage. In order to impress the American dignitaries and the press corps, the Chinese Communist Party officials directed a great theater of the absurd to show how prosperous, bountiful, beautiful, powerful, and everything else China *really* was. These shows are recorded in two of Chen's stories entitled 'Nixon's Press Corps' and 'The Big Fish.'

In 'Nixon's Press Corps,' the narrator, a female teacher at a university in Nanking and 'a returnee from the United States' (Chen 1976: 212), which is also the exact background of the author, is summoned with all her colleagues to an emergency meeting because the provincial authorities have directed them 'to complete preparations for receiving Nixon's press corps' of eighty people, who '*may* pass through Nanking tomorrow for a one-day visit' (ibid.: 209–210, emphasis added). The university official does acknowledge that the possibility of a visit to their school is 'very remote,' but the preparation is necessary because Chairman Mao teaches: 'Do not fight unprepared battles' (ibid.: 210). We may note, incidentally, that President Nixon would never have considered his peaceful and friendly visit to China to be the equivalent of a battle. 'Elaborate preparations' for this 'battle' actually began three months before Nixon's visit was announced. The earlier preparations include 'a general study of all pertinent documents' and assigning 'sample questions that the correspondents might ask' to the street committees 'so that everyone could practice giving appropriate answers' (ibid.: 209). These steps will sound familiar to any reader of *Animal Farm* as they are similar to Napoleon's cover-up schemes. Observing this hoopla, our narrator from the United States, using her own reason and American societal norms, cannot help wondering:

> One would think that after twenty years of attacking 'American imperialism' as the number one enemy, it would be difficult for people to change their way of thinking to such an extent that they would shake hands and fraternize with the President of the United States. But after an intensive reading of all the circulated documents, their thoughts began to fall in line with what they read. No one ever publicly questioned the contradictory statements or this about-face in communist policy (ibid.: 209).

This shows how effectively the communist authorities are able to brain-wash their people and how swiftly the people adapt to their ever-changing political environments. Or to be more exact, this shows, rather, how conveniently and cunningly the communist authorities change their policy and how gullible the people are when presented with contradictory statements by the government.

In another preparation session, one of the university authorities lectures the audience by beginning with comments on how the revolution signals 'the end of the road for American imperialism.' Then, with his 'self-assurance and arrogance'—the diction reveals the narrator's criticism—he says that Nixon has been 'forced to come begging for peace' (ibid.: 210). Surely he forgets to explain why they have to go through such elaborate preparations to welcome a 'peace beggar.' Afterwards, he reminds everyone at the meeting:

> It is of the utmost importance for us to grasp the characteristics of these reporters. They have their 'three excesses'—an excess of running around, an excess of questions, and an excess of picture taking. But we have our ways of dealing with them: We must maintain an attitude neither overbearing nor humble, neither too approachable nor too distant, neither … er, er … in other words, if we maintain an attitude of 'three neithers' in dealing with their 'three excesses' we shall remain invincible (ibid.: 210–211).

The speaker, though not so cunning, is as comic as Squealer. He is obviously unaware of his clownish presentation, which makes the situation even more comic.

The 'elaborate preparations,' however, do not end here. Even though the chance of a visit by the press corps to the school is almost next to zero, the authorities still decide that even the minutest details have to be taken care of. Right after lunch that day, a member of the Neighborhood Committee comes to inform the narrator that they 'have to take down all the drying racks over the windows' for fear that 'the foreign visitors will find them an eyesore.' The response of Chen's narrator to these orders serves as a sensible comment on the preposterous situation: 'Although this struck me as funny to the point of absurdity, I was unable to laugh' (ibid.: 213). The irony is that, after all the fuss, it turns out that Nixon's press corps has 'shown no interest in Nanking' (ibid.: 220) and skips the city.

Another cover-up farce is presented in 'The Big Fish.' The main character K'uai Shih-fu (Master K'uai), an old ironworker at the dockyards in Nanking, returns home much earlier than usual one February day because the afternoon political study session has been changed to a general clean-up to prepare for the visit of 'some American newspapermen,' and his two kind-hearted apprentices are willing to do the cleaning for him. They practically force him to go home to take care of his wife who is sick. They also inform him that because of the American newspapermen, 'the markets will be better stocked than usual' (ibid.: 139). So he takes a long bicycle ride to a famous market, thinking he will give his wife, who has not had a good appetite, a real treat. At the marketplace, the cement floor has 'just been washed' and looks 'spotless.' In fact, every bit of the about-face job has been meticulously carried out for the American visitors. At the fish stall Master K'uai spots several large *ch'ing* fish, 'all shiny and fresh-looking.' He spends a large part of his monthly salary and succeeds in purchasing a big fish even though the stall keeper 'frown[s] at him for some time,' 'shake[s] his head,' speaks to him 'coldly,' gives him 'a hard look,' 'blink[s] his eyes,' etc. (ibid.: 143–145). It is quite obvious that the stall keeper is unwilling to sell the fish to him for some unspoken reason; ironically, in his excitement, the socially well-seasoned K'uai Shih-fu fails to pick up the stall keeper's 'hints' conveyed through physical gestures. Thus, the author presents a comic scene while foreshadowing that something bad will happen to K'uai Shih-fu.

Then old Master K'uai's eyes light up at a vegetable stand because, at the end of February when produce is always scarce, the 'delicacies' such as tomatoes and cucumbers are, like Napoleon's food and grains, 'attractively displayed in separate little baskets placed at the most conspicuous spots in the stand.' He decides to get one of the cucumbers 'whatever the cost' just so his wife can have a taste of her favorite vegetable, but the woman vendor says 'bluntly:' 'The cucumbers are not for sale!' Old K'uai Shih-fu is disappointed, but there is nothing he can do about it. He goes back to his bicycle with the 'impressive looking' fish, his heart 'filled with joy' (ibid.: 145–147). But then a cadreman taps him on the shoulder and orders him to return the fish because it is not for sale:

'What?' K'uai raised his voice. 'Not for sale? Damn it! Then why the hell didn't they say so in the first place? Now you want to snatch it away when it's about to be dropped in the pot!'

At the old man's curses the cadreman's face hardened and he glared at K'uai.

'If they're all sold out, what'll be left to show the foreign visitors when they arrive?' (ibid.: 147–148).

The cadreman's answer is a punch line for the joke and explains everything.

The big fish, then, is all a big lie of the kind that Orwell despised. As Reilly comments: 'In life Orwell dreaded totalitarian propaganda as the supreme iniquity of our time, the throttling of truth even as a theoretic possibility; in the art of *Animal Farm* the image of a pig up a ladder with a paintbrush alchemizes the horror into humor, putting Orwell and the reader in serene control of the situation' (Reilly 1999: 64). The workers such as Master K'uai, though not 'in serene control of the situation,' sooner or later realize the truth beneath the cover-ups.

CONCLUSION

It is not likely that Chairman Mao and other leading communists in China ever read *Animal Farm*, but it is intriguing that the script they followed when they launched the infamous Cultural Revolution is very similar to that followed in *Animal Farm*. Thanks to Chen Jo-hsi and her stories about Yu-lien, Mayor Yin and Master K'uai, we see clearly how common human characteristics such as good looks and vanity, loyalty and devotion, and love of one's wife are exploited in the name of national expediency and the lust for power. As for Orwell, following the success of *Animal Farm*, he returned to this theme of the lust for absolute power in *Nineteen Eighty-Four* when O'Brien states boldly and unequivocally:

> The Party seeks power entirely for its own sake. We are not interested in the good of others; we are interested solely in power. Not wealth or luxury or long life or happiness; only power, pure power ... One does not establish a dictatorship in order to safeguard a revolution; one makes the revolution in order to establish the dictatorship ... The object of power is power (Orwell 1987b: 275–276).

This state of corruption is not what Old Major—or Marx—had promised before the revolution. The revolution is carried out and Mr. Jones and the capitalists are driven away, but the promised state does not materialize and soon Napoleon establishes his reign and the show trials begin. Animals are accused, confess and are 'torn to pieces' by Napoleon's dogs, and Clover, 'her eyes filled with tears,' is silent, but Orwell speaks for her: 'If she could have spoken her thoughts, it would have been to say that ... [t]hese scenes of terror and slaughter were not what they had looked forward to on that night when Old Major first stirred them to rebellion ... [T]hey had come to a time when no one dared speak his mind, when fierce, growling dogs roamed everywhere ...' (Orwell 1987a: 58).

Much like Orwell, Chen Jo-hsi, a believer in the dream of a new socialist China, left the comfort of Taiwan and America to build the workers' paradise in her 'motherland' only to witness Mao's 'growling dogs,' the Red Guards and members of the Neighborhood Committees, roaming all over China and eliminating innocent citizens by the thousands. The damage of the communist dictatorship, as presented in Orwell and Chen, is serious and severe, so much so that Raymond Williams reminds us to remember Orwell: 'not that a period had failed, but that a whole human project had been shown to be fraudulent and, in its consequences, cruel' (Williams 1974: 4). Both Orwell and Chen learned hard-won lessons from these terrifying visions and accomplished works which provide insightful critique to the core problems of communist dictatorship.[6]

NOTES

1. George Orwell, *Animal Farm: A Fairy Story* (1945) in *The Complete Works of George Orwell*, Vol. 8, London: Secker & Warburg, 1987, edited by Peter Davison, hereafter cited by page number in parenthesis.
2. Email interview with Chen, conducted in December 2014.
3. These sessions, also known as 'struggle meetings,' are reported in Fairbank as follows: 'Targets might be required to stand on a platform, heads bowed respectfully to the masses, while acknowledging and repeating their ideological crimes. Typically they had to "airplane," stretching their arms out behind them like the wings of a jet. In the audience tears of sympathy might be in a friend's eyes, but from his mouth would come only curses and derisive jeering, especially if the victim after an hour or two fell over from muscular collapse ... Some preferred suicide' (Fairbank 1986: 336).
4. According to Fairbank, between August and November 1966 Chairman Mao held six rallies which 'brought to Peking ten million Red Guards, with the logistic support of the People's Liberation Army and free rides on trains' (ibid.: 317). Fairbank also comments on the activities of the Red Guards as follows: 'Whatever may have been Mao's romantic intention, the Red Guards turned to destructive activities that have since been called hooliganism, breaking into the homes of the better-off and the intellectuals and officials, destroying books and manuscripts, humiliating, beating, and even killing the occupants, and claiming all the time to be supporting the revolutionary attack on the "Four Olds"—old ideas, culture, customs, and habits. These student youths, boys and girls both, roamed through the streets, wearing their red armbands, accosting and dealing their kind of moral justice to people with any touch of foreignism or intellectualism' (ibid.: 328). The Red Guards were abolished in mid-1968 via action by the People's Liberation Army.
5. This Mr. Whymper is a type of businessman 'represented by Armand Hammer (1898–1990), an American businessman of Russian descent who brokered business deals for both Lenin and Stalin starting in the early 1920s.' It is noted that 'Orwell may not have known of him, but Hammer provides a striking example of the go-between type represented by Mr. Whymper (Quinn 2009: 48, 51).
6. Special thanks to my colleagues Dr. Henk Vynckier, at Tunghai University, as well as Drs Patrick Henry and Mary Anne O'Neil, at Whitman College, for their input and editorial assistance.

REFERENCES

Bloom, Harold (ed.) (1999) *Modern Critical Interpretations: Animal Farm*, Philadelphia: Chelsea House.

Chen, Jo-hsi 陳若曦 (1976) Zixuanji 自選集 (*Selected Stories*), Taipei: Lianjing 聯經.

Chen, Jo-hsi (1978) *The Execution of Mayor Yin and Other Stories from the Great Proletarian Cultural Revolution*, trans. Ing, Nancy and Goldblatt, Howard, Bloomington: Indiana University Press.

Corrigan, Robert W. (ed.) (1965) *Comedy: Meaning and Form*, San Francisco: Chandler.

Dickstein, Morris (2007) *Animal Farm*: History as fable, Rodden, John (ed.) *The Cambridge Companion to George Orwell*, Cambridge: Cambridge University Press pp. 133–145.

Fairbank, John King (1986) *The Great Chinese Revolution: 1800–1985*, New York: Harper & Row.

Frye, Northrop (1970) *Anatomy of Criticism: Four Essays*, New York: Atheneum.

Greenblatt, Stephen J. (1974) Orwell as satirist, Williams, Raymond (ed.) *George Orwell: A Collection of Critical Essays*, Englewood Cliffs, NJ: Prentice-Hall pp. 103–118.

Hsia, C. T. 夏志清 (1976) Chen Jo-hsi de xiaoshuo 陳若曦的小說 (Chen Jo-hsi's Stories), Chen, Jo-hsi, Zixuanji 自選集 (*Selected Stories*), Taipei: Lianjing 聯經 pp. 1–31.

Leys, Simon (1978) Introduction, Chen, Jo-hsi, *The Execution of Mayor Yin and Other Stories from the Great Proletarian Cultural Revolution*, trans. Ing, Nancy and Goldblatt, Howard, Bloomington: Indiana University Press pp. xii–xxviii.

Orwell, George (1987a [1945]) *Animal Farm: A Fairy Story*, Davison, Peter (ed.) *The Complete Works of George Orwell*, Volume Eight, London: Secker & Warburg.

Orwell, George (1987b [1949]) *Nineteen Eighty-Four*, Davison, Peter (ed.) *The Complete Works of George Orwell*, Volume Nine, London: Secker & Warburg.

Quinn, Edward (2009) *Critical Companion to George Orwell: A Literary Reference to His Life and Work*, New York: Facts on File.

Reilly, Patrick (1999) The utopian shipwreck, Bloom, Harold (ed.) *Modern Critical Interpretations: Animal Farm*, Philadelphia: Chelsea House pp. 61–89.

Rodden, John (ed.) (2007) *The Cambridge Companion to George Orwell*, Cambridge: Cambridge University Press.

Rodden, John (2011) *George Orwell and Animal Farm on Three Continents: How 'A Fairy Tale' collided with political realities*. Abstracts and Papers for Conference on George Orwell: Asian and Global Perspectives. Taichung, Taiwan: Tunghai University pp. 6–16.

Rodden, John (ed.) (2013) *Critical Insights: George Orwell*, Ipswich, Massachusetts: Salem Press.

Rossi, John P (2013) *Animal Farm*: Beast fable, allegory, satire, Rodden, John (ed.) *Critical Insights: George Orwell*, Ipswich, Massachusetts: Salem Press pp. 151–165.

Sypher, Wylie (1965) The meanings of comedy, Corrigan, Robert W. (ed.) *Comedy: Meaning and Form*, San Francisco: Chandler pp. 18–60.

Williams, Raymond (ed.) (1974) *George Orwell: A Collection of Critical Essays*, Englewood Cliffs, NJ: Prentice-Hall.

Orwell AND THE Journalistic Imagination

CHAPTER TWELVE

George Orwell AND THE Radio Imagination

TIM CROOK

INTRODUCTION

George Orwell's literary and professional life was situated in the radio age of the twentieth century. His experience of the media was an everyday world in which radio was the dominant mass medium of electronic communication. His death in 1950 marked the year when television's competition for audiences and power was intensifying to a tipping point of overtaking radio.

Orwell was connected through his literary and cultural reviewing and criticism with the world of broadcasting at a period when important experiments were being conducted in sound drama and documentary in terms of their political, social and cultural content and aesthetically. Recorded and synthesized sound blended the margins of factual and fictional representation. Orwell may well have been a regular listener to plays and features when he returned to stay with his parents in Southwold, Suffolk, in the late 1920s after resigning from the Indian Imperial Police in Burma. By this time the BBC had become a corporation and developed the ability to broadcast nationally and regionally. Moreover, his diary gives brief references to hearing dramatic news of Britain's involvement in the Second World War on the radio in public places. He had a battery-powered radio set of his own after the war (Davison 2011).

As a prolific reviewer of the cultural scene, it is possible to imagine him embracing the new medium and enthusiastically listening to modernist commentators such as Harold Nicholson and feature program-makers such as Archie Harding, Lance Sieveking, D. G. Bridson and Olive Shapley. This was a time for avant-garde microphone play experiments by Lance Sieveking (1934) and sound operas and verse plays by Ezra Pound and T. S. Eliot (Fisher 2002; Frattarola 2009).

This chapter argues that Orwell was radiophonic in his writing. There was a style of documentary vision in his prose writing that evoked the sound perspective of radio broadcasting. Indeed, there is a distinct drama-documentary style of prose in books such as *Down and Out in Paris and London* (1933), *The Road to Wigan Pier* (1937) and *Homage to Catalonia* (1938). The first part of Chapter Three of his 1935 novel *A Clergyman's Daughter* reads like a transcript of the 1934 BBC Manchester feature *'Opping 'Oliday*. Both the chapter and the radio feature deal with the now-lost sub-culture of casual hop-pickers traveling to Kent in the late summer. The BBC program was the first documentary feature to use a recording van. The microphone was thus taken out of the studio to record people directly on location.

This 'sonic realism' appears in a considerable amount of Orwell's writing. I think it also accounts for the longstanding success of the adaptation and production of his novels and documentary journalism on BBC radio since the early 1940s. The very fact he joined the BBC as a producer and worked intensively, writing and making programs for two years between 1941 and 1943, means that he was fully professionalized and immersed in a creative public broadcasting institution. Orwell became an expert in making radio for news, editorial propagandizing, and education through entertaining sound dramatization and cultural discussion. It was the equivalent of devising a multimedia syllabus for an Open University of the Air.

Thus, it is crucial to acknowledge the significance of Orwell's completion of a two-week BBC induction training course headed by the former head of feature documentaries at BBC Manchester, Archie Harding, and including on the training staff Felix Felton, the assistant producer of *'Opping 'Oliday* and future author of *The Radio Play* (1949) (Orwell 1998, Vol. 13: 5–9). In this way, Orwell became part of a critical and creative sound program tradition that pioneered and fostered radiophonic and audiogenic story telling.

Four significant legacies emerged out of his full-time broadcasting work during those two years. His direct experience and professional toil at writing talks, documentaries, features and drama for the sound medium amounted to a manifesto for impartial radio and broadcasting news. I argue that the seminal essay 'Politics and the English Language' (1946) arises out of his BBC experience. It is the exposition of a radio journalism communicator.

A second legacy is a creative sensibility about the importance of poetry and radio. Orwell was the first BBC producer to enable T. S. Eliot to read his poetry live on the radio. His essay 'Poetry and the Microphone' (1945) is confirmation of how powerful the radiogenic qualities of sound broadcasting can be for what Eliot defined as the 'auditory imagination.' A third legacy is Orwell's significance as a radio dramatizer, sound playwright and critic of the genre. He would write his own dramatization of *Animal Farm* (1947) that would be produced by BBC Radio several times—most recently in a George Orwell season on BBC Radio 4 in 2013. This dimension of Orwell's exploration of the radio imagination will be addressed by a critical analysis of his adaptation of 'A Slip Under the Microscope,' by H. G. Wells (1943).

This is connected to the fourth legacy. Orwell's undoubted genius as an essay-ist for newspapers and periodicals transferred powerfully to the radio medium as a commentator. Today, the radio commentary retains its intrinsic genre on BBC Radio 3 with fifteen-minute talks called *The Essay* and on BBC Radio 4 and World Service through the iconic series *From Our Own Correspondent*. This pro-vides a platform for foreign correspondents to give background, interpretation and original perspectives on the news stories of the day.

THE RADIOPHONIC *CLERGYMAN'S DAUGHTER*

A Clergyman's Daughter is sometimes described as 'the most adversely criticized of all Orwell's books' (Lee 1969: 23). It was written in 1934 for publication in 1935. Orwell conceded it had a weak ending and he did not want it republished while he was alive. It was subject to considerable censorship in relation to libel and inde-cency. It incorporated a severe denunciation of private education and his publisher, Victor Gollancz, had had to defend libel writs for a previous work of fiction about a school in Kensington (Orwell 1998, Vol. 3: 303–307).

Consequently, it was not clear in the first edition that the reason for the loss of memory by the central character, Dorothy Hare, had been an attempt to rape her. However, Dorothy's entry into the world of down-and-outs in Trafalgar Square and her experiences in the hop fields of Kent are acknowledged by most critics as an example of Orwell's most experimental writing: 'In its use of stream-of-conscious-ness and surrealism, the scene is reminiscent of the Circe episode in Joyce's *Ulysses*' (Lee 1969: 40). Lee argues that the novel's supposed failure 'is usually attributed to its so-called documentary interpolations and its episodic structure' (ibid.: 23). I would argue that this is one of its strengths as innovative radiophonic literature.

It does read as a modernist montage of voices, with a sort of 'literary camera' taking shots of the general scene as in: 'Trafalgar Square. Dimly visible through the mist, a dozen people, Dorothy among them, are grouped about one of the benches near the north parapet' (Orwell 1998, Vol 3: 151) then moving on to the use of the close microphone recording the voices of individual characters singing and talking:

Mr. *Tallboys* (to himself): '*Non sum qualis eram boni sub regno Edwardi*! In the days of my innocence, before the Devil carried me up into a high place

and dropped me into the Sunday newspapers—that is to say
when I was Rector of Little Fawley-cum-Dewsbury ...'

Deafie (singing): 'With my willy, willy, *with* my willy willy ...' (ibid.).

This has all the hallmarks of a post-World War Two Theatre Workshop drama
script developed through social immersion and observation, and the transcription
of improvization by actors. Of course, Orwell's ear and appreciation for the language of this sub-culture as well as the realism of its social reality had been honed
by direct experience. Being down-and-out with the hop-pickers of London and
Kent was the subject of his 1931 diary documentary essay 'Hop-picking.' Scannell
describes it as abrasive. 'While making it clear that the hop pickers had a good
time, the diary brings out the stringent rules imposed by the farmers, their sharp
practices at weighing, and the tactics of the pickers to get fair measure' (Scannell
and Cardiff 1991: 396).

The diary also forms a sort of documentary basis for the novel. His entry for
26 August 1931 hints at how he would later use his aural memory to provide the
foundation for the continuous stream of consciousness sequence of writing in *A
Clergyman's Daughter*:

> The next day I went to Trafalgar Square and camped by the north wall, which is one of the
> recognized rendezvous of down-and-out people in London. At this time of year the square
> has a floating population of 100 to 200 people (about ten per cent of them women), some
> of whom actually look on it as their home (Orwell 1998, Vol. 10: 215).

Orwell's third novel is also a biting satire and attack on the shabby ethics of the
popular Sunday press and its pre-occupation with exposing the sexual hypocrisy
of vicars for his characterization of Mr. Tallboys recognizes the abuse of children:

Mr. Tallboys (to himself): My curate days, my curate days! My fancywork bazaars and
morris dances in-aid-of on the village green, my lectures to
the Mothers' Union—missionary work in Western China
with fourteen magic lantern slides! My Boys' Cricket Club,
teetollers only, my confirmation classes—purity lecture once
monthly in the Parish Hall—my Boy Scout orgies! The
Wolf Cubs will deliver the Grand Howl. Household Hints
for the Parish Magazine, 'Discarded fountain-pen fillers can
be used as enemas for canaries ...' (1998, Vol. 3: 165).

The radio documentary feature movement at the BBC in the early 1930s was
inspired by developments in film. BBC producer Laurence Gilliam sought to imi-
tate the documentary film technique by hiring mobile sound-recording vans. In
the summer of 1934, at the same time Orwell was writing *A Clergyman's Daughter*,
he hired an outside recording vehicle from HMV and made 'the first radio feature

using actuality sound recordings taken on location' (Felton 1949: 99; Scannell and Cardiff 1991: 147). Coincidentally, this incorporated a 'sound picture' of East Enders, and quite possibly some down-and-outs harvesting the hop crop in the Kent fields. '*Opping 'Oliday* was broadcast on 15 September 1934 on the London Regional service. Rather like Orwell's novel, it switched between studio narration and what were coined at the time as 'microphone snap-shots.' It ended with an outside broadcast link-up for a sing-song from a Kent ale-house with the hop-pickers warbling their delight at finishing their end of summer casual and back-breaking work. Scannell says:

> This was the first broadcast programme to realise that populist impulse at the heart of doc-umentary which allows people to speak for themselves. No longer are they merely described by another in a studio talk, or else read a scripted talk from the studio in which they express the viewpoint of 'ordinary person.' Now they speak from their own everyday environment, and produce impromptu talk, via an interview, for the microphone. Broadcasting has gone out into everyday life to capture 'the essence' of that reality as lived by those who speak of it in order to re-present this experience to listeners (ibid.).

Orwell was doing the same in his novel though the language of his fictional char-acters was replete with the dimension of expletives and realistic communication the BBC would not be able to broadcast in the present day. The 1934 BBC radio feature included no de-frocked ecclesiastical paedophiles. Nor were there any encounters with disoriented middle-class women whose memory of attempted rape had also erased their bearings and sense of identity. But the program did relate to Orwell's iconoclastic description of the hop pickers' hardships. It included testimony from an unemployed clerk who worked as a checker/weigh-man and was advised to flee the district by the local police (ibid.: 396–397).

A Clergyman's Daughter may have been intended to reveal other aspects of the underground nature of British society. In his 1931 'Hop picking' diary, Orwell had recorded that Charing Cross Underground station was a great rendezvous for 'homosexual vice in London:'

> It appeared to be taken for granted by the people on Trafalgar Square that youths could earn a bit this way, and several said to me, 'I need never sleep out if I choose to go down to Charing Cross.' They added that the usual fee is a shilling (Orwell 1998, Vol. 1: 96–97).

This was certainly an aspect of Orwell's direct observation that could not be rep-resented in his novel nor any radio program broadcast by the BBC at that time. '*Opping 'Oliday* was designed primarily as its *Radio Times* billings explained: 'An Excursion in Sound to the Hop Gardens of Kent,' including 'sound pictures of work in the hop gardens, and a sing-song celebrating the end of the picking from a village inn in Kent,' and 'a recorded sound picture' of "Arry, 'Arriet, and their families taking themselves off from London's East End for the hopping season' (*Radio Times* 1934, 1937 and 1939).

Despite being regarded as Orwell's weakest novel in terms of plot and characterization, with Orwell himself doing his best to buy up unsold copies in the late 1930s (Lee 1969: 23), the BBC was to recognize its merits as a source of radio story-telling and full sound dramatization. In 1988 it was abridged for *A Book at Bedtime* in ten, fifteen-minute episodes read by the actor George Baker. The abridgement continued to avoid explicit representation of the 'incident' that caused her to leave the shelter of her home, but it is significant that Graham Gauld, the producer of the spoken word representation, focused on 'her progress after that, through the England of the 30s' giving 'George Orwell an opportunity for one of his earliest pieces of social reportage' (*Radio Times* 1988).

Four years later, BBC Radio 4 commissioned an original 90-minute dramatization of the novel in the 'Monday Play' strand. It was produced in stereo by one of the Radio Drama department's in-house young women directors, Celia De Wolff, from a script by John Peacock. It was billed as 'George Orwell's novel about the scandal which rocked a small town when, following an encounter with an elderly free thinker, the clergyman's daughter suddenly disappeared' (*Radio Times* 1992). It was repeated in 1993.

BBC TRAINED AND INSPIRED

George Orwell's witty observations about his self-styled two wasted years at the BBC are often quoted:

> Its atmosphere is something halfway between a girls' school and a lunatic asylum and all we are doing at present is useless, or slightly worse than useless. Our radio strategy is even more hopeless than our military strategy (Orwell 2009: 322).

However, in those two years Orwell produced hundreds of disciplined talk, documentary and creative drama scripts specifically for the sound medium and William J. West argued in 1985 that the two years he spent as a Talks Producer in the Indian Section of the BBC's Eastern Service from August 1941 until November 1943 are the key to his 'evolution from the slightly pedantic and unpolished author of pre-war days' (West 1985: 13). West was emphatic that it was far from the case that these were lost years for Orwell the writer. Orwell's own creative writing continued while at the BBC, and he applied a prodigious force of hard work to achieving something of great cultural value:

> ... nothing less than the setting up of what was in effect a 'university of the air' for students of the Punjab and other Indian universities, coupled with weekly news broadcasts that enabled educated Indians generally to follow the progress of the war around the world (ibid.).

West distilled his view and archival script evidence of the significance of Orwell's BBC years in two edited volumes published in the 1985 *Orwell: The War Broadcasts* and *Orwell: The War Commentaries*. Previously he had contributed to a BBC Radio 4 documentary 'George Orwell at the BBC,' broadcast on 9 October 1984 and produced by Angela Hind. This program argued that Orwell's job as Talks Producer 'was to influence his life and help him become one of the best-known writers of the 20th century' (*Radio Times* 1984). Moreover, on his two years—in Room 101—at the BBC, the editor of Orwell's *Collected Works*, Professor Peter Davison, argues: 'Indeed, given the circumstances his achievements were formidable and had long-term benefits for the institution and those who tuned in to it long after he was dead' (Davison 2011). Certainly, Orwell elevated colonial and proto-postcolonial writers such as Una Marson, Mulk Raj Anand, Balraj Sahni and his wife, Damyanti, to cultural importance when he was a producer in a complex propaganda effort to bring onside young intellectuals in India and elsewhere in the Empire.

The key to Orwell's broadcasting career may well lie in the two-week induction training course he undertook at Bedford College, University of London, in Regent's Park. The course director was the 'guru' of the left-wing radio documentary movement at BBC Manchester in the 1930s, Archie Harding. In the early 1930s he was embroiled in censorship rows and political controversies and according to his protégé, D. G. Bridson, was banished by John Reith to Manchester as Program Director, North Region, with the memorable words: 'You're a very dangerous man, Harding. I think you'd be better up North where you can't do so much damage' (Bridson 1971: 22). It would seem Harding continued his mischief quite happily in Manchester. He headed a department that commissioned two radio plays from Bridson, *Prometheus: A Tragedy of His Ransom and New Power*, in 1934, and *Scourge*, in 1935, which were pulled from transmission in the middle of rehearsals after being billed in the *Radio Times* due to concerns about political controversy and issues of indecency (ibid.: 40, 46–47). He was at the helm when Joan Littlewood teamed up with Olive Shapley in 1939 to produce *The Classic Soil*, a powerful Marxist denunciation of housing conditions for the working class in Manchester. It had the political spirit, iconoclasm, and agitational attitude of Orwell's investigation of the Lancashire coal mines in *The Road to Wigan Pier* (1937). Shapley reflected in later life it was:

> ... probably the most unfair and biased programme ever put out by the BBC. We called it, with a nod to Engels, *The Classic Soil*. Engels had described Manchester as 'the classic soil ... where capitalism flourished.' By recording much of the programme in Salford flea market among an odd little group of families who lived in a condemned warehouse in Pollard Street, we proved to our satisfaction and everyone else's intense annoyance that basically Manchester was unchanged since Engels wrote his famous denunciation of the city in 1844 (Shapley 1996: 54).

One of the staff trainers was Felix Felton who had been assistant to Laurence Gilliam on the Kent hop-picking program of 1934. Orwell was surrounded and nurtured by an agitational and creative culture that accommodated him like a glove made for a prince. One of his fellow trainees was Douglas Cleverdon who would go on to be one of the BBC's most innovative radio feature and drama directors of the 1950s and 60s and was responsible for commissioning and producing *Under Milk Wood* (1954) by Dylan Thomas. Orwell and Cleverdon were in direct contact with Harding and Felton and, as part of their training, had to work on model scripts in order to learn the process of feature research, narrative and production. These scripts included *Dr. Johnson Takes It* by the poet and producer Louis MacNeice and *Arctic Excursion* by the Director of Staff Training himself Archie Harding (Orwell 1998, Vol. 13: 5–9).

The poet and scholar William Empson was another trainee who had, unfairly, condemned it as 'a liar's course' (ibid.). But the course schedule and many of the papers and resources used and annotated by Orwell have survived and been archived at University College London. The documents show that most of the training was concentrated on the art of producing dramatic and documentary radio programs with guidance and inspiration from the leading radio professionals of their day. Felix Felton would consolidate and publish his producing and program-making philosophy in *The Radio Play*, in 1949. On the basis of the course of instruction Orwell took part in, it is very likely he had an opportunity to hear Felton's sophisticated ideas on the use of 'actuality' and location sound recordings (Felton 1949: 103). For Felton advocated a range of narrative and dramatic structuring techniques for documentary that included latent dramatic conflict and musical 'rondo form.' He explained latent dramatic conflict in relation to a program he made on how the Post Office transported a postcard from Euston to the Orkneys:

> Here and there I brought the conflict to the surface by putting the signals against the mail-train, or by giving the pilot some uncomfortable weather; but I did not develop it to such a pitch of intensity that the aeroplane nearly crashed, or the postcard's arrival just averted a human catastrophe (ibid.: 104).

Felton used musical ideas and rhythms to pattern and counter-point his script. The construction of the 'rondo form' was achieved by:

> A principal tune 'A,' followed by another tune 'B.' 'A' is then repeated; then comes a third tune 'C;' then 'A' again; then a fourth tune 'D,' and so on (ibid.).

It is clear that during the first two weeks of his time in the BBC program-making culture rather than bureaucracy, Orwell was engaging with a vast range of narrative and story-telling ideas, concepts and techniques that may well account for the sharpening of narrative and dramatic focus in his two last and most successful novels *Animal Farm* (1945) and *Nineteen Eighty-Four* (1949).

RADIO LANGUAGE AND POETRY

It is perhaps no coincidence that Orwell's two years of toil, industry and creativity at the BBC were followed by the writing of two seminal essays that have had such a powerful influence on radio journalistic writing and the presentation and communication of poetry on the radio. 'Politics and the English Language,' which first published in *Horizon* in April 1946, underpins the professional ethic of impartial, clear, and unpretentious writing in radio news. I believe the stripped down, cautious and spoken word style of broadcasting English reverberated with Orwell's desire to resist the propagandizing and politicization of English communication.

His enduring struggle against academic gobbledygook and determination to fight staleness of imagery and lack of precision is the stalwart aim of anybody writing scripts in spoken English style for the radio. His criticism of a quotation from Professor Harold Laski's essay in *Freedom of Expression* was exquisitely ironic as Laski's constipated expression undermined his purpose in writing it in the first place (Orwell 1998, Vol. 17: 422). Again it is no coincidence that good broadcasting writers avoid 'dying metaphors,' 'verbal false limbs,' 'pretentious diction,' 'meaningless words,' and phrases and unnecessary expressions in foreign languages. As Orwell said, these 'perversions and swindles' debase the language (ibid.: 425).

Orwell's aphorism 'But if thought corrupts language, language can also corrupt thought' is the kind of professional homily present in journalism writing books the world over (ibid.: 428). Orwell's writing six rules that he thought would 'cover most cases' can be extrapolated from, for example, the *BBC's News Styleguide* of 2003 by John Allen:

1. Never use a metaphor, simile or other figure of speech which you are used to seeing in print.
2. Never use a long word where a short one will do.
3. If it is possible to cut a word out, always cut it out.
4. Never use the passive where you can use the active.
5. Never use a foreign phrase, a scientific word or a jargon if you can think of an everyday English equivalent.
6. Break any of these rules sooner than say anything outright barbarous (Orwell 1998, Vol. 17: 430).

Points 1. 3. and 5. are covered in Allen's sections on 'troublesome words,' 'vogue words,' and 'superfluous words and phrases' (Allen 2003: 68–77). They are also clearly referenced in the pages on 'foreign phrases' and 'jargon' (ibid.: 47–50). Point 2. is covered by Allen's page on 'simple words.' (ibid.: 67). No. 4. is covered in the section on 'active and passive' (ibid.: 17–18). On page 23 of the BBC guide, Orwell, its former Eastern Service talks producer, is given pride of place in a quotation on clichés and journalese: 'By using stale metaphors, similes and idioms, you save much mental effort, at the cost of leaving your meaning vague, not only for your reader but yourself' (ibid.: 23). This section is one of the longest in the booklet running to eight pages. In 2003, it could be argued that the BBC's then-Director of News, Richard Sambrook, was conscious of Orwell's rule 4 when he wrote 'Clear story-telling and language is at the heart of good journalism' (ibid.: 3).

Davison argues convincingly in the *Collected Works* that Orwell's seminal essay 'Poetry and the Microphone,' first published in *The New Saxon Pamphlet* in March 1945, was probably written while he was still at the BBC producing the discursive and spoken word-based poetry program strand called *Voice* (Orwell 1998, Vol. 17: 74–80). This was an essay almost evangelical about widening the cultural appeal of poetry by having poets communicate their poems to 'an audience of *one*. Millions may be listening, but each is listening alone, or as a member of a small group, and each has (or ought to have) the feeling that you are speaking to him individually' (ibid.: 76–77). Orwell expresses a fundamental understanding of the radio imagination in this passage.

Orwell's writing and producing of fluid and conversational poetry programs to listeners in the Far East challenged his delightfully expressed metaphor 'Poetry on the air sounds like the Muses in striped trousers' (ibid.: 79). In the sixth *Voice* program, he managed to persuade T. S. Eliot to speak his verse to the microphone for the first time. It is a bizarre irony that the recording of a part of his 43-line poem 'Journey of the Magi' (1927) has survived, but not one recorded word of Orwell himself exists to connect his voice with our radio imaginations.

Orwell's thoughts on poetry and radio endure in the present age of broadcasting where poets still find a happy home in the audio medium which has dispersed exponentially online through podcasting. In 1949, Milton Allen Kaplan published the seminal US text *Radio and Poetry*, published by Columbia University Press. His vision of the future role of poetry in broadcasting would chime precisely with that of Orwell's 1945 essay:

> The fact that the radio is mentioned very often in connection with popular poetry is not accidental. Folk poetry is oral poetry. The rise of the radio verse drama is a happy portent that poetry will be presented once more to the public in a form which it can understand and appreciate. It would seem, therefore, that there is a great future for poetry on the radio, a public poetry that is simple, direct, and clear (Kaplan 1949: 255).

THE AUDIOGENIC DRAMATIST?

It is interesting to examine Orwell's review of the BBC's prestigious production and script publication of Edward Sackville-West's *The Rescue* (Orwell, *Observer*

1945). Orwell was interested in how the Homeric source had been dramatized rather than narrated:

> ... radio has made it possible to revive the soliloquy (no longer tolerable on the realistic stage) and to play tricks with space and time which would be difficult even in a film. On the other hand, the difficulty, in any broadcast involving more than two or three voices, of making the listener understand what is happening where, and who is speaking to whom, has not been fully overcome. It is usually done by means of a Narrator, who ruins the dramatic effect, or by making the characters drop explanatory remarks, which are likely to hold up the action and have to be managed very skillfully if they are to be convincing (ibid.)

Orwell's analysis of *The Rescue* in 1945 is that of an experienced radio writer and former producer who, on reading a script, could quickly spot 'one fact which the microphone brings out is that some stories are much more visual than others.' He argued that the scene in which Odysseus shoots down the suitors with his bow could not be adequately presented unless it took place 'off' the dramatic sound stage (ibid.). Orwell's political antennae were also wise to what he saw as the pervasion of 'official propaganda' through the parallel of Ithaca being occupied by the suitors and Greece occupied by the Germans (ibid.).

Wrigley has analyzed the radiophonic significance of the BBC's production of *The Rescue* as a literary and musical compositional collaboration between Sackville-West and Benjamin Britten: 'The close association of words and music also suggests a reflective awareness of the affinity of radio with the ancient performance of Homeric poetry, whilst encouraging a deep level of interpretative understanding on the part of the radio audience' (Wrigley 2010: 102). Orwell's critical approach and artistic exploration of radio play dramatization rather prioritizes the literary and dramatic rather than musical and sound philosophical point of view.

George Orwell's novels are not normally considered 'modernist,' though he was contemporary with James Joyce, T. S. Eliot, Ezra Pound, and Virginia Woolf, and an active reviewer of their work. Indeed, works by Eliot and Pound were dramatized and broadcast by the BBC in an identifiable modernist tradition of microphone play as explored cogently by Fisher (2002) Frattarola (2009) and Freer (2007). Huwiler has even sought, from a Dutch/German perspective, to theorize radio drama as 'an acoustic art form in its own right' and posit 'a methodology based on semiotic and narratological theories that enables scholars to analyse a narrative radio play by integrating all of its acoustic features' (Huwiler 2005). Accordingly, the sound texts of Orwell's dramatized fiction and non-fiction can be evaluated with an emphasis on 'music, noises and voices and also technical features like electro-acoustical manipulation or mixing' (ibid.). These are useful critical tools to 'signify story elements' (ibid.).

However, Huwiler was not the first academic, practitioner and critic to engage with this methodology though it summarizes and adopts a convincing line and direction of audio-dramatic criticism that is clearly independent and separate from literary studies. She references mainly continental sources in her bibliography though Arnheim (1936) had an impact and influence through the English translation by Herbert Read that was published by Faber and Faber in London. Huwiler enthusiastically and most interestingly engages with the issues of audio dramatization in 2010. She pursues her quest to diverge and cut loose from literary narratology, arguing that 'the positioning of signals within the acoustic space is not a feature with a fixed narrative function, either. Although throughout the history of radio drama production it has been used primarily to indicate the spatial positions of characters in a realistically represented setting, ... it can be used in a much more varied way' (Huwiler 2010: 138). She continues: 'In recent works about English-speaking radio drama, the art form is still being called a literary genre: For Tim Crook it is "one of the most unappreciated and understated literary forms of the twentieth century" (Crook 1999: 3), and Dermot Rattigan calls it "an aural literature" (Rattigan 2002: 3)' (Huwiler 2010: 131). Her conclusion argues convincingly for a separate disciplinary approach to the study of the sound text (as applied here to Orwell's works). Sound drama has its own semiotics, cultural and aesthetic characteristics:

> Regardless of the extent in which language is used in an adapted radio piece, it is never simply a literary work orally told, but always an artistic work in its own right, working with much more varied medial features than only language and creating a story world with its own intrinsic features of the auditive medium (ibid.: 139).

Stanton to some extent anticipated Huwiler in arguing that the art of the audio storyteller rather than the sound playwright moves beyond the words on a page which 'can give only an oblique or partial sense of the play in performance' (Stanton 2002: 105) though this is true of all dramatic texts and musical scores. Stanton went on to stress that the audio play does have an additional radical power:

> ... a radio play—invisible yet aural, allusive, affective—seems to work like a memory trace, possibly like a dream. Its text, borne on multi-layered aurality, effracts the barriers of perception and the unconscious and irrupts into words, into consciousness, where it engages our senses, memories, intellect and emotions. No one is present: neither actors nor audience. The radio play writes us, its auditors, just as it is written—not by the invisible author, but by the interaction of the voices of actors who have already disappeared and sounds that play across and within our memories (ibid.).

All this ties in with Clive Cazeaux's exploration of the phenomenology of audio/radio drama. Sound operates as an aesthetic metaphor that can be perceptually independent of sight reading:

> Sound, instead of being a series of inadequate clues from an unlit world, becomes a medium that opens onto and generates a world and, as a part of this world-generation,

enjoys interaction and conjunction with the other senses. And in manipulating sound to create a world, certain correspondences and tensions will be employed which, from a phenomenological point of view, are among the defining, structural characteristics of expression in art, whatever the medium. This 'whatever the medium' does not reduce all art forms, with their particularities, to a lowest common denominator, but merely reaffirms that the medium of an artwork, be it paint, film, language, or sound, is something that reaches out beyond its own constitution to participate in the invitational relationships at work in perception at large (Cazeaux 2005: 174).

An examination of Orwell's dramatizations while a staff producer and subsequently a successful novelist does not reveal any propensity on his part to experiment with sound and voice consciousness as he did in his novel *The Clergyman's Daughter*. For example his adaptation of the H. G. Wells short story 'A Slip Under the Microscope,' produced by Douglas Cleverdon and broadcast on the Eastern Service 6 October 1943, has an orthodox exposition of traditional narrator and dialogue through characterization (Orwell 1998, Vol. 15: 256–265). The narrative voice is deployed as a lens for the listener and indirect focus for a character's thoughts and feelings:

Wedderburn:	Nobody has read Karl Marx, my dear fellow. He is unreadable. *(Laughter)*
Narrator:	Hill was no good at this kind of conversation, and he knew it. It seemed to him cheap, unfair, and connected in some subtle way with Wedderburn's well-cut clothes, manicured hands and generally sleek and monied exterior.
Hill:	He's got such a mean, sneering way of talking. He never really argues, only tries to raise a laugh. How I wish he'd come to the Debating Society one night! Then I'd smash him.

Orwell was a radio dramatist who preferred to write with clarity rather than play with his listener's cognitive perception. The potential for experimentation with *Animal Farm* must have been great. The allegorical theme combined with the bitter-sweet comedy of a farmer being deposed by his animals who then turn on themselves has a sound tapestry that could extend beyond the binary code of an all-seeing narrative voice switching to and fro with dramatic dialogue and action. Orwell played safe with the narrative convention when adapting his best seller for the BBC in 1946–1947. He thus preserved the integrity of voice and style of the original book in the same way he had with the prose of H. G. Wells's short story.

Bott writes that Orwell was an avid reader of Wells from the age of fifteen and the 'influence of Wells was particularly strong and remained to shape even his last two books' (1969: 5). Yet by the time Orwell worked on 'A slip Under the Microscope' they had become estranged in a bitter row over Orwell's critical writings in *Horizon*, on the BBC and in the *Listener*. Inez Holden described in detail how Orwell's written observation in early 1942 that Wells was 'a shallow inadequate thinker' in his interpretation of the threat posed by the Nazis was countered by Wells's face-to-face verbal insult of Orwell that he was 'a defeatist' (Holden 1972: 244). There had been a temporary reconciliation. But Orwell's broadcast of his BBC talk 'The Re-discovery of Europe: Literature Between the Wars,' with most of the script appearing in the *Listener* in March 1942, drew the public rebuke from Wells that Orwell had been guilty of 'foolish generalizations' about his views on science and mankind (Orwell 1998, Vol. 13: 209–218). In private, Wells penciled a note to Orwell saying: 'Read my early works, you shit' (Holden op. cit.).

Orwell succeeded in separating his admiration for Wells as a writer of fiction whose prose required professional adaptation faithful to the original text with his critical and polemical role as a public intellectual fully aware that 'flattery is no part the job of a literary critic' (Orwell 1998, Vol. 13: 219).

CONCLUSION

George Orwell's adult writing career coincided with the beginnings and development of radio as a powerful and aesthetically pioneering medium for drama and documentary. In his reception of the developing story-telling form in the context of modernist ideas I believe there was a radiophonic and audiogenic influence on his writing imagination that is evident in *A Clergyman's Daughter*. His active and participant role in the radio medium as a professional producer and auteur accelerated his appreciation and expression of sound story-telling to the individual listener. Orwell's experience at the BBC was the source of an evolution in his imaginative understanding of the poetical and political potential of story-telling that informed the allegorical *Animal Farm* and dystopian *Nineteen Eighty-Four*. Broadcast writing and production heightened his literary discipline. He was able to focus on an economy and precision of language.

Far from being a bureaucratic grind of exhaustion and disillusionment, Orwell's experiences at the BBC were predominantly a process of positive creativity and cultural enlightenment both for himself and his audience. The contrasting roles of scripting both factual and fictional programming for the radio served a writer who had the mind of a robust and independent public intellectual and the feelings of the common person. There is nothing particularly illogical in saying Orwell has helped make the BBC as the BBC helped make Orwell. For it was on a BBC Radio program in 1955 that Richard Peters described Orwell as the 'lonely, courageous figure passing with detached honesty and without rancour across the mudbanks of corruption' (*Radio Times* 1955).

REFERENCES

Allen, John (2003) *The BBC News Styleguide*, London: BBC.

Arnheim, Rudolf (1936) *Radio*, trans. Luding, M. and Read, Herbert, London: Faber and Faber.

Bott, George, (1969) *George Orwell: Selected Writings*, London: Heinemann Educational.

Bridson, D. G. (1971) *Prospero and Ariel: The Rise and Fall of Radio, A Personal Recollection*, London: Victor Gollancz Ltd.

Cazeaux, Clive (2005) Phenomenology and radio drama, *British Journal of Aesthetics*, Vol. 45, No. 2, April pp. 157–174.

Crook, Tim (1999) *Radio Drama: Theory & Practice*, London and New York: Routledge.

Crook, Tim (2004) Drama worldwide: Varied traditions of radio narrative, Sterling, Christopher H. (ed.) Chicago Museum of Communications, *Encyclopedia of Radio, Vol. 1*, New York: Taylor and Francis pp. 497–501.

Crook, Tim (2011) *The Sound Handbook*, London and New York: Routledge.

Crook, Tim (2012) George Orwell: Cold War warrior? *Orwell Today*, Keeble, Richard Lance (ed.) Bury St. Edmunds, Suffolk: Abramis Publishing pp. 102–122.

Davison, Peter, (2011) Two wasted years?, March. Available online at http://www.orwellsociety.com/2011/11/22/orwell-at-the-bbc-two-wasted-years-by-prof-peter-davison/, accessed on 4 June 2012.

Esslin, Martin (1987) *The Field of Drama: How the Signs of Drama Create Meaning on Stage and Screen*, London: Methuen.

Felton, Felix (1949) *The Radio Play: Its Technique and Possibilities*, London: Sylvan Press.

Fisher, Margaret (2002) *Ezra Pound's Radio Operas: The BBC Experiments, 1931–1933*, Cambridge; Massachusetts and London: The MIT Press.

Frattarola, Angela (2009) The modernist 'microphone play': Listening in the dark to the BBC, *Modern Drama*, Winter, Vol. 52, No. 4, pp. 449–468.

Freer, Scott (2007) The mythical method: Eliot's 'The Waste Land' and *A Canterbury Tale*, *Historical Journal of Film, Radio and Television*, August, Vol. 27, No. 3, pp. 357–370.

Guthrie, Tyrone (1931) *'Squirrel's Cage' and Other Microphone Plays*, London: Cobden and Sanderson, incorporating the scripts *Squirrel's Cage*, *Matrimonial News*, & *The Flowers Are Not for You to Pick*.

Guthrie, Tyrone (1934) Radio drama, *BBC Annual 1935*, London: BBC.

Hand, Richard J. and Traynor, Mary (2011) *Radio Drama Handbook: Audio Drama in Context and Practice (Audio Drama in Practice and Context)*, New York and London: Continuum.

Holden, Inez (1972) Orwell or Wells? Letters to the editor, *Listener*, 24 February.

Huwiler, Elke (2005) Storytelling by sound: A theoretical frame for radio drama analysis, *The Radio Journal—International Studies in Broadcast and Audio Media*, Vol. 3, No. 1, pp. 45–59.

Huwiler, Elke, (2010) Radio drama adaptations: An approach towards an analytical methodology, *Journal of Adaptation in Film & Performance*, Vol. 3, No. 2, pp. 129–140.

Kaplan, Milton Allen (1949) *Radio and Poetry*, New York: Columbia University Press.

Keeble, Richard Lance (ed.) (2012) *Orwell Today*, Bury St. Edmunds, Suffolk: Abramis Publishing.

Lea, Gordon (1926) *Radio Drama and How To Write It*, London: George Allen & Unwin Ltd.

Lee, Robert A. (1969) *Orwell's Fiction*, London: University of Notre Dame Press.

Orwell, George (1945) In fields of air, *Observer*, 5 August 1945.

Orwell, George (1975) *The Collected Essays, Journalism and Letters of George Orwell, Volume 1, An Age Like This 1920–1940*, edited by Orwell, Sonia and Angus, Ian, Harmondsworth: Penguin.

Orwell, George (1998) *The Collected Works, Vols. 3, 10, 13, 14, 17, 18,* edited by Davison, Peter, London: Secker & Warburg.

Orwell, George (2009) *Diaries,* edited by Davison, Peter, London: Penguin.

Radio Times (1923–2009) Programme billings. Available online at http://genome.ch.bbc.co.uk/, accessed on 5 January 2015.

Rattigan, Dermot (2001) *Theatre of Sound: Radio and the Dramatic Imagination,* Dublin: Carysfort Press.

Sackville-West, Edward (1945) *The Rescue: A Melodrama for Broadcasting Based on Homer's* Odyssey, London: Secker and Warburg.

Scannell, Paddy and Cardiff, David (1991) *A Social History of British Broadcasting: 1922–1939,* London: Wiley.

Shapley, Olive (1996) *Broadcasting a Life: The Autobiography of Olive Shapley,* London: The Scarlet Press, in association with Christina Hart.

Sieveking, Lance (1934) *The Stuff of Radio,* London: Cassell.

Stanton, William (2004) The invisible theatre of radio drama, *Critical Quarterly,* December, Vol. 46, No. 4, pp. 94–107.

West, William J. (1985) *Orwell: The War Broadcasts,* London: Duckworth/BBC.

West, William J. (1985) *Orwell: The War Commentaries,* London: Duckworth/BBC.

Williams, Raymond (1971) *Orwell,* London: Fontana.

Wrigley, Amanda (2010) A wartime radio *Odyssey:* Edward Sackville-West and Benjamin Britten's *The Rescue* (1943), *The Radio Journal: International Studies in Broadcast and Audio Media,* Vol. 8, No. 2, pp. 81–103.

RADIO PROGRAMS

A Clergyman's Daughter, BBC Radio 4, *A Book At Bedtime,* 11 April 1988.

A Clergyman's Daughter, BBC Radio 4, *The Monday Play,* 9 March 1992 and 22 March 1993.

George Orwell at the BBC, BBC Radio 4, 9 October 1984.

The 'Opping 'Oliday', London Regional, 15 September 1934, 15 September 1937, 15 August, 1939.

Through the Eyes of a Boy, BBC Home Service, An impression of George Orwell by Richard Peters, 9 September 1955.

CHAPTER THIRTEEN

Orwell AND THE War Reporter's Imagination

RICHARD LANCE KEEBLE

INTRODUCTION

In late December 1936, George Orwell (under his real name of Eric Blair) arrived in Barcelona to report on the civil war between the Republicans and the fascists led by General Franco.[1] Orwell had originally contacted the Communist Party with the aim of reporting from the side of the International Brigades. But, as Richard Baxell reports (2012: 183), Harry Pollitt, its general secretary, was irritated by the writer's upper middle class background and suspicious of his politics, so 'flatly turned him down.' Orwell immediately turned to the Independent Labour Party which was offering support to the Partido Obrero de Unificación Marxista (POUM)—a small, anti-Stalinist party based mainly in Catalonia in northeast Spain. But once he arrived in Spain and became overwhelmed with the revolutionary spirit he witnessed there, Orwell dropped his idea of reporting and resolved on fighting for the Republican side along with the POUM militiamen. His experiences in Spain until he fled (along with his new wife, Eileen O'Shaughnessy, who had come to support him on the frontline) for his life in June 1937 formed the basis for *Homage to Catalonia*.

Orwell planned to write 'the truth about what I have seen' (Crick 1980: 339n) for his normal publisher, Victor Gollancz. Back in England he had found that many of those men he had been fighting alongside 'were being falsely accused.' 'If I had not been angry about that I should never have written the book' (1970 [1946]: 29). But Gollancz objected to Orwell's links with POUM and the anarchists and so it was eventually published by Fredric Warburg on 25 April 1938. While generally well reviewed—by the *Times Literary Supplement, Manchester Guardian, Listener, New English Weekly* and *Time and Tide,* though savaged in the Communist *Daily Worker*—it sold only 700 copies during Orwell's life and there was no US edition until 1952 (Lucas 2003: 45).

This chapter will argue that *Homage* is a wonderfully confident piece of eye-witness reportage that embraces a wide range of literary techniques. In contrast, the pieces of war reporting which Orwell contributed to the *Observer* and *Manchester Evening News* from 15 February to the end of May 1945 lacked that assurance and highlighted his 'difficulties in finding an appropriate voice' (Keeble 2001: 404). Significantly, in writing *Homage* Orwell was in no way constrained by the demands of professionalism: he was an outspoken, activist journalist—but these demands later intruded into his reporting style while on assignment at the end of the Second World War.

PROFESSIONALISM OR ACTIVISM?

In Spain, Orwell made no attempt to associate with fellow journalists. As Meyers comments (2000: 143), 'he remained an outsider in Spain.' He is not included in David Deacon's seminal study of journalists in Spain (2008) and he is given only a few passing references in Paul Preston's exhaustive study of foreign correspondents during the civil war (2008). Orwell does not appear in the famous painting, 'Bar in the Hotel Scribe (Paris)' by Floyd Davis alongside such journalists as Ernest Hemingway, Robert Capa, the *New Yorker* reporter Janet Flanner, and William Shirer (see https://www.flickr.com/photos/bootbearwdc/3278872594/). Nor does he feature in Amanda Vaill's glitzy, romantic account of the adventurous journos (such as Ernest Hemingway, Martha Gellhorn, Robert Capa and Gerda Taro) and press officials (Arturo Barea and Ilsa Kulcsar) who congregated at the Hotel Florida, Madrid, during the conflict (Vaill 2014). All this is in no way surprising. Orwell spent his time fighting in Spain—and only wrote about it afterwards. Significantly, Deacon speaks of the 'pressures on professionalism' for the reporters in Spain and comments on war reporting (2008: 58): 'Journalists often struggle to determine where their professional obligations end and their patriotic duties begin. Although such factors are evident in peacetime, it is during war that they acquire acute intensity.' He continues:

> Journalists have most professional discretion in conflicts that have no direct implications
> for their nation of origin. Conversely, the graver the threat to national security, the more
> journalists will be expected to subordinate their independence to the propaganda needs of
> the nation. It follows therefore that the greatest tensions between professionalism and pro-
> paganda in war reporting tend to occur in those conflicts where serious national interests

are at stake but not matters of national survival. The Spanish Civil War was precisely such a conflict for British and North American journalists (ibid.).

Deacon divides journalists into four main sections (ibid.: 59–64): propagandists, partisans (those passionately committed to one side but with an associative rather than formal relationship with a cause of a party), sympathizers (those whose identification with a cause or party was 'more measured and conditional than the partisans') and agnostics (focused in particular on the war's intrinsic news value).

Orwell did not face these 'professional' dilemmas while in Spain. Indeed, he stood deliberately outside the journalists' pack even joking about his meeting a suspected fat Russian agent in the Hotel Continental in Barcelona after the fighting ended there on 6 May 1937 that, 'it was the first time that I had seen a person whose profession was telling lies—unless one counts journalists' (Orwell 1962 [1938]: 135). Sections in the book are also given over to detailed critiques of the press coverage of even pro-Republican newspapers such as the Communist *Daily Worker* and the liberal *News Chronicle*. Later he wrote (in 'Looking Back on the Spanish War,' in *New Road*, 1948):

> No event is ever correctly reported in a newspaper, but in Spain, for the first time, I saw newspaper reports which did not bear any relation to the facts, nor even the relationship which is implied in an ordinary lie. I saw great battles reported where there had been no fighting, and complete silence where hundreds of men had been killed.

He also commented: 'It is the same in all wars, the soldiers do the fighting, the journalists do the shouting' (Orwell 1962 [1938]: 65). But according to Richard Baxell (2012: 290) Orwell is unfair here since a number of foreign journalists were killed while covering the war including photographer (and girlfriend of Robert Capa) Gerda Taro, and three correspondents accompanying Kim Philby—later revealed as a Soviet spy after rising high in British intelligence (see Knightley 2003)—whose car was hit by a Republican shell on New Year's Eve 1937.

HOMAGE AND THE JOURNALISTIC IMAGINATION

Orwell wrote the book in a state of 'white hot anger' during the second half of 1937 and this helps account partly for the extraordinary freedom of his writing, its flair, outspokenness, its creative, imaginative, literary richness—and its use of an eclectic range of fictional techniques (see Keeble and Tulloch 2012 and 2014). It is reportage but it also amounts to art. As Orwell commented in 'Why I Write' (1970 [1946]: 28): 'What I have most wanted to do throughout the past ten years is to make political writing into an art.' Indeed, drawing on the work of Max Saunders (2010), Nick Hubble (2012: 36) argues that *Homage* amounts to a 'prime example' of the genre of autobiografiction since it blends two established forms: autobiography and fiction.

Bernard Crick, the author of one of the most celebrated biographies of Orwell, strangely failed to note the wide range of literary techniques and genres evident in *Homage* (1980: 318) and stressed its 'factuality':

> *Homage to Catalonia* is closer to a literal record than anything he wrote; for in order to controvert the many existing false accounts (he was not breaking new ground, only in the way he wrote) he had to get the facts right and give himself no artistic licence. It poses no general problem of genre, only lesser problems of some particular questionable judgments; and while he warns his readers that Catalonia was not the whole of the Republican Spain, he did not always take his own advice.

Yet one of the book's most striking aspects, in fact, is the range of literary genres and tones Orwell incorporates into the text. For instance, there are profiles (of individuals, cities, groups), sections of very direct, personal, emotional writing (conveying an earnestness to represent authentic/real experience); elements of background description, generalizing comment and concrete experience; and personal commentary together with eye-witness reportage informed by a social political awareness. In addition, there is a journalistic emphasis on the extraordinary and the contradictory; confessional writing; a practical, down-to-earth awareness/ sensibility; press content analysis/critique; political analysis (however reluctant); wit, irony, humor; there's the droll debunking of the heroism of war and the claims of history—and political analysis/commentary. All of that packed into little more than a couple of hundred pages. George Woodcock even raves, perhaps a little over-the-top (1967: 134): 'The great virtue of *Homage to Catalonia* is not merely that it brings the period back to life in one's mind, but that it does so with such exceptional radiance.'

PROFILES

Michael Waltzer argues (1998: 185):

> At bottom, he was always Eric Blair, the 'lower upper middle class' Englishman who went to school at Eton and who joined, and left, the Burmese police ... He was not easily a comrade, never a proletarian. One can find in *Wigan Pier* and *Homage to Catalonia* idealised portraits of individual workers, but the authorial voice in the two books is consistently that of the middle class (lower, upper) reporter.

Take a look at the much-anthologized opening paragraphs of *Homage* where Orwell describes so vividly meeting an Italian militiaman. He begins in traditional journalistic style: spelling out concisely, emphatically the 'where,' ('in the Lenin Barracks in Barcelona') the 'when,' ('the day before I joined the militia') the 'who,'

('I') and the 'what,' ('saw an Italian militiaman standing in front of the officers' table') (1962 [1938]: 7). As Lynette Hunter comments (1984: 71):

> It is an abrupt start to the book. There is no introductory prelude for the 'I' who writes. The reader is thrust into a situation which he is supposed, in some way, to recognize: the detail is so concrete it assumes our familiarity with it.

Orwell then describes/profiles the militiaman. There is extraordinary intensity in his gaze, perhaps with an element of homo-erotic excitement in it, as he dwells on the violence of the man: he stresses he was 'a tough-looking youth of twenty-five or six, with reddish-yellow hair and powerful shoulders. His peaked leather cap was pulled fiercely over one eye ... Something in his face deeply moved me' (1962 [1938]: 7).[2] He says there were 'both candour and ferocity in it.' But then a somewhat patronising, contemptuous tone emerges (perhaps from his educated, Old Etonian, 'lower upper middle class' background) as he mocks his 'pathetic reverence that illiterate people have for their supposed superiors' (ibid.). Orwell is not hiding his feelings here. The mockery continues: 'Obviously he could not make head or tail of the map; obviously he regarded map-reading as a stupendous intellectual feat.'

Yet, paradoxically, the man's ignorance adds to his allure which is matched by Orwell's own confessed ignorance. He writes: 'I hardly know why, but I have seldom seen anyone—any man, I mean—to whom I have taken such an immediate liking.' As Hunter observes (1984: 72): 'The lack of knowledge, combined with ignorance, paradoxically creates for the reader an elusiveness similar to the response to the Italian soldier and points to the past narrator's inability to define the situation.'

Having gazed at a distance at the man, Orwell propels his dramatic narrative towards closer, more intimate contact: first, they engage in awkward, clipped dialogue as the Italian raises his head:

> '*Italiano?*'
> I answered in my bad Spanish [notice how Orwell assumes the persona of a self-effacing, linguistically incompetent newcomer, using the familiar voice: *tu*, the French equivalent rather than the more formal *vous*]: 'No, *Inglés. Y tú*'
> '*Italiano*' (ibid.).

From gazing and dialogue the intimacy quickly moves on to the level of touching, and there is a certain 'violence' in the contact which Orwell clearly finds attractive: 'As we went out he stepped across the room and gripped my hand very hard.' And then he comments: 'Queer, the affection you can feel for a stranger!' This generalization serves two purposes: from the isolated incident Orwell is able to draw out an observation about the human predicament and at the same time avoid the personal voice. Perhaps Orwell felt for a moment a certain embarrassment/shame about the intensity of his feelings for the stranger. Significantly, he quickly returns to the personal voice stressing the 'utter intimacy' of the contact: 'It was as though his spirit and mine had momentarily succeeded in bridging the gulf of language and tradition and meeting in utter intimacy. I hoped he liked me as well as I liked him.' The battlefront had, then, became the traditional site for male bonding.

Looking back on the incident, Orwell reflects, with a certain sadness: 'But I also knew that to retain my first impression of him I must not see him again; and needless to say I never did see him again' (ibid.). And from the personal he shifts to the impersonal, generalized 'one' voice—as if to distance himself from a certain pain: 'One was always making contacts of that kind in Spain.' As Hunter says (1984: 71–72):

> The movement from optimistic fervour to criticism alerts the reader to a duality of naïve commitment yet clear detachment in the narrative. The duality is primarily one of chrono-logical difference. There are two narrative voices: the earlier, immediately experiencing voice of the past, and the older, more reflective voice of the present.

Orwell moves on to profile, in effect, Barcelona, including personal impressions and vivid observations—while the emotional intensity of the writing captures both his own exhilaration and the extraordinary nature of the events witnessed. He quickly moves from the 'I' voice to that of the passionately engaged eye-witness:

> It was the first time that I had ever been in a town where the working class was in the sad-dle. Practically every building of any size had been seized by the workers and was draped with red flags or with the red and black flag of the Anarchists; every wall was scrawled with the hammer and sickle and with the initials of the revolutionary parties; almost every church had been gutted and its images burnt … Waiters and shop-walkers looked you in the face and treated you as an equal. Servile and ceremonial forms of speech had temporar-ily disappeared (Orwell 1962 [1938]: 9).

Orwell, the narrator of the past here, is deeply inspired politically by what he sees. Looking back, he is able through the benefit of hindsight to acknowledge his ignorance: 'There was much in it that I did not understand, in some ways I did not even like it, but I recognized it immediately as a state of affairs worth fighting for' (ibid.). And he admits to his innocence and naïveté: 'Also I believed that things were as they appeared, that this was really a workers' State and that the entire bourgeoisie had either fled, been killed, or voluntarily come over to the worker' side' (ibid.). The voice of the more reflective, present narrator adds: 'I did not realize that great numbers of well-to-do bourgeois were simply lying low and disguising themselves as proletarians for the time being' (ibid.). This tension between detachment and involvement (and between past and present narrators) is a constant feature of the reportage.

Yet, Meyers (2000: 143) is critical of Orwell suggesting that his 'intoxica-tion' with the radical politics he witnessed in Barcelona meant that he failed to acknowledge adequately the atrocities that accompanied the raising of the red and black flags: 'Despite the shocking desecration of the churches, the persecution and murder of priests and nuns, Orwell was intoxicated by the atmosphere of Barcelona.'

THE POLITICS OF THE 'HUMAN INTEREST'

The human interest bias has been built into the routines of Western journalists—certainly since the emergence of professionalism in the second half of the nineteenth century. As John Taylor sums up (1991: 2): 'The concept of news as human interest has remained staple because it has consistently sold newspapers. These stories are the most widely read in both tabloids and broadsheets. Their appeal carries across the differences between men and women, young and old, middle class and working class.' While usually pursued unproblematically by journalists, the human interest focus stills serves many complex ideological purposes (Keeble 1997: 65). As Curran, Douglas and Whannel argue, human interest is not simply a neutral window on the world but embodies a particular way of seeing (1980: 306). Accordingly, the possibility of basic structural inequalities is rejected while non-historical forces of 'luck, fate and chance' are represented as dominant within a given naturalized world. This view is reinforced by Sparks (1992: 39) who argues: 'The popular conception of the personal becomes the explanatory framework within which the social order is presented as transparent.' The media fail to convey the 'social totality' comprizing 'complex mediations of institutional structures, economic relations and so on.' Similarly Chibnall (1977: 26) suggests that the personalization of politics and the media is 'perhaps the most pervasive product of cultural fetishism of modern society.' Issues are increasingly defined and presented in terms of personalities 'catering for the public desire for identification fostered by the entertainment media.'

Yet these 'human interest' conventions are profoundly challenged by Orwell in *Homage*. While it is essentially a highly personal account of his time on the frontline in Spain until his flight from the conflict in late June 1938, his personal predicament is always placed within a broader historical and political context. All of Chapter 5 (Orwell 1962 [1938]: 46–70) is, in fact, given over to an attempt by Orwell to explain the political and historical background to the conflict. Political analysis mixes with personal impressions: war reportage blurs into memoir which then blurs into political analysis from an activist stance.

Lynette Hunter (1984: 2–3) identifies a dualistic epistemology (a way of understanding knowledge) that over the last three hundred years has dominated Western thinking which has stressed the 'divisions between subject and object, fiction and fact, novel and documentary.' And she concludes: 'Orwell's search for a valid voice through experimentation with genre was a search for writing that would be able to move outside the dualisms that surrounded him.' For Orwell fact and fiction were not always divided from each other but could rather be viewed 'fruitfully as part of a continuum' (ibid.: 5).

In keeping with his efforts to present himself authentically as an 'innocent' in the crucial process of political education, Orwell addresses his readers directly at the start of Chapter 5:

> If you are not interested in the horrors of party politics, please skip; I am trying to keep the political parts of this narrative in separate chapters for precisely that purpose ... When I came to Spain and for some time afterwards, I was not only uninterested in the political situation but unaware of it. I knew there was a war on, but I had no notion what kind of war ... The revolutionary atmosphere of Barcelona had attracted me deeply, but I had made no attempt to understand it. As for the kaleidoscope of political parties and trade unions with their tiresome names—PSUC, POUM, FAI, CNT, UGT, JCI, JSU, AIT— they merely exasperated me. It looked at first sight as though Spain were suffering from a plague of initials (ibid.: 46–47).

From then on he patiently outlines the stances of the various parties—as he understood them—and how both the left- and right-wing press in Britain had both 'dived simultaneously into the same cesspool of abuse' (ibid.: 65). Originally he had preferred the communist strategy as the one most likely to bring victory, but then he came to detest the communists for their attacks on POUM:

> The POUM was declared to be no more than a gang of disguised Fascists, in the pay of Franco and Hitler ... This implied that scores of thousands of working class people, including eight or ten thousand soldiers who were freezing in the frontline trenches and hundreds of foreigners who had come to Spain to fight against Fascism, often sacrificing their livelihood and their nationality by doing so, were simply traitors in the pay of the enemy (ibid.: 63–64).

In effect, through outlining his own process of political education he is encouraging his readers to engage in a similar process. But for Orwell knowledge is never fixed, always conditional on time and place. As he writes of his early times in revolutionary Barcelona: 'I was breathing the air of equality and I was simple enough to imagine that it existed all over Spain. I did not realize that more of less by chance I was isolated amongst the most revolutionary section of the Spanish working class' (ibid.: 66).[3]

HUMOR

Orwell is often associated with failure, pessimism, guilt and the terror of torture. The very word 'Orwellian' has come to be associated, in part, with the gloom, authoritarianism and oppressiveness of the Big Brother society as described in his celebrated dystopian novel, *Nineteen Eighty-Four* (1949) where the state invades the most private aspects of the individual's life (Keeble 2015a forthcoming). So it is easy to ignore the fact that humor and satire appear as constant features of his writing. Indeed, throughout *Homage*, the reportage is infused with a droll, self-deprecating wit: military cynicism mixed with military knowhow. Of his time on the frontline fighting for the Trotskyite POUM militia against Franco's forces, he writes: 'It is curious, but I dreaded the cold much more than I dreaded the enemy' (Orwell 1962 [1938]: 21). On the Russian gun he wrote: 'Its great shells whistled over so slowly that you felt certain you could run beside them and keep up with them' (ibid.: 83). And notice his brilliantly down-beat, anti-heroic description of being shot through the neck on 20 May 1937, a model of journalistic clarity and conciseness drawn from personal experience:

> The whole experience of being hit by a bullet is very interesting and I think it is worth describing in detail ... Roughly speaking it was the sensation of being at the centre of an explosion ... Not being in pain I felt a vague satisfaction. This ought to please my wife, I thought, she had always wanted me wounded which would save me from being killed when the great battle came (ibid.: 177).

He assumes he is about to die and continues: 'It is very interesting to know what your thoughts would be at such a time. My first thought, conventionally enough, was for my wife. My second was a violent resentment at having to leave this world which, when all is said and done, suits me so well' (ibid.: 178). He adds: 'No one I met at this time ... failed to assure me that a man who is hit through the neck and survives is the luckiest creature alive. I could not help thinking that it would be even luckier not to be hit at all' (ibid.).

He describes a cathedral as 'one of the most hideous buildings in the world.' 'I think the Anarchists showed bad faith in not blowing it up when they had the chance' (ibid.: 214). Chapter 11 includes a detailed account of the fighting in Barcelona in May 1937 after the government ordered the anarchists to surrender their arms which he viewed from a roof overlooking the main avenue, the Ramblas—and the distorted coverage in the Spanish and British press. But notice his droll, dead-pan debunking of the lofty claims of History:

> When you are taking part in events like these you are, I suppose, in a small way, making history and you ought by rights to feel like a historical character. But you never do because at such times the physical details always outweigh everything else. Throughout the fighting I never made the correct 'analysis' of the situation that was so glibly made by journalists hundreds of miles away. What I was chiefly thinking about was not the rights and wrongs of this miserable internecine scrap but simply the discomfort and boredom of sitting day and night on that intolerable roof and the hunger which was growing worse and worse ... If this was history it did not feel like it ... (ibid.: 134).

Amidst all the horror of trench warfare (when it flares up), Orwell also manages to inject some humor into his narrative. For instance, Orwell is involved in a rare attack on the fascist lines and he sees 'a shadowy figure in the half-light' (ibid.: 90). He continues:

> I gripped my rifle by the mall of the butt and lunged at the man's back. He was just out of my reach. Another lunge: still out of reach. And for a little distance we proceeded like this, he rushing up to the trench and I after him on the ground above, prodding at his shoulder-blades and never quite getting there—a comic memory for me to look back upon, though I suppose it seemed less comic to him (ibid.).

AFTER SPAIN: ORWELL'S COMMITMENT TO THE ALTERNATIVE PRESS

For most of his journalistic career, Orwell chose deliberately to direct his writings to alternative/non-mainstream outlets. Following his experiences in the Spanish Civil War, he wrote in 'Why I Write' (1970 [1946]: 28): 'Every line of serious work that I have written since 1936 has been written, directly or indirectly, *against* totalitarianism and *for* democratic socialism, as I understand it' (italics in the original).

In this way, he engaged in the crucial debates with the people who mattered to him: activists and intellectuals of the broad left. He may have disagreed with many of them, but they were an authentic audience compared with what Stuart Allan (1999: 92) calls the 'implied reader or imagined community of readers' of the mainstream media. So most of Orwell's journalism and essay writing was either poorly paid or done entirely free for such small circulation, literary or left-wing publications such as *Adelphi, New Statesman and Nation, New English Weekly, Fortnightly Review, The Highway, Time and Tide, Controversy, New Leader, Left Forum, New Writing, Horizon, Tribune, Left News, Polemic, Progressive, Focus, Persuasion, Contemporary Jewish Record, Politics and Letters* and *Gangrel* (see Marks 2011). In the United States, he chose not to contribute to the prestigious *New York Times* but to the left-wing *Partisan Review* and *Politics*. From this engaged, activist stance came some of the greatest journalism of the last century (Keeble 2000).

ORWELL'S AWKWARDNESS IN THE MAINSTREAM

Thus, when in 1945 Orwell went to Paris in 1945 on a reporting assignment for David Astor's *Observer* and *Manchester Evening*, distinctly mainstream newspapers, he was straying from his normal practice. He may well have been prepared to make the compromises for a number of reasons. It is very probable that his main purpose for the trip was to work on an intelligence assignment for David Astor, who was then serving on a unit of the Special Operations Executive liaising with the resistance in France (Keeble 2010 and 2012). Significantly while in Paris Orwell attended the first conference of the Committee for European Federation, bringing together resistance groups from around Europe (Dorril 2000: 457). W. J. West (1992: 122–124) suggests that Orwell's main motive was to earn a 'large lump sum' to help pay for his family's move to the remote Scottish island of Jura.

From Paris Orwell moved to Cologne where he became ill and had to enter hospital on 24 March. Then he suddenly had to leave the hospital to return to England following the sudden death in an operating theatre of his wife, Eileen, on 29 March. By 8 April he was back in Paris, moving afterwards to Nuremberg, Stuttgart and Austria. These were, indeed, traumatic times for Orwell and it remarkable that he was able to complete the assignment. In all he sent 14 articles (each roughly 1,000 words long) to the *Observer* (though the final two, of 27 May and 10 June, were composed on his return to London) and five to the *Manchester Evening News*. Perhaps most reflective of his awkwardness was his constant reference in the pieces to his being a 'newcomer'. In one respect, it follows from the position he outlined in 'Why I Write' in which he stressed the importance for the writer to acknowledge subjectivity and bias: 'The more one is conscious of one's political bias, the more chance one has of acting politically without sacrificing one's aesthetic and intellectual integrity' (Orwell 1970 [1946]: 28). In his war reporting in 1945 he makes no pretence of being the omniscient observer. He sees with the fresh and somewhat surprisingly innocent eye of the outsider.

Yet, the references to 'newcomer' can perhaps be seen to represent a part of Orwell's troubled efforts to conform to dominant journalistic conventions. He does not say: 'I, the newcomer.' Rather he becomes the generalized newcomer and so distances himself from his observations. In effect, he is laying claim to some kind of objectivity. In his first article for the *Observer*, of 25 February, he writes: 'The first remark of every newcomer is that Paris manages to put a very good face upon its miseries' (see Orwell 2014: 332). And in his 28 February *MEN* despatch, he comments: 'A newcomer notes how alike all the papers are' (Keeble 2001: 397). In his 4 March *Observer* piece he writes: 'One of the first things that strike a newcomer is that almost any Frenchman has a far tougher attitude towards Germany than almost any Englishman' (ibid.). Then in his first report from Austria, on 20 May, he comments: 'In some places a newcomer must get the impression that Austria is being occupied not by the Allies but by the Germans' (ibid.). Generalizing can be an important aspect of journalistic writing but in these examples—as a strategy, it could be argued, largely to overcome a sense of insecurity—it tends to oversimplify and to be too emphatic.

According to David Astor, Orwell 'didn't do well' on the assignment because, in part, away from book reviewing and comment pieces, he was unsure about straight reporting to deadlines.[4] Orwell's first article in the series for the *Observer*, dated 25 February 1945 and headlined 'Paris puts a gay face on her anxieties' is particularly revealing since it reflects the writer struggling to deal with his new assignment, unsure in his subjective stance and uncertain about his relationship to his audience (Orwell 2014: 332–334). First he is the generalized 'every newcomer.' Then he shifts to the I' voice which he had developed to such effect in his 'As I Please' columns in *Tribune* (Keeble 2007a), reporting that 'in several days of wandering to and fro in all kinds of quarters I have not seen a barefooted person and not many who were conspicuously ragged.' Next he speaks as an impersonal 'one' ('When a pale tree on the side-walk is lopped one sees elegantly dressed women waiting to collect bundles of twigs.'). He moves on to speak through the 'you' voice ('On the Metro they eye your foreign uniform.'); then returns to 'one' ('One is not even asked for cigarettes.') and finally returns to the 'I.'

Yet Orwell achieves some kind of resolution in the final section (Keeble 2001: 396). Here his individual voice emerges confidently. The reader accompanies Orwell around the French capital comparing in meticulous detail the sites with those he had known during his previous stay in 1937 on his way back from the Spanish Civil War. 'Almost as soon as I set foot in Paris I returned, as anyone would, to the quarters I had known best in the days before the war. Round Notre Dame it was almost the same as ever. The little bookstalls along the river were just the same, the print sellers were even selling the same prints: the innumerable anglers were still catching nothing, the minders of mattresses were as busy as ever on the quays.' Next he observes: 'In the big Montparnasse Café, instead of a cosmopolitan mob of artists there sat middle class French families thriftily sipping at glasses of fruit wine.' Through the build-up of details, the reader is drawn into Orwell's travels which conclude in 'delight.' He writes, wittily: 'Then, to my delight, I came upon a little bistro which I used to know and which had not changed hands. The proprietor welcomed me with open arms, refused to take more than half the cigarettes I offered him and bought a bottle of something that was very drinkable though it was not what its label declared it to be.' Then Orwell suddenly shifts focus and tone. From a feeling of 'delight' he becomes aware of the appalling suffering behind the Parisian façade and ends: 'Across the street the tiny hotel where I used once to live was boarded up and partly ruinous. It appeared empty. But as I came away from behind the broken window pane of what used to be my own room I saw two hungry-looking children peeping out at me just like wild animals.' This is far from dull prose (ibid.).

CRITICAL RECEPTION OF THE 1945 WAR REPORTS

In the many studies of Orwell's work, these articles are either ignored (as in, say, Woodcock 1967; Fyvel 1982; Lewis 1981; Hunter 1984; Wykes 1987; Meyers

1991) or dismissed as untypically drab. Bernard Crick, in his biography, says the reports were 'not distinctly Orwell.' 'He earned his salt but he did not shine.' Similarly, Stephen Ingle comments (1993: 67): 'Indeed, it is true to say that, thoroughly competent though his reporting was, his few months in Europe produced no writing of any great note.' Meyers follows the consensus (2000: 232) and describes the war articles as 'curiously flat, lifeless and impersonal.' Significantly, the *Collected Essays, Journalism and Letters*, edited by Sonia Orwell and Ian Angus and published by Penguin (1970), fails to include any article from the war series; Shelden, in his biography (1991: 421–422) makes a brief reference to only one of the articles while Peter Davison, in a collection of Orwell's journalism (2014) only includes two of the despatches and makes no comment about the assignment in his 'Introduction' (ibid.: 1–8).

There are a number of reasons for this lack of analysis. Journalism until quite recently has not been considered Literature (with a capital 'L') and worthy of serious attention due to a range of complex factors—historical, cultural, ideological, political (Keeble 2007b: 3). Since their emergence in the early seventeenth century in Europe's cities, particularly London, the 'news media' (variously known as corantos, diurnals, gazettes, proceedings and mercuries) have been associated with scandal, gossip and 'low' culture. And by the early eighteenth century the derogatory term 'Grub Street' had come to be associated with all forms of struggling, low-level publishing—and the term stuck even when much of the mainstream press moved to Fleet Street. John Tulloch suggests that another reason for the low status of journalism in Britain has been its perceived lack of creative control by the author compared to the control allegedly associated with the 'artist.' He argues (2007: 60): 'Arguably one of the malign effects of Romanticism in British culture was to define the "true" artist's status as not having a patron but a soulful relationship to the audience that precluded writing for anything as vulgar as the market.' Paradoxically, Orwell was somewhat dismissive of his journalism, describing it as 'mere pamphleteering' and a 'lesser' form of literature (cited in Bromley 2003: 125). He had a horror of hack reporting and despised the 'dreary subworld of the freelance journalist' (ibid.).

CONCLUSIONS

As for Orwell's relatively poor journalistic performance on the continental frontline in 1945 there are a number of complex reasons. His thoughts may not have been entirely on the job of reporting. As already stated, he may well have been engaged in some kind of intelligence mission; he was ill and had to enter hospital; he then had to rush back to the UK to attend the funeral of his wife—and equally rapidly return to the continent. All this must have been somewhat distressing and distracting.

An alternative analysis might argue that while Orwell's voice is somewhat uncertain yet still some of the best elements of his style—immediacy, clarity, a sense of urgency, an ability to highlight the most interesting, the paradoxical, the most tragic; a facility both to generalize effectively and to focus on the specific, relevant detail; an economy of language, even within colorful, eye-witness, descriptive reporting; a political and moral stance and an openness to conflicting views—are apparent in some of his despatches (Keeble 2001: 404–405).

However, at the core of Orwell's dilemma in 1945 was the difficulty he faced in finding an appropriate voice as a *mainstream* reporter. As Phillip Knightley, author of the seminal history of war reporting (2000), comments: 'At that late stage of the war in Europe there were dozens of battle-hardened war correspondents covering the last days of the fight against Germany. They were confident about what they did. Orwell was feeling his way. He was troubled, diffident and insecure in his reporting. Should he allow his emotions free rein? Could he insert his political views? Could he refute the propaganda some of the others had been writing? He never found the answers.'[5]

Compare this to the writing of *Homage to Catalonia*. Here, Orwell was free from any of the constraints inhibiting his 'professional' colleagues. One is even tempted to generalise from this and suggest that the best reportage—both in the past and today—has come from the alternative media! (see Keeble 2015b forthcoming).

NOTES

1. *En route*, he had stopped over in Paris to meet the author Henry Miller. Colls (2013: 72) comments: 'He did not get much encouragement from the American about going for a soldier except a warm corduroy jacket which was maybe encouragement enough …'

2. The homoeroticism appears in the poem 'The Italian Soldier Shook my Hand' Orwell composed in 1939 about the experience: To meet within the sound of guns/But oh! What peace I knew then/In gazing on his battered face/Purer than any woman's. See Colls 2013: 73. Available online at http://theorwellprize.co.uk/george-orwell/by-orwell/poetry/the-italian-soldier-shook-my-hand/, accessed on 20 February 2015. The poem was first published in Looking back on the Spanish War, *New Road*, 1943.

3. Orwell's analysis of the Spanish conflict, of course, has not escaped criticism. For instance, Raymond Williams (cited in Hitchens 2002: 37) wrote: 'Most historians have taken the view that the revolution—mainly anarcho-syndicalist but with the POUM taking part—was an irrelevant distraction from a desperate war. Some, at the time and after, have gone so far as to describe it as deliberate sabotage of the war effort.' This view was, in turn, challenged by Hitchens who criticises Williams's 'pseudo-objectivity' (ibid.: 38).

4. In a conversation with the author at his London home, 21 December 1999.

5. In an email to the author, 12 November 2000.

REFERENCES

Allan, Stuart (1999) *News Culture*, Buckingham/Philadelphia: Open University Press.

Baxell, Richard (2012) *Unlikely Warriors: The British in the Spanish Civil War and the Struggle against Fascism*, London: Aurum Press.

Bowker, Gordon (2003) *George Orwell*, London: Little Brown.

Bromley, Michael (2003) Objectivity and the other Orwell: The tabloidisation of the *Daily Mirror* and journalistic authenticity, *Media History*, Vol. 9, No. 2, pp. 123–125.

Chibnall, Steve (1977) *Law and Order News*, London: Tavistock.

Colls, Robert (2013) *George Orwell: English Rebel*, Oxford: Oxford University Press.

Crick, Bernard (1980) *George Orwell: A Life*, Harmondsworth, Middlesex: Penguin Books.

Curran, James, Douglas, Angus and Whannel, Garry (1980) The political economy of the human interest story, Smith, Anthony (ed.) *Newspapers and Democracy: International Essays on a Changing Medium*, Cambridge, Massachusetts: MIT Press pp. 288–316.

Deacon, David (2008) *British News Media and the Spanish Civil War: Tomorrow May be Too Late*, Edinburgh: Edinburgh University Press.

Dorril, Stephen (2000) *MI6: Fifty Years of Special Operations*, London: Fourth Estate.

Fyvel, Tosco R. (1982) *George Orwell: A Personal Memoir*, London: Weidenfeld & Nicolson.

Hitchens, Christopher (2002) *Orwell's Victory*, London: Allen Lane: The Penguin Press.

Hitchens, Christopher (2002) *Unacknowledged Legislation: Writers in the Public Sphere*, London: Verso.

Hubble, Nick (2012) Orwell and the English working class: Lessons in autobiografiction for the twenty-first century, Keeble, Richard Lance (ed.) *Orwell Today*, Bury St. Edmunds: Abramis pp. 30–45.

Hunter, Lynette (1984) *George Orwell: The Search for a Voice*, Milton Keynes: Open University Press.

Ingle, Stephen (1993) *George Orwell: A Political Life*, Manchester: Manchester University Press.

Keeble, Richard (1997) *Secret State, Silent Press: New Militarism, the Gulf and the Modern Image of Warfare*, Luton: John Libbey.

Keeble, Richard (2000) George Orwell—the Journalist, *Press Gazette*, 21 January.

Keeble, Richard (2001) Orwell as war correspondent: A reassessment, *Journalism Studies*, Vol. 2, No. 3, pp. 393–406.

Keeble, Richard (2007a) The lasting in the ephemeral: Assessing George Orwell's 'As I Please' columns, Keeble, Richard and Wheeler, Sharon (eds) *The Journalistic Imagination: Literary Journalists from Defoe to Capote and Carter*, Abingdon, Oxon: Routledge pp. 100–115.

Keeble, Richard (2007b) Introduction: On journalism, creativity and the imagination, Keeble, Richard and Wheeler, Sharon (eds) *The Journalistic Imagination: Literary Journalists from Defoe to Capote and Carter*, Abingdon, Oxon: Routledge pp. 1–14.

Keeble, Richard Lance (2010) Hacks and spooks—close encounters of a strange kind: A critical history of the links between mainstream journalists and the intelligence services in the UK, Klaehn, Jeffery (ed.) *The Political Economy of Media and Power*, New York: Peter Lang pp. 87–111.

Keeble, Richard Lance (2012) Orwell, *Nineteen Eighty-Four* and the spooks, Keeble, Richard Lance (ed.) *Orwell Today*, Bury St. Edmunds: Abramis pp. 151–163.

Keeble, Richard Lance (2015a forthcoming) Orwell's humour, Keeble, Richard Lance (ed.) *The Pleasures of the Prose*, Bury St. Edmunds: Abramis.

Keeble, Richard Lance (2015b forthcoming) Secrets and lies: On the ethics of conflict coverage, Robinson, Piers, Seib, Philip and Froehlich, Romy (eds) *Routledge Handbook of Media, Conflict, Security*, London: Routledge.

Keeble, Richard Lance and Tulloch, John (2012) *Global Literary Journalism: Exploring the Journalistic Imagination Volume 1*, New York: Peter Lang.

Keeble, Richard Lance and Tulloch, John (2014) *Global Literary Journalism: Exploring the Journalistic Imagination Volume 2*, New York: Peter Lang.

Knightley, Phillip (2000) *The First Casualty: The War Correspondent as Hero and Mythmaker from the Crimea to Kosovo*, London: Prion Books.

Knightley, Phillip (2003) *Philby: KGB Masterspy*, London: Andre Deutsch.

Lewis, Peter (1981) *George Orwell: The Road to 1984*, London: Heinemann/Quixote Press.

Lucas, Scott (2003) *Orwell*, London: Haus Publishing.

Marks, Peter (2011) *George Orwell the Essayist: Literature, Politics and the Periodical Culture*, London/New York: Continuum International.

Meyers, Jeffery (2000) *Orwell: Wintry Conscience of a Generation*, New York/London: W. W. Norton.

Meyers, Valerie (1991) *George Orwell*, Basingstoke, Macmillan.

Orwell, George (1938) Why I joined the Independent Labour Party, *New Leader*, 24 June (see *Collected Letters Essays, Journalism and Letters*, Vol. 1, Harmondsworth, Middlesex: Penguin Books 1970 p. 338).

Orwell, George (1970 [1946]) Why I Write, Orwell, Sonia and Angus, Ian (eds) *Collected Essays, Journalism and Letters*, Vol. 1, Harmondsworth, Middlesex: Penguin Books 1970 pp. 23–30, originally published in *Gangrel*, No 4, summer 1946.

Orwell, George (1962 [1938]) *Homage to Catalonia*, Harmondsworth, Middlesex: Penguin.

Orwell, George (1970) *The Collected Essays, Journalism and Letters*, Orwell, Sonia and Angus, Ian (eds) Harmondsworth, Middlesex: Penguin.

Orwell, George (2014) *Seeing Things as They Are: Selected Journalism and Other Writings*, edited by Davison, Peter, London: Harvill Secker.

Preston, Paul (2008) *We Saw Spain Die: Foreign Correspondents in the Spanish Civil War*, London: Constable.

Saunders, Max (2010) *Self-Impression: Life Writing, Autobiografiction, and the Forms of Modern Literature*, Oxford: Oxford University Press.

Shelden, Michael (1991) *Orwell: The Authorised Biography*, London: Heinemann.

Sparks, Colin (1992) Popular journalism: Theories and practice, Dahlgren, Peter and Sparks, Colin (eds) *Journalism and Popular Culture*, London: Sage pp. 24–44.

Taylor, John (1991) *War Photography: Realism in the British Press*, London: Routledge.

Tulloch, John (2007) Charles Dickens and the voices of journalism, Keeble, Richard and Wheeler, Sharon (eds) *The Journalistic Imagination: Literary Journalists from Defoe to Capote and Carter*, Abingdon, Oxon: Routledge pp. 58–73.

Vaill, Amanda (2014) *Hotel Florida: Truth, Love and Death in the Spanish Civil War*, New York: Farrar, Straus and Giroux.

Waltzer, Michael (1998) George Orwell's England, Holderness, Graham, Loughrey, Bryan and Yousaf, Nahem (eds) *George Orwell: Contemporary Critical Essays*, Houndmills, Basingstoke: Macmillan Press pp. 182–202.

West, W. J. (1992) *The Larger Evils: Nineteen Eighty-Four: The Truth Behind the Satire*, Edinburgh: Canongate Press.

Woodcock, George (1967) *The Crystal Spirit: A Study of George Orwell*, London: Fourth Estate.

Wykes, David (1987) *A Preface to Orwell*, London/New York: Longman.

Afterword

Why Orwell Is More Relevant Today Than Ever Before

PETER STANSKY

In many ways Orwell is more relevant today, sixty-five years after his death and a hundred and twelve years after his birth, than he has ever been before. Not that we should try to speculate on what he might think about the present but rather how his writings are not only valuable in themselves but enable us to better understand our present situation. We should not try to decide what Orwell might say today. This happened to a degree in the Orwell bonanza year of 1984 when Christopher Hitchens led the charge for Orwell of the left and Norman Podhoretz for the Orwell of the right. On a lesser scale it was also true in the centenary year of his birth, 2003, when Christopher Hitchens was the lead proponent of Orwell of the right, particularly in terms of the Iraq war, and others, such as Stephan Collini and Louis Menand in their attacks on Hitchens, for the Orwell of the left.

These are lively and at times relevant debates. But it is far better, in my view, to read Orwell in the context of his own time. For those such as Podhoretz, his most famous books, *Animal Farm* and *Nineteen Eighty-Four*, demonstrate that socialism was a bad thing and it was bound to lead to disastrous results. For others, such as myself, those books show that Orwell, though a committed socialist, as he had firmly become through his experiences in the Spanish Civil War, saw how easily socialism could go wrong and fall into the hands of those whose primary interest was simply power and the oppression of others. There is no question, however, that those books were weapons, indeed in many ways legitimate ones, against the Soviet Union during the Cold War. The reissue of his brilliant book about his experiences in Spain, *Homage to Catalonia*, in 1952 reinforced this position. (It had only sold 700 copies when first published in 1938.) Yet his writings can quite dramatically shed light on our present experiences, strikingly enough more perhaps at this time than at any other point since his death.

In many ways, our world is more 'Orwellian' than it ever has been before. There is a nice paradox in the popularity of that term. I suspect (violating my dictum that we should not say what we think Orwell would have thought today) he would have disapproved of its popularity. The use of 'Orwellian' is in many ways a short-cut to thinking. It is perhaps also a little sad that the name of that wise and wonderful writer should now be taken to stand for the grimness to be found in his two last novels. But our world is, I believe, more 'Orwellian' now than it was in the period of the Cold War. Or to put it another way, the world may well have been 'Orwellian' then but now more than in the past governments and others have the tools to make it even more so.

This is first of all true domestically. Governments have always, I believe, wished to spy upon us far more than they are prepared to admit. The British government spied upon Orwell from the time he was in Paris in the late 1920s although admittedly its file on him is not very extensive. It is striking how obsessive and paranoid governments can be. I am at work on a biography of the writer Edward Upward who became a 'person of interest' to MI5 and had a file established on him in 1931, three years before he joined the Communist Party. That year he made a contribution to a fund that supported the *Daily Worker* and the state began its file on him. As the Edward Snowden revelations make clear, governments' ability and wish to spy upon their citizens are far more far-reaching than we might have thought. In our age of terrorism there is some legitimacy to these efforts but it is far from clear that the extent of the spying is justified by its results.

Governments, it seems, would like to spy on us as extensively as possible on all aspects of our life. In *Nineteen Eighty-Four*, one is observed through the mandatory telescreen in Winston Smith's flat and also, as it turns out, in his love nest in Mr. Charrington's cosy curiosity shop, where, indeed, Mr. Charrington himself is an agent of the Thought Police. (As Henk Vynckier discusses in his essay in this collection, the shop reflects Orwell's interest in collection curios.) What is striking, as Florian Zollmann makes clear in his piece, this surveillance is as characteristic of democratic states as it might be in totalitarian societies. And although it hasn't played as prominent a role in our present concerns, what *Nineteen Eighty-Four* also predicts through Winston Smith's job at the Ministry of Truth is how comparatively easy it is in our digital age to rewrite the past through the *ex post facto* alteration of documents.

THE RELEVANCE OF ORWELL'S DEPICTION OF THE SOCIAL STRUCTURE OF SOCIETY

Perhaps a less obvious way that Orwell may be more relevant today than he was more than fifty years ago was in his depiction of the social structure of society. In the early years of the war itself, most notably in his great pamphlet, *The Lion and the Unicorn* (1941), he argued that Britain would have to become a socialist state, perhaps through a violent revolution, in order to win the war. As he later admitted, he was wrong and the welfare state that came into being in Britain in the years after the war was far less than he had hoped for. But it came about in a perfectly peaceful way, although the war had helped bring it into being. It was a step in the right direction, and it seemed then that in many parts of the world we were heading towards more egalitarian societies.

Although there now may be more safety nets in place than there were before, there is a greater gap than after the war between the rich and the poor, those with money and power and those without, as was to be found in the society of *Nineteen Eighty-Four*. As John Newsinger suggests in his essay, there might be some hope that the 'proles' will rebel but it seems a fairly faint possibility. Orwell wished that it might be true but he is deeply pessimistic. Even if there is such a revolution, as there was in Russia in 1917, the only hope for it being successful, he felt, would be if its leaders were almost immediately replaced by others. This would need to happen continually for the goals of the revolution to be preserved. Otherwise, inevitably, the leaders of the revolution are corrupted, and, as O'Brien says, and as the pigs demonstrate in *Animal Farm*, the lust for power and probably profit as well doom the promised egalitarian society.

Another way in which the times have, so to speak, sadly caught up with the world that Orwell depicted is that we exist in a world of continual warfare, in various parts of the world, but in a sense at a secondary level. The major powers are not directly fighting one another—the United States, the Western nations, Russia, China—but rather in some rather unclear proxy way, primarily in the Middle East, but elsewhere as well. Is the West fighting Russia in Ukraine? Is the West fighting Islam in the Middle East? Yet as terrorism makes clear, this is also a war that is fought on Western soil as well ranging from the fall of the Twin Towers to the dreadful deaths of the *Charlie Hebdo* journalists in Paris in January 2015. For some tragic reasons societies seem to need warfare, enemies to be demonized in a 'Two Minute Hate.'

In our present concerns, it would seem that George Orwell's predictive powers of the sort of world we now live in are very much to the fore. But in my view, it is always essential to remember that a primary aim for him was to be as fine a writer as he could possibly be, as he made clear in 1947 in his great essay, 'Why I Write.' As he stated there: 'Every line of serious work that I have written since 1936 has been written, directly or indirectly, *against* totalitarianism and *for* democratic socialism, as I understand it ... What I have most wanted to do throughout the past ten years is to make political writing into an art ... *Animal Farm* was the first book in which I tried, with full consciousness of what I was doing, to fuse political purpose and artistic purpose into one whole.'

Perhaps his novels, with the exception of *Animal Farm*, are less skilled than his other writings. *Homage to Catalonia* is a great book of reportage and also plays the major role in his becoming George Orwell, the disillusioned believer in socialism. His greatest writings, in my view, are his essays for their ideas and for their style. He gave up the police life in Burma in order to be a writer, to put forth his ideas and to succeed aesthetically. And he did.

Contributors

Paul Anderson is a lecturer in journalism at Brunel University and University Campus Suffolk. He was deputy editor of *European Nuclear Disarmament Journal* (1984–1987), reviews editor (1986–1991) and then editor (1991–1993) of *Tribune*, deputy editor of *New Statesman & Society* (1993–1996), news editor of *Red Pepper* (1997–1999) and deputy editor of *New Times* (1999–2000). From 2000 to 2012 he was a journalism lecturer at City University London. He has worked as a sub-editor on the *Guardian* since 1999. He was editor (with Mary Kaldor) of *Mad Dogs: The US Raid on Libya* (Pluto, 1986), and co-author (with Nyta Mann) of *Safety First: The Making of New Labour* (Granta, 1997).

Richard Blair is Patron of the Orwell Society (www.orwellsociety.com).

Philip Bounds is a historian, journalist and critic. He holds a PhD in Politics from the University of Wales and is the author of a number of books, including *Orwell and Marxism* (2009), *British Communism and the Politics of Literature* (2012) and *Cultural Studies* (1999). His most recent book is a memoir of life on the British left entitled *Notes from the End of History* (2014).

Tim Crook is Reader in Media & Communication at Goldsmiths, University of London and Visiting Professor of Broadcast Journalism at Birmingham City University. He has written a number of books on radio, media law and other subjects as well as having a journalism career that spans nearly four decades.

Sreya Mallika Datta is a final year undergraduate student of English Literature at Presidency University, Kolkata, India. She is interested in Postcolonial

Studies and would like to base her future academic career on African literature. Academic presentations include an International Symposium on George Orwell at Lincoln University, UK, a Postcolonial Studies seminar at RKMRC, Narendrapur, and a seminar on travel writing at Aliah University. She is also interested in creative writing. Her writings have been featured in a number of international, national and regional publications including the *Sahitya Akademi Bi-Monthly Journal*, *Inspired by Tagore*, *Inspired by My Museum* (anthologies launched by the British Council and Sampad South Asian Arts) and *Desde Hong Kong: Poets in Conversation with Octavio Paz*, published by Chameleon Press.

Richard Lance Keeble is Chair of the Orwell Society and editor of *Orwell Today* (Abramis 2012). He has been Professor of Journalism at the University of Lincoln since 2003. Before that he was the Executive Editor of the *Teacher*, the weekly newspaper of the National Union of Teachers and he lectured at City University London for 19 years. He has written and edited 29 publications on a wide range of subjects including peace journalism, literary journalism, journalism ethics, practical reporting skills, investigative journalism, the coverage of US/UK militarism and the secret state. He is also joint editor of *Ethical Space: The International Journal of Communication Ethics* and the winner of a National Teacher Fellowship in 2011—the highest prize for teachers in higher education in the UK. In 2014, he was given a Lifetime Achievement Award by the Association for Journalism Education. He is currently editing five texts: on profiling and the 'human interest' bias in the media, on the BBC today—and on humor in journalism.

Peter Marks is Associate Professor of English Literature at the University of Sydney. He is the author of more than twenty articles and chapters on topics including George Orwell, surveillance, literary periodicals, and utopias. His books include *British Filmmakers: Terry Gilliam* (2009), *George Orwell the Essayist: Literature, Politics and the Periodical Culture* (2011) and *Imagining Surveillance: Eutopian and Dystopian Literature and Film* (2015).

Utsa Mukherjee is a final year undergraduate student of English literature at Presidency University, Kolkata, India. His areas of interest include Postcolonial Studies, the sociology of childhood and gender studies. Academic presentations include the British Conference of Undergraduate Research 2014 at the University of Nottingham; the international symposium on George Orwell at Lincoln University, UK; a Childhood Studies conference at the University of Northampton, UK; 'Everyday Life in Contemporary India' international conference at the University of Madras; a Postcolonial Studies seminar at

RKMRC, Narendrapur, and a seminar on travel writing at Aliah University. His poems have been published in the Sahitya Akademi bi-monthly journal, *Indian Literature, Taj Mahal Review* and *Inspired by My Museum*, an anthology launched by the British Council and Sampad South Asian Arts.

John Newsinger is Professor of Modern History at Bath Spa University. He is the author of *Orwell's Politics* (1999) and of numerous articles on George Orwell. His most recent books include *The Blood Never Dried: A People's History of the British Empire* (2010), *Fighting Back: The American Working Class in the 1930s* (2012) and *Jim Larkin and the Great Dublin Lockout* (2013).

Marina Remy Abrunhosa is currently completing her PhD at the Sorbonne, Paris, where she also taught British literature, history and translation. Her research focuses on English literary journalism, from the Victorians to George Orwell. An alumnus of the Ecole Normale Supérieure in Lyon, Marina has also taught French at Royal Holloway. She has taken part in three conferences of the International Association of Literary Journalism Studies and contributed to De Gruyter's 2014 volume on *Narrating Poverty and Precarity in England*, edited by Barbara Korte and Frédéric Regard. She currently teaches at a university level in a Classe Préparatoire aux Grandes Ecoles in Besançon, France.

Luke Seaber currently teaches on modern European culture at University College London. He has degrees from the Universities of Oxford and Turin, and between 2012 and 2014 was a Marie Curie Research Fellow at UCL. He is the author of a book on G. K. Chesterton's influence on Orwell, as well as various articles and chapters on nineteenth- and twentieth-century British literature. His chief research interests include incognito social investigation texts, the relationship between literature, roads and walking and late nineteenth-century British Gypsiologists.

Peter Stansky, Emeritus Professor of History at Stanford University, is the co-author of *The Unknown Orwell* (1972) and *Orwell: The Transformation* (1979).

Adam Stock is Lecturer in English Literature at York St John University. He is currently preparing a monograph to be published by Routledge (2016) entitled *Modern Dystopian Fiction and Political Thought: Narratives of World Politics*. Formerly, he was Network Facilitator for the Leverhulme International Research Network 'Imaginaries of the Future' at Newcastle University and Co-Investigator on the AHRC 'Care for the Future' Developmental Award (2014–2015), 'Re-configuring Ruins: Materialities, Processes and Mediations.' He is honorary treasurer of the Utopian Studies Society.

Henk Vynckier is Associate Professor in the Department of Foreign Languages and Literatures at Tunghai University in Taichung, Taiwan. His interests in research include George Orwell; the literary legacy of Sir Robert Hart and the Chinese Maritime Customs Service; and collecting as a literary theme and cultural practice. He co-edited, with John Rodden, 'Orienting Orwell: Asian and Global Perspectives on George Orwell' (special issue of *Concentric: Literary and Cultural Studies*, March 2014), and his articles and book chapters have appeared in *History of European Ideas, CLC Web: Comparative Literature and Culture, Biography: An Interdisciplinary Quarterly*, and *Sinographies: Writing China* (2008).

Shu-chu Wei is John and Jean Henkels Endowed Chair and Professor of Chinese, emerita, Whitman College, Washington, USA. She earned her PhD in Comparative Literature from the University of Massachusetts, Amherst, and is currently Visiting Professor at the Foreign Languages and Literature Department, Tunghai University, Taiwan. Her fields of interest include Chinese-Western comparative literature, classical Chinese drama and children's literature.

Florian Zollmann is a Lecturer in Media at Liverpool Hope University, UK. Previously, he worked as a lecturer at the German Sport University Cologne and the University of Lincoln, UK. He holds a PhD in Journalism Studies from the University of Lincoln. Florian is contracted to write a monograph on international news coverage of human rights issues during a range of contemporary conflicts for Peter Lang of New York (to be published in 2016). Additionally, he is conducting research on the ethical implications of surveillance in liberal democracies and press-state relations in the 21st century new media environment. With Richard Lance Keeble and John Tulloch he jointly edited *Peace Journalism, War and Conflict Resolution* (Peter Lang, 2010).

Index

Lee B. Becker, *General Editor*

The Mass Communication and Journalism series focuses on broad issues in mass communication, giving particular attention to those in
which journalism is prominent. Volumes in the series examine the
product of the full range of media organizations as well as individuals
engaged in various types of communication activities.

Each commissioned book deals in depth with a selected topic, raises
new issues about that topic, and provides a fuller understanding of it
through the new evidence provided. The series contains both single-
authored and edited works. For more information and submissions,
please contact:

Lee B. Becker, Series Editor | *lbbecker@uga.edu*
Mary Savigar, Acquisitions Editor | *mary.savigar@plang.com*

To order other books in this series, please contact our Customer Service
Department at:

(800) 770-LANG (within the U.S.)
(212) 647-7706 (outside the U.S.)
(212) 647-7707 FAX

Or browse online by series at www.peterlang.com